THE NAKED MANAGER
FOR THE NINETIES

THE NAKED MANAGER FOR THE NINETIES

Robert Heller

LITTLE, BROWN AND COMPANY

A *Little, Brown* Book

First published in Great Britain in 1995
by Little, Brown and Company

Copyright © Heller Arts Ltd 1995

The moral right of the author has been asserted.

A CIP catalogue record for this book
is available from the British Library.

ISBN 0 316 9113 48

Typeset by Solidus (Bristol) Limited
Printed and bound in Great Britain by
Clays Ltd, St Ives plc

Little, Brown and Company (UK)
Brettenham House
Lancaster Place
London WC2 7EN

To Jane,
my managing daughter

Contents

Contents

Contents

Acknowledgements

The Naked Manager could not have been started without the help, direct and inadvertent, of the many, many managers I have met and talked with over the years. Nor could it have been written without the education received from Sir Gordon Newton, my first editor. I am permanently in his debt, not least for sending me as a correspondent to the US.

His chairman at the *Financial Times*, the late Lord Drogheda, among many kindnesses, encouraged me to start *Management Today*. At that magazine I was taught as much about business as journalism – thanks largely to colleagues such as the late Jim Hunter, Michael Heseltine, Lindsay Masters and Geoffrey Foster. The genesis of the book lay in the fortnightly column, *Management in Action*, published in the *Observer*, for which I am everlastingly grateful to David Astor, then the editor, and to Anthony Bambridge, then business editor.

Leopold Ullstein, the managing director of Barrie & Jenkins, thought of the book almost before I did; and so did my then agent, Hilary Rubinstein, who buoyed me up at moments when buoys were badly needed. I owe many other debts I can never fully repay: among others, to Sheila Black; to John Davis of the *Observer*; to Hugh Parker of McKinsey &

Company; to Wally Olins of Wolff Olins; to Lord Weinstock of the General Electric Company; to the late Tommy Wilson of the London Business School; to John Diebold; to Peter Drucker, who has set the standard of perfection in writing about management; and to John Thackray, whose articles on US business in *Management Today* were as invaluable as they are brilliant.

I am also grateful to all those who have commissioned the work which has helped me to produce this revised version of the original *The Naked Manager*. In particular, I must mention the editors of *Management Today*, the partners in Executive Interim Management, and Redwood Publishing. As ever, like any student of the management scene, I am indebted to its principal drama critics: the *Financial Times*, *Business Week*, and *Fortune* magazine.

Finally, like everything I write, this book should really be dedicated to the late David Roberts, senior history master at Christ's Hospital.

Prologue:
The Age of Cut and Thrust

This book is dedicated to all those executives who did the right thing for the wrong reason, and were acclaimed as geniuses and heroes; and to all those who did the wrong thing for the right, the wrong, or no reason at all and still hold their overpaid jobs.

There are less of the latter around than there used to be, though. There are many more managements which actually do the right thing for the right reason. Recession and foreign companies have wonderfully concentrated the managerial mind – and wonderfully concentrated many a business on its real business as described in these pages: which is to manage the affairs of the company so that everybody involved (employees, stockholders, customers, communities) has good cause to be profoundly thankful for management's work.

In the process of concentration, too, more and more managements have decried the nonsense nostrums I describe; have thrown the rubbish out of the window; have set out, often with stunning and sudden success, not to do likewise – to make a break with the over-managed, under-productive past. But nothing exceeds like excess. Just as the conglomerate cons and the merger mania of the late 1960s were the product, the oil slick if you will, of the Kennedy-Johnson boom, so the Reagan-Thatcher pseudo-renaissance generated, and is still posthumously generating, a new collection of excrescences every bit as bothersome as any managerial nudity of the past.

Actually, the faults and the dangers are always the same. The dialogue and the actors may change, but every time the business cycle peaks, it's basically the same stupid plot. Only think back to that dedication to 'those who still hold overpaid jobs' they don't deserve. Well, maybe more managers actually deserve their positions – but even Americans are now rightly questioning (though to absolutely no avail) whether executives deserve their pay, or rather over-pay.

Men (women haven't yet got into this act) who have never laid their own fortunes on the entrepreneurial line are making themselves multi-millionaires, at the stockholders' expense, with no more trouble than it takes to arrange a bonus deal or stock option scheme. If as much ingenuity had been spent on getting more productive collaboration from the rest of the workforce, maybe the managerial élite would have presided over fewer losses of jobs and markets.

In many cases, the over-pay became still more excessive, merely because the corporation had been swollen by one of many mega-mergers. These have passed with astonishingly little adverse comment – even at a time when the managements of earlier merged creations, still in sackcloth and ashes, are busy dismantling failed agglomerations. Was there truly any economic point in BAT buying Eagle Star, or Eastman Kodak buying Sterling Drug, or General Motors shelling out $2.5 billion for Electronic Data Systems?

Weren't corporations such as these already supposed, long ago, to be too big for their own managerial good (setting aside the good of the community)? Or has the hardship and reshaping of the recession years so improved managerial competence and attitudes that the latest mega-deals, and the host of lesser corporate combinations of unrelated businesses, will genuinely create new wealth elsewhere than in the stock market?

There are no prizes for the right answers, which are very

obvious. Indeed, the new conventional wisdom holds that agglomeration is the total contradiction of effective modern management, which aims for the minimum size of unit with the maximum amount of independence and informality. Set the people, or at least the business, free – and wonders will follow. That is part of the rationale for the LBO: the leveraged buy-out. But behind the façade of the LBO, other time-dishonoured acts of managerial folly were repeated on a still grander scale – a debt spree of unprecedented size.

It used to be thought imprudent to borrow more than half the worth of the company's equity. Some of the LBOs entered life as independents with 80% or more of their capital in the form of high-interest debt. The size of the deals, once confined to quite small spin-offs, usually from deconglomerating mergers, waxed greater and greater, too – numbers in the billions didn't frighten the greedy US bankers who financed the deals, and who waxed rich on the LBO proceeds. If the British players waxed less rich, it was merely because their deals were inevitably smaller.

Quick-draw operators, the spiritual heirs of the conglomerators, continued to flourish. In 1984 one executive used an LBO to create a $115 million fortune for himself out of thin air – while trebling his holding in the company. In 1994, Barry Diller, once Rupert Murdoch's prime mover in the creation of the Fox network, had his ace trumped while bidding, on behalf of QVC, his home shopping business, for CBS. Defeat enriched Diller by an estimated $75 million.

Once again, the economic justification of such phenomena is hard to find. Once again, the gunslingers cloak their activities with the current language of fashionable management theory – in the case of the LBOs, merely the latest version of an old nostrum: managing a business as if it's your own. The trouble is that too many managements have begun to treat the corporation as if it really were their own: another misdeed of the discredited past. The bad old days, though, threw up nothing that was more discreditable than today's golden parachutes (paid on departure), golden handshakes (paid on arrival) and greenmail (merely paid).

God save the shareholder indeed (that being the title of

one of the following chapters) when executives can write themselves contracts that shower them with wealth should anyone unwanted (or even wanted) acquire the company: devices so deplorable that even the Reagan Administration rightly (but to no avail) attempted action against them. These golden parachutes had no justification of any kind, save in the minds and pockets of those who devised them.

Greenmail, on the other hand, is not a situation of the executive's own choosing. The villains of these pieces are the predators – the corporate raiders who, using the easy availability of bank money for merger operations, launch or even threaten a feasible bid for some constipated giant (like Gulf Oil, BAT or ICI) and place the victim's managers in a terrible fix.

Either, one, they let the whole corporation pass (with themselves aboard) into the captivity of someone they dislike and perhaps despise: or, two, they find a white knight to buy the company instead, as Gulf found Socal, in which case their independence still goes: or, three, they massively rearm the corporation, skunk-like, to repel attackers; or four, they buy back the predator's stock at a premium. The predator cleans up a lot of loot for a little trouble. But that money must come from somewhere: and that place, again, is often the stockholder's pocket.

As some of the afflicted have begun to argue – long, loud and legally – if the board of, say, Walt Disney was prepared to pay Saul Steinberg of Reliance a fat premium on his stock to get rid of him, why shouldn't other holders get the same price? The answer, of course, is usually that the stock isn't worth it, and may be worth still less if, during the greenmail battle, the management has bought up companies (as Warner did Chris Craft) with the motivation of making the attacker's task more difficult.

These are only the more conspicuous ways in which history has, unfortunately, repeated itself. The point shouldn't need stressing that the excesses of the late 1960s were followed by, or led into, the period of American management's most abysmal post-war performance, as technology and market leadership, in industry after industry, passed to other companies, mostly Japanese ones – events that once nobody would have thought remotely conceivable.

Could it happen again? Management in America, demonstrating anew the great national talent for regeneration, bloomed again in the early 1990s, as the new entrepreneurs in Silicon Valley and elsewhere, in high technology and low, were joined by big corporation managers determined to right the wrongs of their predecessors. Even the laggards of Detroit, buoyed by booming demand and protected by a sinking dollar, began to match the Japanese for quality and productive efficiency.

There are many examples, large and small, of top-class, well-dressed management all over the West: of executives not afraid either to recognise reality or to act on its imperatives. It isn't, of course, that the truth of the direct approach to management, as recommended in these pages, and drawn from observed best practice over a quarter of a century, has suddenly been revealed to managers. The big corporations are reacting not so much to challenge as to threat – and the threat hasn't gone away.

That threat, the fact that American and European companies can no longer rely on the vast riches of safe home markets to maintain their world market share, is the biggest single reason for supposing that it won't happen again: that the excesses of the Great Greed of the mid-1980s (always more conspicuous in the Anglo-Saxon world) aren't a preliminary to another lethal bout of managerial complacency and industrial under-performance.

The folderols and hot flushes of greed, too, have little to do with the lives and concerns of the younger managers who are going to carry the ball for Western management, whether their seniors like it or not. The sheer volume of new technology, the shortening time between innovation and imitation, the speed of change in the market and the workplace – all these demand by their nature that responsibility be pushed down the company into the hands of those who most need to exercise it.

These coming generations of management are the people who have shown most impatience with the dominant traditions of the big corporation. Maybe their impact on managerial life will, one day, turn this account of the follies and foibles of management into an historical document, like a record of the Great Plague. Maybe not, though – for management is an entirely human activity, and its failings are human ones. Look at the overall statistics, in fact, and you see clear evidence that the all-too-human managers running big business are not emulating the thrusters mentioned above.

The naked manager pays lip-service to fashionable ideas – like the need for higher investment in modern plant and innovation. But what's actually done is a very different matter: American management has been spending billions upon billions in completely sterile operations which, just like those cons of the conglomerate era, have the sole purpose of elevating, not true performance, but untrue earnings per share.

For a main instance, tens of billions went, totally without economic justification, on buying back corporations' own stock. That outweighed tenfold the amount, still vastly too large for comfort, lavished on LBOs and roughly equalled the gigantic sums disbursed for other mergers and acquisitions. Both the M & A expenditure and the stock buybacks were many, many times the money which the venture capitalists (supposedly the stars and leaders of the new American economy) invested in start-ups.

Worse still, spending on research and development, the fount of innovation, has lagged in the West. Spending on innovation, as every manager must surely know by now, has to be backed up by capital investment. Yet capital spending by manufacturers has remained low, too: it's the service industries which have raised their investment. And that's not good enough. In fact, as British manufacturers have found, it's deadly dangerous: so dangerous that in 1994 their output was much the same as two decades before.

In an era of unparalleled competitive cut and thrust, those who don't thrust stand a strong chance of being cut to pieces. That's why thrusters and non-thrusters alike need to ponder the myths of management and its realities more than ever before. It isn't a question of may the best men and women win. They will.

BOOK I:
POWER GAMES

Introduction:
The Management Revolution

Read any book about management, listen to any management guru, and you will be made aware that a revolution is under way in management theory – and, as always, theory reflects real changes in practice. As always, true, the action lags far behind the language. But the new emphasis on words like 'innovation', 'vision', 'empowerment', 'teamwork', 'customers', 'quality', 'service' and 'focus' is a reaction to the real forces embodied in another much-used, much-stressed word: change.

The management of change has become the dominant theme of the century's final decade. Of course, change has always been endemic: the history of any business is one of constant flux in customers, employees, competition, suppliers, products, processes, markets, technologies, and many other crucial factors – for example, business cycles and government policies. The difference today, however, is that the nature of management itself is being altered radically by the pace and force of change.

You can try to manage in the same way, but you won't succeed – not when customers are becoming more demanding: when satisfying their needs hinges on involving, integrating and satisfying everybody who works in the business;

when beating the competition means widening your vision outside the company to embrace the whole business system; when lags in products or processes can be fatal within months in markets of great volatility; and when the only safe position in technology is the leading edge.

One technology is universal and especially influential: computery in the broadest sense. The majority of companies are still operating without the benefits of the networked PC. By the turn of the century that will be a minority. By then most managers will be used to working in self-managed, project-based teams linked by the network. It won't matter where they are located geographically. Wherever they are, they will have instant access to every colleague and all needed information. This isn't futuristic, either. Several companies operate in this mode in the here and now.

Information isn't creating the managerial revolution: but information technology (IT) is powerfully enabling and enhancing trends which began independently. Flattening hierarchies, empowering workers and getting close to customers with better standards of quality and service have been enforced responses to the pressures of competitive change. You can't afford layers of management and long chains of command when speed to market and in the market-place are vital; you can't get to the highest levels of quality and service without the active and enthusiastic cooperation of everybody who works in or for the business.

This degree of change plainly has a powerful impact on the careers of individual managers. Getting familiar with the PC is the least of the changes. Another is becoming one of many 'reports', instead of a few, but that's less important than it sounds: the normal line relationship matters much less when managers spend much of their time in changing multi-disciplinary, inter-departmental teams which work horizontally, not vertically. Job titles, too, mean much less than work content: there's one high-flying manager in an American company who rejoices in the title, 'Manager in charge of getting things done'.

The shock of the new, not surprisingly, is most apparent in those companies whose products are spearheading the IT revolution. If, like Intel, you're producing a whole new family of microprocessors, each vastly more powerful and speedy than its predecessor, every two years, there must be a premium on creativity and energy. As an Intel manager told *Fortune,* 'Even as a manager you have to add value ... You just can't say, "Well, I am a manager so I will just manage and coordinate these people." People don't require that kind of management any more.'

The advice from another IT high-flier, Sun Microsystems, is that corporate executives must assume responsibility for their own careers. That means thinking of themselves as a business, and, like any business, determining their area of expertise and their target market. They must offer their 'customer' a 'value proposition' and deliver high quality to achieve the customer's satisfaction. Thoroughgoing professionals, they maintain mastery of their trade by constant updating. They develop new products and services for their customers, and they're willing to shift from business to business.

Whatever happened to the organisation man? As described above, the new managerial career sounds much closer to consultancy or interim management than to the historic climb up the hierarchy. But if there's little or no hierarchy, there can't be that many climbers. Flat organisations imply many flat or lateral moves from assignment to assignment. The manager's rising rewards, prospects, and authority depend on personal, portable skills and their successful use for specific purposes. Permanent and temporary employment really are fusing.

What brings them together is the pressure of change. If the environment and the competition are altering, companies which don't shift their strategies and tactics are still changing, whether they like it or not. Their *relative* positions are altering in ways that are being controlled by others. Winning strategies demand taking control, using creativity and innovation to create differentiation. Without innovation, strategy means either staying with existing policies or being a me-too: neither is the way to win in today's environment.

Differentiation has become crucial because of the success

of the catch-up programmes of the past decade. As a manager at Robert Bosch says, 'Quality is getting more and more equal all over the world, products are getting more and more equal, the procedures by which they are made are more and more equal, even the machinery on which they are produced is more and more identical.' In these conditions, only creativity can provide a competitive edge – and that's where the Japanese are now trying to shift their emphasis.

Is a high-creativity, innovation-led organisation different in kind? If the comparison is with the traditional pyramid, topped by an all-powerful chief executive, the answer is uncompromising. The creative company inverts the pyramid and enlarges it to cover the entire business system. The customers form the apex, and the boss is at the bottom to signify that he and senior management as a whole act as supports. Rather than 'empowering' the other layers, they act as enablers – a task which is more demanding than the obsolescent culture of order-and-obey.

Since creativity is no respecter of rank, relationships within highly innovative firms are fluid and based on the authority of expertise. Bureaucracy favours rigid structures and the authority of position; so the creative business keeps central staff (and overheads) to a minimum by the highest effective degree of contracting-out. This matches the increasing division of work with outside contractors in the supply chain: some IT 'manufacturers' make virtually nothing themselves.

'Virtual' (meaning the ability to respond instantaneously to satisfy specific customer demand) is becoming a key word in the new order of management. The high-creativity, increasingly virtual company is the template for all organisations that want to achieve ends that are highly pragmatic. The essence of the management revolution is to achieve such practical breakthroughs, and there's general agreement among the gurus, and among the managers who both feed the gurus and feed from them, on what must be done.

But the manager is still naked. There's a kind of managerial schizophrenia, with one state of mind recognising what's just been described, and the other mandating the self-defeating actions described in these pages. All managers say they want to work with people at all levels who are self-motivated, team-working achievers in an innovative environment that isn't averse to risk, embraces change and is action-oriented. That's what managers *say*. Most even know what must be done to achieve this outcome. But they don't actually do it. And that's why they still don't have enough clothes.

1
Why Successes Flop

The naked emperor in Hans Christian Andersen's story was magnificently dressed, not only in the public's mind, but in his own. The business manager, ruler of economic empires richer than many nations, has gone one better. The public believes in him: he believes in himself; but his clothing is not simply that of personal prestige and power (though both can be great); the manager is wrapped in a rich and seamless garment, which, going by the name of management, has become a pervasive religion of our time. But management, like the emperor's clothes, does not exist; the prime myth of management is that it does.

Management's non-existence explains why there are so many confused and conflicting attempts to define a pastime that all but monopolises the waking hours of earnest men, many of them able, creative, and industrious; many of them none of these things. Any definition of management must be right, because almost any definition must fit something so amorphous and shifting. 'Achieving results through other people' is one of the more popular definitions. It applies to the president of General Motors, but it also fits the madam of a brothel. And she is an executive facing real problems of personnel selection, marketing, and accountancy – not to mention her tax and legal arrangements.

The president of GM may not fancy the idea that a madam is in the same business, but she is – the business of business. All executives are in this racket, organising something or somebody in such a way that somebody else, somehow or other, will pay for it. The job of a big business executive is basically the same as that of a small shopkeeper: turning a (more or less) honest penny. And executives forget this (as they often do) at their peril.

Efficient businesses and brilliant executives are those who turn the most pennies, make the most money. The public never bothers about the methods. It accepts the results as evidence of their excellence. And this seems perfectly right and proper. So the good executives are the effective ones, and the effective executives are the good ones – or are they?

Effectiveness means more than goodness, but not much more. This little difficulty explains how a professor of management could write: 'Effectiveness is best seen as something an executive produces from a situation by managing it appropriately.' Substitute 'effectively' for the last word in that mish-mash, and you have a sentence that means exactly the same, i.e. nothing. There is no absolute criterion of managerial achievement. A manager is good and a company efficient only because others consider the results of their work good: their so-called goodness endures only as long as this good opinion holds.

Ivar Kreuger, the European match king, and Samuel Insull, the American utilities magnate, are early figures in a line that stretches to the crack of corporate doom. Leader after leader, honest and less honest, has been turned into a hero-figure, sometimes even without benefit of assiduous publicity. Behind the great collapses of companies and reputations – Maxwell Communications, Drexel Burnham Lambert, Bond Corporation, etc, etc – are collapsed heroes, feet-of-clay names which, if not yet forgotten, will be.

Among fallen-idol companies, some, like Litton, ITT or Rolls-Royce, would be too conspicuous to forget even if they hadn't survived; others slid so far from grace that nobody remembers either their names or the exact astronomical height of their former price/earnings ratios. In management, wonders nearly always cease. One day, events will surely expose any executive, in all his nakedness, for what he is: a fallible human being trying, with the help of others, who are equally fallible, to cope with circumstances that are constantly changing.

In the kingdom of the uncertain, the one-eyed manager makes mistakes. And that is why corporate goodness, even measured on the standard scales, is infrequent. Any study of leading companies will show that few can claim to be good – if you define goodness as doubling profits in real terms in a decade, maintaining return on stockholders' equity over the ten years, and having only one off-year. In any ten years, you won't need three hands to count the good, thus defined.

The average performance of big companies is just that – average. In the United States, half of the 500 largest companies had annual earnings per share growth of less than 7% in the period from 1973–83; and any company that couldn't double its earnings in a grossly inflationary era, in which all manner of juggles for the painless boosting of earnings per share were still available, has no claims to any managerial skills, even low cunning.

What about the next decade? Was there any sign that the Reagan years had inspired management to new heights of achievement? Alas, over this ten-year period 70% of the *Fortune* 500 failed the same none too exacting test. If you take total return to investors, which is dominated by capital gains, 272 of these large companies had at least doubled their shareholders' money over the decade. All that proved, however, was that 1993 ended with the stock market on a high, for reasons of its own.

Executives are not always to blame for mediocrity. Running large corporations, or middling, or small, is never easy: to run them excellently is always tough, and is sometimes impossible. This explains the management that is excellent in everything except its results – as in aluminium. You won't find a nicer, harder-working, keener, better-educated, cleverer, better-developed bunch of managers anywhere than in companies such as Alcoa and Alcan (heaven knows why, since aluminium is the world's second most boring industry, after cement).

Yet the result of all their effort and massed brainpower is an insignificant return on capital and profitless growth. Alcoa, the fifty-fourth largest industrial company in the US, earned 0.1% on both sales and its stockholders' equity in 1993. The industry also has a terrible proneness to accident. Alcan, possibly the most expert of the groups erecting aluminium smelters in Britain, naturally had the project that went most grievously awry; and the whole industry has an uncontrollable urge to plunge into excess capacity.

A former boss of Alcoa once made the immortal remark, 'There is no over-capacity, only under-selling' – another of those management sayings that read the same backwards or forwards. Executives are bad judges of their own actions, their own talents, their own stock prices. Every member of the board thinks his company's shares are too cheap, although few are foolish enough to buy them (they don't mind having them free). Whenever a company boasts of its managerial excellence, sell the shares; and if you own the firm, regard the boss with deepest suspicion.

Bids bring out the worst in executives. They can't judge their own ability fairly, which is understandable. But they can also be awful judges of other managers. When you hear a chief executive say, 'You should not forget that in buying a company we are buying management as a primary asset' (to quote one merger fanatic), run for the hills. Management does not exist, and here's this colossus paying good money for the invisible and evanescent.

You can't buy management, but you can very easily buy trouble. Better executives can, and often do, walk out; and sometimes, after the reality emerges from the image, the worse ones have to be fired. An American group bought a red-hot British growth company for a tycoon's ransom and discovered subsequently that '(a) it does not have good reporting and control data, (b) the production output per person employed is very poor, (c) it has too many people for the job they are doing, (d) it has never really set good targets, and (e) it is much too diversified'.

Otherwise, the buy was in pretty good shape. The incident was echoed when Ford Motor bought Jaguar Cars for a pretty penny, only for the American-appointed managing director to discover that he controlled the worst car factory he'd ever seen, with the exception of a Russian plant at Gorky. Yet Jaguar had been one of the cynosures of Mrs Thatcher's alleged economic renaissance, an exemplar of the meaning of fitness and leanness.

The optical illusion of goodness arises from the one-idea phenomenon. Sigmund Freud called *The Interpretation of Dreams* his greatest work, noting that inspirations of this order only came to a man once in his lifetime. Companies and chief executives are subject to the same law. A company such as Apple has a large notion about small computers and a couple of brilliant men who can make it work. In the process, the company's worth – and their fortunes with it – can swell in half a dozen years from peanuts to ten figures.

All this proved, not that the Apple crew are super-managers, but merely that their one super-idea was good, wonderfully good. The managers will look good as long as the big idea does; but so will all their other ideas, including the foolish ones, until – as happened to Apple when the personal-computer market was invaded in overwhelming force by IBM – the profits are poleaxed and new men must be imported to remake the management and the success.

Scepticism in the face of success is an impudent posture. But corporate history must foster the sceptical approach. The eye-opener lies in the way that respectable, established, conservative corporations and their no less clean and decent executives start off in one direction and end up facing the other way, with equal ardour for both postures. Sad examples here are diversifying managements like BAT's, which once threw fortunes into the laps of other people to add new sectors to their businesses; and then, under pressure from predators, discovered the virtues of the concentration they had sought to flee.

In corporation land, you learn rapidly that there are some villains, but no heroes. I once had to write the profile of an oilman reputed to be the hero-genius behind one of the world's greatest companies. Research showed that, after an incomparable early career battling against the arch enemy, he had long since sat on the sidelines. In despair, I asked the real boss to say what the hero did. 'Well,' he said, after deep thought, 'he has the office next to mine.' The profile, inevitably, perpetuated the legend.

Nobody would have believed the reality – any more than most people would believe that Herbert Hoover Jr., famed (falsely) for internationalising an introverted Midwest business, was once so claustrophobic that he held conferences in an open bus. Cured by his shrink, he then became so agoraphobic that he could work only in a windowless room. Neither strategy helped the Hoover company, which descended from leadership in Europe to the ignominy of an accident-prone, also-ran conglomerate subsidiary.

Men like Hoover, or the Cunard chairman who never took a ship to America, are the human factors, the real stuff of management – eccentric to the point of lunacy in a few cases, and generally odd enough in multitudinous smaller ways. Time and again, what happens in corporations cannot be explained by economics. It can only be understood by realising that, naturally enough, men express in their work the same motive forces that drive them in their ordinary lives.

Management is an arena for human behaviour at its most naked – under stress, but freed from many restraints of civilisation. A man can yell and scream at a subordinate in a way that would not be tolerated even by a wife. You can force a man to lose all his assets, though you wouldn't trespass on his lawn. You can tell lies, but if the lies are good enough, they will be applauded as universal truth. You can behave with total inhumanity – and *Fortune* magazine may well applaud you as one of 'America's toughest bosses'.

This is the background against which one Harry Figgie can be seen as a real management hero of our times. Figgie, a manager of brilliant reputation, had won high academic respect and an avid stock-market following for his 'nucleus theory of growth', which he applied to Automatic Sprinkler. The nucleus theory proved to be an empty sham. The reality was that in rapid succession Figgie bought a fire-hose nozzle company whose profits promptly fell from $939,000 to $76,636; a vacuum-cleaner firm whose sales methods were outlawed just before acquisition; and a metal-bending defence contractor that managed to lose $8 million on a $6.3 million Pentagon contract.

There are no theories of growth, nuclear or non-nuclear. There are only actions – intelligent, not so bright, and stupid. And the only thread binding the intelligent actions is that they work, as Figgie himself tried to show after these dismal events. His company has changed its name since those days, first to ATO, and then to Figgie International Holdings, and at one stage achieved fair non-nuclear success. But it's still no great shakes; in 1993 it managed to lose $180 million on $769 million of sales.

The trouble is that in management, nothing succeeds like success – if you define the latter as winning a high, wide and handsome management reputation. But pride goeth before a flop, as *Business Week* discovered, retreading the ground covered by *In Search of Excellence* only a few years after publication. It found that 'at least 14 of the 43 "excellent" companies' highlighted in that booming bestseller 'have lost their lustre'. Since then the number of the fallen has swollen – led by the biggest and brightest of the *Excellence* champions, IBM.

Worse still, several of the alleged champs shouldn't have been in the book at all; notably Atari, a firm so appallingly mismanaged that it infringed all eight of the book's 'attri-butes', or rules of management, and very nearly bust its miserable owners, Warner, in the process. But what does all this prove? First, that there are no universal rules of success: thus, Hewlett-Packard, which, as the magazine noted 'stum-bled badly' in the critical microcomputer and super-mini-computer markets, obeyed all eight commandments.

Second, past success by no means equates with either future triumph or excellent management – and neither does past failure. The very same Hewlett-Packard was widely and properly acclaimed in the 1990s for its ability to grow its sales at an astonishing rate of $4 billion a year; that growth alone is equivalent to the total sales of a large and successful competitor like Sun Microsystems. In the right company, as with the right athlete, 'stumbling' can simply be an incident on the way to the winning tape.

So what else is new? Speaking (or writing) personally, I've stressed both the above self-evident truths of success *ad infinitum* (if not *ad nauseam*) for three decades. But nothing will ever stop managers, especially at times of great uncertainty – to which modern man is condemned – from seeking, and over-valuing, examples of apparent certainty. All the same, the *Business Week* analysis cited above is valuable, maybe more so than the original *Excellence* study.

For instance, eight of the Fourteen Flops didn't stay close to the customer – companies like Avon, Disney, Revlon, Tupperware and Levi-Strauss, which are practically synonymous with consumer satisfaction. Take the last-named. So long as the world-wide jeans market was booming, Levi's management could afford, paradoxically, to ignore it. 'For so long we were (always) sold out. Our time was prioritised on getting more product, new factories, more raw materials. We were internationally oriented.'

As for the customers, 'we let the relationship with our retailers fall into a sad state of disrepair, the company completely missed the powerful (and profitable) trend towards fashion jeans'. Direct, in-the-home sellers Avon and Tupperware similarly failed to spot or react to the obvious consequences of more women going out to work. Disney went on flogging clean and decent – and unimaginative – entertainment into an increasingly less wholesome and more excitable market-place.

Yet turn the clock back a decade and what proved to be crucial defects were being hailed as heroic virtues. The very different policies which Levis and Disney adopted to become shining stars of the 1980s have been cited in their turn as wonder-working formulae. Theories or methods of management can work wonders in individual companies at individual times – but only because they suit the way in which individual managers like to act in individual markets. The methods that Robert Townsend, of *Up the Organisation*, used to run Avis were a marvellous way for Robert Townsend to run Avis. But they might paralyse a different company with different men and women – even Hertz.

Yet executives, beset by corporate ailments, reach for a theory formed in a different context as if it were a broad-spectrum antibiotic, a wonder drug. They see their businesses as suffering patients requiring medical treatment: though there is seldom anything wrong with a company that better, or better-directed, executives won't cure. Executives, however, will undergo almost any treatment rather than amputation of themselves.

But self-amputation is far more effective for the stockholders. I know of two companies, one large, one gargantuan, which found themselves with cuckoos in the nest – two tough, aggressive, ruthless entrepreneurs whose drive, hunger for profits, and magical rapport with figures couldn't live with the passive, profitless vagueness on the existing board. Laying their own heads on the block, the older directors voluntarily handed the axe to the new men. In the next few years, both companies grew by such prodigious bounds that some of the superannuated oldies became very wealthy – and they deserved every penny. They followed the golden rule: if you can't do something yourself, find somebody who can, and then let them do it in their own sweet way.

In contrast, many cures that less self-effacing boards purchase are subject to the same objection as psycho-analysis: they are expensive, they take a lot of time, the patient does all the work, and there's no way of telling that he wouldn't have got better, anyway, with the mere passage of the years. If it takes two years (to take one example from the past) to draw up a new shop-floor management structure in a car company, the problem won't be the same at the end as it was at the beginning. That's why, in the discontinuous present, speed has become of the essence. You not only have to fix it today, you must fix it fast.

Any improvement, however, can always be looked at two ways. You can stroke yourself on the back (as most executives do) for your brilliant advance, or you can kick yourself for the imbecility that made improvement necessary. If executives don't like one view through the telescope, they can turn it round and look through the other end – precisely because management is not a scientific and objective activity, but a subjective historical process, full of ifs and buts.

Thus Roy Ash, when president of Litton, forced to explain how the management wasn't to blame for errors that wiped out billions in stock-market value, had no trouble at all: 'Operationally, we could have made sure of never facing the problem by never undertaking the venture.' Nothing ventured, nothing lost, in fact. That's like the guilty party in a mid-air collision offering as excuse that, if he had never learned to fly, the accident would never have happened.

The literature and history of companies like Litton or ITT bear careful reading by anybody who believes that the emperor-manager is wearing clothes. In this history, although there are no heroes, there are Goodies and Baddies. The Baddies range from leading actors – the men who brought giant companies like IBM, General Motors, American Express, and Eastman Kodak nearly to their knees – to a strong supporting cast of lesser lights, whose badness is of the same ilk: the damage done by arrogant managers to innocent stockholders.

In addition to the Baddies, the Heavies – such as Du Pont, Procter & Gamble, ICI, Ford, Exxon, Philips, Volkswagen and all too many others – have at all times been conspicuous under-performers: companies whose enormous potential for goodness was constantly frustrated by their own bad habits. In extremis, some of the Heavies have proved in recent years, with Chrysler leading the bunch, that the under-performance was indeed culpable – they changed their awful habits, and that enormous potential came bursting through into the bottom line.

Writing back in 1985, I noted that there were Goodies, too, in my books: 'men (and there are many of them) who (unless and until I am proven wrong) can be trusted with the stockholders' money to the last line on the balance sheet'. The evidence of the intervening years shows that this trust will be misplaced as often as it is justified. Today's Goodie quickly becomes tomorrow's Heavy: and tomorrow's Heavy may be the day after's Baddie – think only of IBM.

Think before you act; the money isn't yours – the First Truth of Management – is a home-truth. But management is a far more homely business than its would-be scientists suggest, more closely allied to cookery than any other human activity. Like cooking, it rests on a degree of organisation and on adequate resources. But just as no two chefs run their kitchens the same way, so no two managements are the same, even if they all went to the same business (or cookery) school. You can teach the rudiments of cooking, as of management, but you cannot make a great cook or a great manager by teaching.

In both activities, you ignore fundamentals at grave risk – but sometimes succeed. In both, science can be extremely useful, but is no substitute for the art itself. In both, inspired amateurs can outdo professionals. In both, perfection is rarely achieved, and failure is more common than the customers realise. In both, practitioners don't need recipes that detail timing down to the last second, ingredients to the last fraction of an ounce, and procedures down to the last flick of the wrist; they need reliable maxims, instructive anecdotes, and no dogmatism. This is a cookbook for managers who want to get their clothes back.

2
The Shareholder Finagle

To hear them tell it, big company directors on both sides of the Atlantic are quite dedicated to the shareholder. Strangely, devotion turns to irritation, almost a sense of betrayal, if the love object asks offensive questions about the company's performance at the annual general meeting. The shareholder whom the directors love is better than a good Victorian child or a chairman's yes-man, neither seen nor heard: one who merely collects his dividend (if any) and dutifully returns his proxy form if, by some mischance, one of the directors' projects needs a democratic rubber-stamp.

Most top executives are sincere men. When they say they hold the shareholder dear, they really and truly mean it – because they truly can't imagine any conflict between the shareholders' interests, as seen by the directors, and the directors' own desires. What's good for the board of General Motors is good for the shareholders, and *vice versa*, more or less sums up the philosophy. Suppose that the shareholders would be better off with a whole new management: the existing managers won't share the horrible idea, and they won't protect shareholders by lopping off their own heads.

The shareholder is not expected to criticise. It's enough to know that managements, in deciding what they want, will have general objectives that directly promote the share-holders' everlasting comfort – or will they? Rich targets for growth in earnings per share were once standard corporate objectives. (That was before a series of disasters, starting with the late-1960s recession and proceeding, through oil-price shocks, hyper-inflation and the great deflation of the late 1970s, to the competitive wars of the 1980s gave business hell – and brought it down to earth.)

In happier days the hotter US giants dreamed of a 15% annual compound increase in earnings per share. The number was plucked out of the air: 10% looked too small, and 20% (doubling every three and a half years) absurdly large for a swollen corporation. A steady 15% clip, doubling monotonously every five years, would surely guarantee a high price/earnings ratio for all eternity.

But this corporate target has a secret advantage for the men in charge of companies. Earnings per share are engineered by dividing profits attributable to ordinary share-holders (that is, after tax and minority interest) by the number of shares in issue – which is a beautifully elastic sum on both sides. For instance, if Wonder Company A buys Wonder Company B with shares, kindly valuing B at the same noble price/earnings ratio as its own, the earnings per share of A (now A plus B) stay exactly the same. But if A uses money borrowed at fixed interest, any margin between B's profits and the interest paid comes through as a straight, juicy increment in earnings per share.

As the conglomerates of the 1960s were first to note, many tricks can be worked around this basic dodge – simply buy earnings without diluting the equity, and by a stroke of the computer, management seems to achieve the results of years of honest toil. This cult of earnings per share has never been worshipped quite so widely in Britain as in the US, where management has elaborated much the same concept into something, still widely used, called 'return on invested capital' or 'stockholders' equity'.

The notion behind invested capital is that only the money that belongs to the stockholder counts. So you conveniently forget about loans, however overpowering, and take the often much tinier sum of stockholders' capital. This in turn relates to balance sheet values that have been shrunk by so-called depreciation over the years. To this much skinnier residue, you apply the net-profit figure – and the result is a much zestier index of performance than could be got in any other way. For example, General Motors earned a massive 44.1% on stockholders' equity in 1993 (the ninth largest ratio in the *Fortune* 500). As a percentage of assets, the figure shrank to a miserable 1.3%.

At one of America's most praised corporations, General Electric, the return on the shareholders' loot was a handsome enough 16.7%. The return on assets figure? Only 1.7%. At Philip Morris, the tobacco-led giant, an awesome equity return of 26.6% shrinks to a mere 6% on assets. At Coca-Cola, which takes its earnings on capital very seriously indeed, the equity return was no less than 47.5% – but that on assets, while high at 18.1%, was less than a third of the exalted equity figure.

Few managements consciously fix their figures in the most flattering light – but that's what happens when they define their objectives by shareholders' finances alone. It's dangerous. It sustains the myth that high debt is good for the company, and it also misrepresents the motivation of the board. Though the directors chatter about the shareholder as the owner of the company's assets, they don't really see the investor as a proprietor – and still less as a member of the company. The members, in the director's inner mind, are those sitting on the payroll, above all the upper management itself.

The shareholders are remote licensors. They get a cut of any profits, and in return they license the managers to do as they please with the assets. More, they let managers do what they like (apart from outright theft) with the value of the shares. If the management longs to dilute those famous earnings per share by some over-priced acquisition, the shareholder can seldom kill the deal. And if the management wants to change the entire business of the company, the shareholder is expected to sit tight and watch, clapping loudly.

The tobacco companies, faced with evidence that they were merchants of death, could have taken their profits, remitted the maximum loot to the stockholders for as long as the going was good, and then folded into graceful liquidation. No law ordained that Imperial Group (*née* Tobacco) or R.J. Reynolds had to be preserved in perpetuity. Yet the company's executive officers (who would otherwise have liquidated themselves out of good jobs) proceeded to act as if in slavish obedience to such a law.

At all costs, the corporate entity must be perpetuated. So the shareholders, like it or not, were swiftly switched from owning a lucrative cigarette manufacturer, with minor diversified interests, to possessing heavily diversified companies with interests in tobacco. Nor did the tobacco giants, after their heavy plunge into strange waters (and liquors), achieve any miracles of growth: neither Philip Morris nor American Brands could manage much above 3% annual growth in earnings per share in the decade to 1993.

As for Reynolds, that's an even more cautionary tale. Though it heroically reduced the cigarette to under half its sales, the effort was full of appallingly expensive mistakes (like a $1.6 billion shipping line eventually given away to shareholders) and costly pain – thus, at its canner, Del Monte (purchased at a price of $618 million), Reynolds had to close twelve businesses and thirty-eight plants. Its food and beverage buys included the equally troubled Kentucky Fried Chicken (where just about everything that could go wrong had done so).

The dénouement came when the Reynolds management, by then presiding over something called R.J.R. Nabisco, decided to play the predatory role themselves, launching the biggest buyout bid in history – only to have their ace famously trumped by Kohlberg Kravis and Roberts. To the victors, not the spoils, but the pains: the buy lost a quarter of its market value in 1993, despite massive restructuring and selling-off (including the whole of the afore-mentioned Del Monte).

At Imperial Tobacco, a decade of massive buying also meant radical surgery, plus poor growth that left sales only doubled in those ten years – and left Imps desperately vulnerable to external predators. Bought on the cheap by Hanson Trust, the conglomerate was promptly dismembered.

Like it or not, those shareholders who stuck with the tobacco companies had to go along with the board's creation, through years of travail, of what managements fondly saw as consumer-products colossi. The chief beneficiaries were the non-tobacco men hauled in to handle the transformation from the great corporate seminaries of branded goods. The big switch from cigarette men who wrongly thought themselves whizzes at consumer marketing to marketing men who reckoned they could also sell cigarettes was marvellous for the managers concerned. (It was especially so for F. Ross Johnson, the chief executive officer, whose punishment for the torment of R.J.R. Nabisco was a $50 million pay-off). But along the way the shareholders were forced by corporate managers to pay prices for independent provision merchants that made the latter's shareholders drool.

Management's liberties are guaranteed by the weakness, apathy, and ignorance of shareholders, by the shareholders' lack of time to harass bad management, and by the stockholders' perpetual freedom, if disenchanted, to sell out. However, not all shareholders are weak, apathetic, and ignorant; at least, they shouldn't be. The directors' real masters are institutions – investment concerns and foundations that control the dominating chunks of the equity; the banks that hand over short- and medium-term finance; the investment banks and merchant banks that are pipelines to the long-suffering investing public.

These solid institutional citizens are not always shareholders – the banks in Britain and the US do not, as in Europe or Japan, own industry. But in several respects, the banks' interests are no different from the shareholders', individual or institutional: since they want their booty back, the banks, like the shareholders, need to ensure that inefficient management doesn't drain or dribble the money away.

Yet the institutions, on both sides of the Atlantic, have generally been almost as supine as the little old lady in Toledo, Ohio, or Melton Mowbray, Leicestershire. When they do zero in on a lagging management, the move is ponderous and far too late. That's been true in every generation. Take Lockheed as an example from the 1970s (though you could just as well take Chrysler, Massey-Ferguson, Burmah Oil or British Leyland – and there are plenty of others).

In 1975 Robert Abboud, chairman of the First National Bank of Chicago, found himself alone in demanding that Daniel Haughton, the aircraft manufacturer's chairman, be fired for the incompetence that had landed Lockheed with the Tristar jetliner and also, at that point, with a desperate need of $595 million just to stay alive. Bankers Trust led the other banks in total opposition to Abboud; he only won, eventually, not because of the proven failure of the Haughton management, but because of its proven propensity to bribe foreign potentates – including the Prime Minister of Japan and Prince Bernhard of the Netherlands.

Move on to the 1980s, and who were the most faithful friends and latest critics of the corporate destroyers who weren't just incompetent, but crooked? Behind Robert Maxwell and his awful ilk stood the respectable banks and the dead straight institutions. True, some of the latter made a splash in the 1990s by putting pressure on boards to abandon failed CEOs at great companies like IBM, General Motors and Eastman Kodak – but only after unconscionably long periods of self-evident error and severe shareholder damage.

Why did the dog take so long to bark? The executives who lead financial institutions are, if anything, more conservative, more deeply dyed in tradition, happier to rest on seniority and security, and more thoroughly inbred than industrial directors. They have a vested interest in stability at the top, especially a top manned by personal friends or men of higher rank in the arcane lists of business snobbery. Those who run mammoth banks and insurance companies don't like boats being rocked – especially their own (and banks were, of course, shipping water heavily in the early 1990s).

In any event, most financial men are not especially knowing about business and business management, in their own trade, or in other people's. Financial institutions are better at burying their million-pound mistakes in billion-dollar aggregates than at displaying commercial drive, managerial acumen and marketing enterprise. The expertise needed on Wall Street or in the City of London is not that of the industrial executive suite – and the financier's judgment of directors is therefore fallible.

That is why banks lend gigantic sums to managements of bewildering incompetence and proven dishonesty, and on propositions of worse than dubious worth – like the dud US loans to real-estate investment trusts, less-developed countries, and over-leveraged buy-outs. The unsureness of investment managers and their bosses about how to judge management in industry partly explains their profound reluctance to tackle non-performing boards – and of those there is never any shortage.

Even if you use their own soft criterion of growth in earnings per share, the top fifty US companies made a feeble showing from 1973 to 1983: in four cases, earnings per share fell over the decade; in seven further cases, they rose by less than 2% compounded annually; ten others grew by less than 10%; the magic 15% mark was hit only four times. The 250 UK largest were no more inspiring. After allowing for inflation, 206 showed declines; another thirty-four grew by less than 7%; and only forty-six managed 15%.

The 1980s showed no improvement. Among the fifty largest US companies with a ten-year record, a dozen had negative growth in earnings per share: four grew by less than 2% compounded annually: sixteen advanced by less than 10%: a mere nine had managed the 15% level which a corporate strategist might well claim as success. In 1993, a marvel for growth in profits, there were eleven US firms in the top fifty whose earnings per share were worse than in the previous year: and only seventeen which showed gains.

As for return to investors, in which the stock price is dominant, 40% of the 500 biggest US companies produced a negative figure in both 1993 and for the decade; over the longer period stockholders had not obtained a 7% annual return on their investment in half these cases. Yet few knives have leaped out; nothing has disturbed the slumber in the executive suites of companies such as the once-mighty Du Pont (with a *negative* 1983–93 change of 6.4% annually for its earnings per share).

Unless companies are on bankruptcy's brink (in which case the directors have other anxieties), dozing managements have little cause to fret about their mighty, weak shareholders. They only need watch out for a few uncommon enemies of their species. There's the corporate gadfly who seeks a fortune by harassing managements on behalf of aggrieved shareholders: and the corporate raider, whose pounce may be sincere (he really wants the company), or cynical (he only wants the greenmailing profits).

These two predators can overlap, as when a greenmailed board of directors (like Disney's in 1984) goes to such self-abasing lengths to escape one hunter, the raider, that the other scourge, the gadfly, gets handed a strong case for a stockholder suit. But such animals are by definition rare, even in the corporate jungle. Even though their numbers multiplied in the 1980s, the Great Crash of 1987 cleared out much of the undergrowth.

There's a third foe of supine managements – the rich and determined individual investor. Some of these, like T. Boone Pickens, whose group picked up a billion from the corpse of Gulf Oil, bow out with the alacrity of any greenmailer: but others insist on having their investment managed to success. Thus, coal tycoon George H. Love injected new management into Chrysler (he jacked it up high enough to plunge right back into disaster).

Thus, too, Chicago financier Colonel Henry Crown twice intervened to arrest General Dynamics' slide into bankruptcy. Thus, to descend from the great to the middling, and from the public to the private, Victor Kiam turned a million of his own money into $12 million of pre-tax profits from Remington, whose previous owners, Sperry Rand, couldn't make a dime from the razor company.

Note, however, that both General Dynamics and Chrysler had recurrent bouts of financial nausea. Maybe even effective intervention by rich shareholders has its limits; it often comes too late, when too much vitality and cash have already been sucked away by years of travail. The Kiam experience points the moral. It's when the rich shareholder also takes a stake in the management that you can more confidently expect miracles; when a Carlo de Benedetti puts in $12 million of his own cash as he takes managerial control of Olivetti, and turns his nest-egg into a veritable cornucopia – for a time, that is, and for the proprietor above all.

In such cases, the other shareholders are strictly along for the ride, as long as it lasts, which in Olivetti's case was until the boss bungled the microprocessor revolution. The execrated Robert Maxwell was briefly a hero of the City establishment after buying three-quarters of the moribund British Printing Corporation for £12 million – and in a scant eighteen months managing and masterminding the stake up to £200 million. It took several years before Maxwell staged his criminal spectacular and bared his reality: the managing proprietor too commonly acts on the principle that the gods help those who (literally) help themselves.

Can anybody else save the shareholder? Investors could save themselves by trying to avoid companies that on past performance can't outdo the returns from an American savings and loan company or a British building society. But most individual investment in shares goes via the insurance companies and investment companies, anyway, and the sheer weight of the money that they must invest presses them to buy into big companies, and with little discrimination.

Only the heavyweights have enough shares on the market for heavy buying, and only large-scale purchases are any use to a large fund. Big companies and big investors are locked into each other by nature, which is one good reason why the investment record of the great funds is generally so insipid; they are stuck with insipid investments.

The myth that men who run investment funds or manage companies can always do more with shareholders' money than the latter could for themselves still stands – despite its destruction by all manner of evidence. A theory of stock markets has, almost irrefutably, shown that stock prices follow a haphazard statistical pattern known to mathematicians as the 'random walk'. If so, all the beavering 'fundamental' analysis designed to prove that a company's share price must soar is beside the point. In reality, security analysts, however closely they nuzzle up to an industry, judge the favoured managements too kindly; being articulate men themselves, the analysts especially fall for executives who can actually talk.

It also follows that the expert is no more likely than the inexpert to pick a growth stock that grows. One year, top American investment professionals picked Viatron, an electronics outfit, and a company called National Student Marketing as the two hottest growth prospects of the year. Both slid down a slippery slope. In the 1980s such examples of slithering became too common to count, largely because of the high-tech phenomenon. Outsiders have no real means of judging the management (or for that matter the technology) in a fast-moving business like computers – and since many such companies have gone down with large quantities of supposedly expert venture capital clinging to the wrecks, it doesn't seem that insiders are necessarily any better placed.

One of the biggest start-ups greatly proves the point. Trilogy Systems raised a towering $230 million to finance an IBM-crunching number-cruncher and a monstrously powerful monster-chip. Its ambitions surfaced in 1980: in August 1984, in swift and disorderly succession, Trilogy, strapped for cash, abandoned both the giant computer and the gigantic chips. So much for the sharp insiders who financed, found and finagled Trilogy's quarter of a billion dollars precisely to pay for these two goodies.

The funniest tale in this genre is that of a data-processing company that had a rousing reception on Wall Street – until its sponsors saw the prospectus. Unlike other similar gee-whiz ventures, which were all losing money handsomely, this one was making profits. The sight of its price/earnings ratio, up over the 100 mark, so terrified the sponsors that they sold out of the stock; had it reported losses, they would happily have held on for some later deluge.

The fall-back argument is that all equity investment, taking the lean years with the fat, will wax rich. First, the money purchases productive assets that (however inept their management) become worth more year after year through the simple magic of inflation: second, the company can do massively what the individual can seldom do – get 'leverage' by borrowing at fixed interest, achieving double the financial horsepower from the same engine.

Both arguments rest on one unsafe assumption: that management will, year in, year out, boost earnings by a statistically significant amount. If, as in most companies, it doesn't, the market value of the shares, which is all that matters, may slump below the book value of the assets – let alone their supposed inflation-proof real value. And all that leverage which is mathematically bound to accelerate the profit decimates them when, as happens more often than not, the company steps firmly on a banana skin.

Maybe there is a haphazard statistical pattern, a 'random walk', in profits. Since in most human affairs there is only a fifty-fifty chance of being right, half the actions of any company are likely to be wrong. Certainly the records of many corporations (after extracting the impact of acquisitions) look more random than planned; and in such circumstances the highly geared company is a menace to one and all.

Surveys by *Fortune* in the US and *Management Today* in Britain showed conclusively long ago that the most profitable companies have the least debt and that the most indebted are the most likely to be unprofitable. *Fortune* found that the fifty highest-debt corporations among the 500 biggest companies in the US included fifteen in the lowest bunch for profitability and not one in the top fifty; the fifty lowest-debt companies included twenty-three, nearly half, in the top lot for profitability and not one in the bottom. In Britain *Management Today* noted that the twenty lowest-debt companies had an average profitability that was 70% higher than that for the twenty highest-debt firms.

Like many earth-shaking management finds, this one

enshrines childish logic. If a company generates great profits, it rarely needs to borrow; if it needs to panhandle heavily, the overwhelming odds (as with an individual) are that it is earning too little. In most cases, it never will earn enough, either – the borrowing becomes a permanent burden on the sore backs of management and unwitting or witting shareholders.

The combined impact of prolonged recession and mismanagement in the later 1980s demonstrated the hard truth about soft debt in two especially dramatic ways. First, management after management concentrated on 'degearing' – cutting back the debt to equity ratio – as fast as their financial situation would allow. Second, the worst-hit (and worst-run) companies piled up such monstrous debts that their all-too-numerous bankers couldn't afford to let the borrowers go bust and the loans go dead.

In the now-classic case of Chrysler, of course, the two phenomena were combined. Lee Iacocca skilfully used the corporation's $2 billion debt overhang to pressure the bankers and the government to give him the time and space needed to degear on a heroic scale. Financial institutions don't, however, pause to wonder why they lend most generously to managements that show themselves least capable of making the money grow.

Without its friendly neighbourhood bankers, for instance, Lockheed would have gone to the wailing wall long ago. Yet (as noted) the banks, on all external evidence, went on showing nothing but confidence in Lockheed's Daniel Haughton and his merry men as nine-figure sum after nine-figure sum was literally sunk into the company – as it was into many other mighty miscreants.

Lockheed's partner in calamity, Rolls-Royce, soaked the City of London for money time and again on the strength of a balance sheet that would have worried Mr Micawber. And yet the big-business executive, who finds it relatively easy to get around the allegedly sharp-eyed men with the big money, says that he is genuinely concerned about the little shareholder in the shires. He can safely leave the shareholders to look after themselves; nobody else will.

3
The American Daydream

Great ideas commonly turn false when they are most widely promulgated, applauded, and received. For a decade Europeans groaned under what J. J. Servan-Schreiber nicknamed *The American Challenge*. Super-efficient Americans were supposed to deploy the bottomless riches of magnificently organised corporations to trample, take over, and mesmerise European competition. But the thesis, promulgated in 1967, was untrue even then – and it got further from reality with every passing transatlantic flight.

In reality, American executives turned out to be no abler than Frenchmen, Germans, or even Englishmen – and notably less effective than the Japanese. US corporations, including the most highly praised, suffer from all the same inefficiencies as their competitors. American technology, in most fields, is not some magical, insuperable advantage, and (so much for Servan-Schreiber) many European firms – even in Britain – outgrew the Americans by a mighty margin in the decade after *Challenge* appeared. The beauty of the invader lay only in the eyes of the invaded.

For a start, the awesome figures of American invasion overstated the challenge. Take away oil and cars, and US investment dwindles severely; and almost all the original investment in these capital-hungry industries dates back well before the Second World War. Even in computers, the most typical, most publicised, and most glamorous post-war industry, American dominance was based not on the miracles of Pentagon-financed technology, but largely on IBM's pre-war lead in punch-card machines; the Watson family business had 80% to 90% of this market back in 1935, more than it ever managed in computers.

In the personal-computer era, European firms tried to meet the challenge, not just of IBM, but of newcomers like Apple, Compaq, Digital Equipment, Intel and Microsoft. Here, the Europeans lost out decisively. But in other industries in which transatlantic hostilities have begun since the peace – chemicals, say, or convenience foods – Europeans have often had little trouble defending themselves, and Americans even less difficulty in losing inglorious sums. Much of the superior quality of American management in Europe in fact consisted of this endearing ability to suffer losses that would have sent most Europeans to the poorhouse.

While admirable, in its way, the attribute is not on the curriculum of the Harvard Business School. But that seminary, and its like, were launching-pads for the most truly challenging American invasion. More pervasive, and more profitable, than the computers of IBM are the acolytes of American management technology. They came and still come from all sides – highly motivated professors of motivation, consultants commanding the world's highest fees, visiting lecturers of every posture, sellers of packaged management development aids – witch-doctors whose spells, if they can't cure all corporate ailments, will definitely provide hours of harmless, profitless diversion.

The arrival and acceptance of this flood seemed logical enough. When a powerful commission under Lord Franks, a former British ambassador to Washington, compared the defects of British management with American virtues, it saw one prime difference. The Americans had myriad business schools, Britain none. *Ergo*, build British business schools, native imitations of Harvard, and British management would improve. Nobody unkindly observed that the Germans, whose managers have also handily outstripped the British, had no business schools either; nor did the Japanese.

The Franks theory rested on two improbable or at least unprovable notions: that American business management actually was more efficient and that the business schools had been critical in creating this lead. The grains of truth are only that management, as a body of theoretical knowledge, is almost entirely an American creation, and that business management, as a professional racket, attracts far more highly educated US citizens than Britons or Frenchmen.

It is also true that American business, chasing the economies of scale in the richest market in creation, and in a society that is indulgent towards high profits, has spawned corporations of variable but often immense success and, for all practical and some highly impractical purposes, unlimited resources. Some of these resources have been invested in some brave, sometimes despairing, attempts to combat the disadvantages of scale by constructing new corporate systems. And these are truly built with a thoroughness and theoretical justification worthy of that great free-enterpriser, Karl Marx.

But a system, or a management theory, or a posse of business-school graduates, are only as good as their achievements. Even at the height of the *Challenge* mystique, there was a long string of American disasters in Europe – the Betty Crocker cakes, the Dial soap, the Gerber baby foods, the Frigidaire refrigerators, the Campbell's soups (those lost $6.1 million in a single year as the obstinate British refused to change their tastes), and so on, and so on. Forgetting these, and later failures like Ford of Europe's relapse into large losses, consider instead events back home in corporations that, by common consent, are among America's finest.

Nobody can wander through the thickets of management lore for long without bumping into General Electric and American Telephone & Telegraph. GE is virtually a free business school; its investment in management theory, organisation, and development is legendary. AT&T's fame spreads from the invention of the transistor in its Bell

Laboratories via experiments in human relations and job organisation to the courteous efficiency of the phone service. At least, that was the story until the New York telephone system had its coronary in 1969, and simply broke down.

Move on to 1984, and the communications colossus, with its arms, legs, fingers and toes all missing after the legal amputation of its domestic telephone network, rated the following abrasive comment from *Business Week*: 'Product shortages and customer defections have plagued the company's equipment-manufacturing arm, while its long-distance unit has lost business to rivals and service snafus.' Not surprisingly, the new, streamlined AT&T had missed its financial targets by several miles – earning only $1 billion in the first nine months of a year that was supposed to produce twice as much.

At GE, matters had improved since the 1960s, when its record would have shamed any company. Between 1963 and 1969, while its sales doubled, its profits budged scarcely an inch – and over the decade from 1960, GE's rise in earnings per share was a pitiful 4.8% annually. That this was bad management, rather than possession of bad business, was amply demonstrated by GE's sharp improvement under sharper managers from 1973 to 1983, when earnings per share rose by an average 10.74%. All the same, that was only 127th among the *Fortune* 500: not much of a score for so supposedly expert a body of executives.

Nor are these criticisms the gibes of an ill-informed outsider. At both giants, management itself fully accepted the indictment. Under Jack Welch and Bob Allen respectively, the companies were reviewed and revised from top-to-bottom in recognition that the previous systems had simply failed. When Welch took charge, he looked at GE's strengths and weaknesses and found only one of the former (the balance sheet) and a mass of the latter: including inadequate cash flow, slow productivity growth, sluggish decision-making, and excessively inward focus.

The malfunctions of these two giants are in no way extraordinary; running a business with GE's then workforce of 340,000 employees (the old unsplit AT&T had twice as many) is a crucifying task. Welch dealt with that problem in part by savagely reducing the numbers, which won him the nickname of 'Neutron Jack': like the neutron bomb, he killed off the people, but left the buildings standing. Since then both he and Allen at AT&T have been in the vanguard of seeking methods that exploit people's strengths – rather than simply exploit people.

The oddity, though, is that no gleaming theory that the two giants tried to implement in the failed past was soiled by their self-evident lack of success. The poor records had little to do with the damage inflicted on US growth by Nixonian economics and the oil sheikhs. Right through the Kennedy-Johnson boom, the performance of GE was inferior: its management of its computer business, stuck out on a limb in Arizona, was a nightmare of decentralised failure that only ended with a humiliating sell-out. AT&T in New York was brought low, not by a shortfall in demand, but by inability to cope with the expansion that it stimulated through its own homely and costly advertising.

As their more recent resurgence shows, neither GE nor AT&T lacked management talent at the time or lack it now. Very few American leviathans do. They all claim otherwise, but many consultants outside the US agree that the American corporation, unchecked, used to multiply executives like mice. Just as paperwork breeds paperwork (every memo demands at least one answer), so one executive bred more executives (every executive vice-president needing at least two vice-presidents reporting to him).

This overbreeding and interbreeding of executives, mostly assembled from the business schools, went into reverse in the 1980s, when 'downsizing' to cut costs became a mandatory fashion, and middle-management ranks contracted. But the previous ungoverned expansion was the root of the tendency that reached its apotheosis at the end of the 1960s and is still the dominant mode in 1994. That is the corporation decentralised on product lines, with management responsibility devolved to profit centres within profit centres, bound together by tight financial controls and meticulous forward planning, activated by regular reviews of plans and progress.

The system, imitated slavishly by one European corporation after another, seems a sensible answer to diversity and to the problems of maintaining individual responsibility and initiative inside the whole. With the rose-coloured spectacles off, the system can be seen as a monumental bureaucracy, with veins made of paper, subject to bloodclots at any point. To work at all, the system demands more layers of management, a great burgeoning of staff work, and heavy expenditure of line managers' time, simply to cover the control, planning, and review. Much of this managerial time is frittered away on meetings for 'coordination', 'consultation', and 'approval' – in other words, in committees.

Take AT&T's macabre New York fiasco, as detailed by the *Wall Street Journal*. Under pressure for good figures, the New York 'profit centre' pushed up earnings by 16% and 10% in successive years – and cut capital spending significantly in both of them. Down the line, each subsidiary profit centre was under strict budgetary control. This meant that in one area, grossly overworked men were transferred from repairs to installations (a separate profit centre on a separate budget) 'to get them off the maintenance account'. The installers, in turn, were the bottom of a line of command that ran through foremen, service superintendent, divisional superintendent, assistant vice-president, and operating vice-president to the president.

This was the long, long trail up which the bad news about New York's overload wound its way. AT&T executives, being human, were reluctant to face the facts – and the consequences for their budgets. A former sales manager from the main disaster area, Wall Street, told the *Wall Street Journal*, 'We were well aware that these problems were coming, and we kept passing it up the line.' But nothing much seemed to happen. The story has been repeated, and will go on being repeated, in many companies, with similar dire results. In this case, 1,500 expensive technicians were imported six months too late and an additional $200 million was pumped in as capital spending – also belated.

But Americans have a wondrous talent for regeneration. The big company is swinging to other fashions, trying to cast into outer darkness the kind of decentralisation that isolated AT&T's top management so effectively from what it was supposed to be managing. The brightest business-school graduates are impatient with climbing the mountainsides of corporate bureaucracy. Recession and recovery have sharpened the reflexes of the American executive, too, shaken off some of the bonds, and flexed the managerial muscles. But the renewed might of management and money, coupled with America's wizard technology, partly financed by the taxpayer through defence contracts, has still not enabled US business to win again as it always has done – or was supposed to.

That, though, was another American daydream. Some bitter US disappointments of the recent past (GE, General Dynamics, Litton Industries, Lockheed, Ling-Temco-Vought, etc) were all leading recipients of federal largesse. Although the US spent so enormously on research and development, supplies defence plant and equipment free (with working capital thrown in) and gave most of its bounty to relatively few lucky companies, it got a great deal of pain for its bounteous billions.

The annals are replete with cases like the helicopter programme which showed a doubled unit price, even though precious little had been changed; or the three years during which the time the Pentagon had to wait for A-10 and F-15 warplanes lengthened by ten months. A similar stretch-out for the F-16 cost $4.7 billion. The M1 tank programme was a disaster in its first four years, with terrible quality and cost problems; its price soared from a planned few hundred thousand to $2.5 million a throw.

The situation was no better in the shipyards; not judging by a US Maritime Administration complaint that US shipyards lacked thirty-nine out of seventy new technologies important for civilian shipping – which makes it easy to understand why the Trident missile-carrying submarine programme, for just one example, overran on both cost and time. Worst still, this lavishly financed technology has often not worked, or not worked well. Very little has been directly useful in civilian markets, either; this deficiency became painfully apparent when the ending of the Cold War chilled the Reaganite fever for defence spending.

The real gee-whiz stories, such as Xerox or Polaroid in their heyday, or Microsoft and Intel of late (plus their ace customers in PCs), were private ventures; and even in industries that US firms do still lead in volume world-wide, such as chemicals or cars, the few technological advances have mostly been made outside America. American defence contractors, like government-financed firms everywhere, have stumbled over the myth of their own efficiency, forgetting that the market-place is no respecter of legends.

Lockheed was so fabled a defence performer that its executives never conceived that they could flop over military projects or even make civil bloomers – even though their earlier Electra turbo-prop airliner, several years too late and accident-prone, was an awesome augury. The Cheyenne helicopter, SRAM missile, and Galaxy super-transport military disasters were promptly compounded by over-stretching what was left of Lockheed's resources on the Tristar jet airbus. Almost from take-off, the Tristar flew far in the vapour trail of its Douglas rival.

Yet in beautiful downtown Burbank, Lockheed's directors seemed oblivious of onrushing financial doom. They could neither see nor admit that any management error lent a hand to the $2 billion (or 60%) excess on the Galaxy. 'We've asked ourself what we did wrong,' said one executive, 'and we concluded that there really wasn't anything.' However rich Lockheed was in usable technology, blind conceit made it as vulnerable in management terms as any European corporation stuck in the fog of its between-the-wars mentality.

Look down the list of prime American defence contractors – very few (Boeing being the prime exception) have made any significant new impact on post-war European markets. Where their technology was relevant, their cost structure was often too high. Once upon a time, the Americans could trust greater productivity to offset higher costs, but that possibility was eroded long ago.

Companies operating in highly unionised Megalopolis, USA, faced horrendous problems even in maintaining productivity, let alone accelerating its rise. Gigantic ploughback of funds into new capital equipment was supposed to offset declining productivity of labour. Despite blatantly protective devices, such as 'voluntary' import quotas, which brought 40% of US trade in manufactured goods under constraint, events showed that, especially in comparison to the Japanese, US plants had lagged fatefully in their modernisation programmes.

Countries with cheaper currencies had no real disadvantage against the armies of US management – armies which sent ten men to do one executive's job. Faced with imports of Japanese cars and steel, the US lack of competitiveness, just as much as the high valuation of the dollar, was responsible for the massive trade deficits with which the 1980s began. By the same token, the resurgence in US exports which started at the end of the decade owed much to the dollar's low valuation.

About half of the export improvement is credited to the cheap dollar. Much of the rest, however, is explained by sharp rises in productivity, which stemmed from 'downsizing' heavily to reduce labour numbers and costs (coupled with a successful assault on unionisation in many industries). The impact on profits as well as productivity was spectacular: on *Fortune's* figures, profits for the 500 biggest US groups showed growth of 15.1% in 1993. Sales, however, barely budged, which lends support to the verdict of Harvard professor Henry Porter, coiner of the concept of 'competitive advantage': that top managements were 'hunkering down, streamlining, focusing – not building, pioneering, innovating'.

The American performance was also flattered by the fact that Western Europe, led backwards by Germany, and Japan, in political and economic disarray, were providing less unflattering comparisons than at the start of the 1970s, when the largest non-American companies were outgrowing the leading Americans by four to one. This divergence was the first statistical proof that the American challengers were actually on the defensive, and that no managerial alchemy, taught at business school or anywhere else, could overcome basic facts of economic life. These have continued to rule the international roost ever since.

The threat posed by non-American competition, above all that from Japan, has become a cliché of American business journalism and management books. In a sudden access of inferiority complex, spurred on by the clear evidence that, on many objective counts, when measured against Japanese competition, they really were inferior, American managers went to excesses of imitative fervour: a centuries-old work on swordsmanship by a Japanese master, of all things, became a bestselling text for US managers in search of Eastern salvation.

The productivity revival indicates that much of this fervour has paid off handsomely. Whether the pay-off goes as far as *Fortune*'s encomium is another matter; by 1994 the 'bold, lean' companies of the US were supposedly setting the pace with 'cheaper, faster and better' methods of manufacture and management. Certainly, concentration on 'core competencies' and exploitation of information technology have closed many gaps between American firms and their leading competitors; but that has brought them back into the game, rather than winning new victories.

The obvious truth is that American executives share all the normal human qualities, including incompetence. Where their own myth had made them over-confident, they proved just as vulnerable as Europeans wrestling with their far longer-standing managerial inferiority complexes. All the same, Europeans have found this hang-up hard to shift. Whatever the growth figures, doesn't American business remain more profitable than European? And don't American subsidiaries in countries such as Britain tend to earn more than the local bumpkins? Aren't Japanese growth records distorted by protection, cheap finance and government manipulation of markets and money?

On the last point, while all these factors have contributed to Japan's successes in world markets, every expert study has come to the same conclusion: that the real explanation for Japan's greater competitiveness is greater quality of management. As for the margin between the US invaders and the locals, that narrowed as American satellites became more mature and could no longer live so easily off the technology and output exported cheap or free by their ever-loving parents.

These Americans, by definition, are offshoots of the more aggressive, better-heeled and better-equipped US corporations. It would be shameful if they couldn't out-perform the mass, gloomy average of local industry. Yet some US subsidiaries don't even manage that. Few records are as grim as European newcomer Dow Chemicals' $43.3 million write-off on the Phrix joint venture in textile fibres with Germany's BASF. Dow, in its despair, even asked an American competitor what production standards should apply to the Phrix operation. 'We don't know,' came the answer. 'We've never seen a plant that small.' That collapse was only the precursor of several American chemical come-uppances, culminating with such traumatic events as the total withdrawal of Gulf from the European market.

Both newcomers and veterans provide examples of mediocre performance. Quaker Oats had been in Britain since the turn of the century – yet in the 1970s it achieved (or didn't achieve) what one writer tactfully describes as 'gentle volume decline', not just in one bad spell, but for an amazing seven or eight years. Hoover is a more awful case in point. While the annals of British marketing are littered with lost causes, few are more heart-rending. Once upon a time, Hoover was as invincibly generic as Frigidaire (another collapsed cause – and also American-owned). The company's one-time reputation rested, not just on its vacuum-cleaners, washing-machines or steam irons, but on the belief that here was an urgent example to the rest of British industry: market-oriented, export-hungry, low-cost and profit-conscious – and, of course, US-led. What went so wrong?

Over the decade to 1980, the company's earnings before tax fell by no less than 31% on a 259% sales rise, reducing it to the point where the American parent (no great management shakes itself) had to pick up the shattered pieces, before itself succumbing to takeover. What can possibly explain so extreme a failure? No less a person than Professor Ted Levitt, whose 'marketing myopia' thesis shaped a whole generation of marketing thought, argues that Hoover was weak precisely where US companies were supposed to be strongest: the marketing concept.

Faced by inadequate home demand and limp exports, the Hoover men asked themselves the classic marketing question: what do the customers want? Unfortunately, they didn't get the right answer. In Levitt's view, Hoover's boob was not to offer a 'simple, standardised high-quality' automatic machine at a price between the market extremes. As it was, Hoover got the three critical pillars of marketing – price, promotion and product – all hopelessly wrong; not just once, moreover, but for the best (or worst) part of two decades.

The destruction of the conglomerate myth is another telling saga. The conglomerate was an American invention, founded on the supposed supremacy of modern management, nurtured on business-school graduates, fuelled by theories such as 'the free-form corporation' or the effective use of high debt. Non-Americans watched in awe as the conglomerate star rose, but didn't draw the obvious moral as it sputtered and exploded. That passage through the corporate heavens was symbolic of the whole American challenge. It was founded, not on real managerial, technological, and financial supremacy, but on passing circumstances, myth, and the infinite capacity of people for self-delusion.

By the same token, the comeback of American management in the 1980s and 1990s, especially its strong leadership in the new industries of electronics and biotechnology, doesn't result from any innate human superiority. Rather, it reflects the innate vitality of an economic society which reacts rapidly to challenge, dearly loves an opportunity, and abounds in the human and material resources needed to seize chances like these offered by the large-scale integrated circuit and recombinant DNA.

Leadership in these industries, though, isn't founded, like the expired and exploded American challenge, on the massive weight of expensive installed capacity. The new leadership rests on technology and still more on its application – and this in an era when economies of scale, thanks again to technology, have come to count for much less. These days passing circumstances don't just pass. They change drastically overnight – and managers, American or not, who think otherwise are victims of the most dangerous myth of all.

That applies doubly to managers who attribute superior Japanese performance to anything other than superior management. This isn't because the Japanese government didn't aid and abet Japanese business with all the guile it can muster – it did. It isn't because the Japanese banks didn't extend credit to business on highly advantageous terms – they did. It isn't that there are no bad managements and no bad managing in Japan (there's plenty), or that Japanese social strengths haven't helped – of course they have.

But none of that explains why in 1991 Japan had 2,620 industrial robots per 100,000 people, and the US only 174 (on a par with Austria and France, and vastly fewer than Singapore and Sweden). Once the wisest of them started taking Japanese managerial success at face value, American managers were driven to raise their own standards higher – without raising excuses. Give a manager an excuse for bad performance, and he'll take it; and that's no way to create the chastened and recharged Western management that the 1990s and the new century demand.

4

Marketing Make-Believe

No question has influenced management more, or for more years, than this: 'What business are we in?' The question was put by Theodore C. Levitt in a *Harvard Business Review* article entitled *Marketing Myopia*. He cited the US railroads, which chugged off into penury under the delusion that their business was railways, not transportation. And there was a myopic buggy-whip company that went bust because it too had defined its business by the product, not by the market.

Levitt's thesis sounded plausible, although it did raise certain questions. Would dumb-headed railroad proprietors have been any brighter at managing truck companies or airlines? And what if the buggy-whip firm had decided that, instead of being in transport accessories or guidance systems, it was in flagellation?

But executives love a new panacea; so companies all over the world chugged off, as the American railroads didn't, into the business of defining their business. The bigger the company, the greater the pain – because large firms, like rocks acquiring barnacles, build up an encrusted deposit of unrelated activities over time. In the US, for instance, the

49

biggest conglomerate, in the sense of operating in the most different markets, was not Charles Bluhdorn's Gulf + Western or Harold Geneen's ITT or Royal Little's Textron. It was good old General Tire, one of the unselect few among America's leading companies, be it noted, whose earnings per share in 1983 were actually lower than a decade before.

The search for definitions led off in strange verbal directions. Of all odd results, the old Tube Investments had the most alliterative and meaningless – 'metal manipulation'. This fine phrase can cover everything from the tubes that provided most of the group's profits to hairpins, which it didn't make; but the company's products did include some that used no metal, and others, such as gas heaters, in which manipulating metal was about the least important factor.

Dunlop, deeply influenced by the McKinsey consultants, who in turn were then majoring on the marketing concept, came up with an equal beauty to explain its confusion of activities. 'What do rubber and its successors do?' asked the chairman of the day rhetorically. 'They absorb shock. They cushion. They grip. They bounce. What binds us together is the extension of these kind of things.'

A binding that grips mattresses, tennis-rackets, anti-skid devices and slippers is not tight; nor did the definition help Dunlop to absorb the shocks delivered to its system by its own incompetence – shocks so severe that in 1983 it quit forever the European tyre business where it had begun and (once) prospered.

Any diversified giant's business is seldom logical. It is nearly always founded on one basic well-defined market – such as tyres, which made up roughly two-thirds of Dunlop. The logic of Levitt, if strictly applied, would lead here to one of two conclusions. Either everything unrelated to the cushioning and care of transport equipment should be dropped as time-wasting diversion; or Dunlop should be treated, not as homogenous, but as a bunch of different and unrelated businesses.

Neither course is attractive. Company directors never (or hardly ever) voluntarily reduce their imperial sway; failed conglomerates have been slow to reduce their mass, or deconglomerate, until under acute financial pressure. If a big company does dump a major interest (as GE and RCA did with their computers), there are usually only two explanations: either the disposed fragment was losing money in floods, or the trust-busters (as with ITT and Avis or AT&T with its regional phone companies) have forced the issue.

In 1994, the tune has changed somewhat. While many of the businesses dropped in the previous decade, in the greatest fire-sale in corporate history, were indeed losing money, some were less mistakes than misfits – businesses bought in the era of conglomerate diversification. In the new age of concentration around so-called 'core businesses' or 'core competencies', these buys suddenly seemed out of place. Some of the most spectacular offloading came from disenchanted conglomerates (the disenchantment being shared by managers and stockholders alike).

No case was more remarkable than the selling spree on which Gulf + Western embarked almost immediately after its creator, Bluhdorn, was killed in a plane crash. What man had wrongly put together, it seemed, man must take asunder – and better had if the corporation wanted to meet any goals worth having. At one bankrupt outfit, the seven companies put on the block in a dying spasm had mainly only just been bought. And at Consolidated Foods, the new logic meant the management selling half an astounding bundle of 125 businesses, reshaping itself into six distinct core activities, and changing its name to Sara Lee.

Separate and strengthen, divide and conquer: whatever the description, the principle is hard to gainsay and makes much better sense than the old principle of join and justify – which so often ended up with the junction showing no justification at all. The record-breaking surge in divestment, of course, has been battling against an equally unprecedented wave of mergers, ranging from routine multi-million-dollar buys (of exactly the kind that bloated Consolidated Foods in the past) to billion-dollar bonanzas (bonanzas for the shareholders at the receiving end, that is).

The mega-mergers of the 1980s provided some new, instant episodes of divestment under duress. Having paid a barely believable $2.8 billion for Esmark, Beatrice Foods was forced into a sell-off programme to a total value (even less believable) of a billion dollars in a single year. But mostly the duress is that imposed by inadequate results. That explains, for example, why Bowater's North American newsprint interests, long the very heart of the corporation, were set adrift. The company had two horses pulling in different directions on opposite sides of the Atlantic. While the split-up (spectacularly successful in stock market terms, as sell-offs, significantly, often are), the British management back home couldn't escape from one basic problem: its remaining interests were still highly diversified – i.e. a ragbag.

Most executives are not happy accepting the fact that they have a ragbag, which cannot be managed as one company in one way by one group of top men. They have mostly risen through the one homogenous business that makes sense for the company. They used to manage that business positively, by day-to-day involvement. In the 1960s and 1970s, they would not admit that their skills were of little help to the companies clustering round the mother planet. So they interfered and produced some concept of the company that lent rhyme and reason to their fiddling (as, in most cases, top managers still do).

The marketing-myopia question thus inadvertently nourished a policy of widening spread, which is the antithesis of the marketing concept – although that isn't wholly unforgivable. Marketing has attracted piles of unenlightened prose. Its definitions wander into long, echoing sentences littered with the ugly word 'orientation'. Marketing seems to mean finding out what the customer wants, putting on the market something which meets that need at a price the 'punter' (a horribly condescending word) is ready to pay, producing whatever it is for a cost that yields a fat profit at the price demanded, and knitting in the distribution and advertising with the marketing idea.

That's all very sound and satisfying – until you ask what a non-marketing company is up to. Reversing the definition, that kind of company makes things whether anybody wants them or not, prices them any old how (except at the right price for the market), manufactures without any thought of the market, and distributes and promotes the result at random. Many companies are guilty of all these sins, but it isn't their marketing that is at fault. It's their entire management.

Marketing's definitions end up describing every activity of top management, including even mergers, and stopping short only at personnel relations (on which top management has traditionally spent too little time, anyway, except when there are strikes). If marketing equals management, and bad marketing equals mismanagement, why all the fuss? And why, if marketing is a non-existent mystery, have companies hired graduates wholesale from firms such as Procter & Gamble that are supposed to have the knack?

Good books or articles on marketing are suspiciously thin on the ground. Except for recondite areas, such as the impenetrable equations of market research, there isn't much to write about – merely general management. One executive turned marketing professor, now retired, believes that marketing as a subject will eventually wither away, as executives finally master, once and for all, the outlandish notion that they have customers. That idea is the foundation of Total Quality Management, which in its pursuit of the satisfied or (far better) delighted customer is supposed to link every function and person in the company to that cause.

Marketing (not successful marketing, but marketing as the provision of bright ideas) is the easiest function in business management – which is why smooth-talking confidence artists have created such havoc. An ex-soap man, whose impeccable credentials included creating near-chaos in his first non-lather post, proceeded to tie up nearly all his next employer's working capital in the unsold stocks of just one division. The employer learned too late that any fool can produce a plan to capture 20% of the market.

The excruciating job is making products that work at a cost that brings reasonable profits within earthly possibility. You can (the Germans did) successfully flog a well-made product for decades without having a marketing man or marketing notion on the premises. But nobody, for more than the shortest period, can market mangled goods – no matter if every marketing consultant ever to wing the Atlantic is massed on his side. In a way, the old, despised production orientation had more logic. Any business has to be adept at its basic physical operations; without that, nothing is possible.

That's the lesson which the late W. Edwards Deming, the great guru of quality control, preached to the Japanese (who lionised him) for over thirty years; and then to the Americans (who had ignored him most of that time), once the US had woken up to the threat of Japan's productive lead. Apply Deming's ideas on quality control and manufacturing organisation, and you get, not just lower costs, but much better performance in the market-place.

That seemed to be the lesson of the Pontiac Fiero, according to *Fortune*, 'the first US car produced from scratch according to the Deming way'. It started off by breaking all US sales records for a two-seater car. One of Deming's key principles is that companies should not choose suppliers on the basis of price alone, but instead should consider quality. 'In one extraordinary leap of faith in Deming, Pontiac chose a single supplier for each item it buys for the Fiero, without competitive bidding. By GM's internal ratings, Fiero quality is the best in the corporation, even though the Fiero plant has no on-line inspectors.'

Unfortunately, the Fiero flopped after its splendid start, the victim of monumental mismanagement and mismarketing. But bad production, as much as bad marketing, is what opened the garage door to the Japanese. What Western car companies, as opposed to their Eastern competitors, consistently got wrong were questions of engineering design, cost of production, purchasing policy, balance of productive capacity, manpower deployment and compatibility of components.

In a period when British industry was being lashed for marketing lapses, its sins of production were far more heinous. Historically, Americans were more deeply indoctrinated in the arts of marrying engineering and manufacture to meet product and profit requirements. But the old black

54

magic fled, possibly because of all US specialisations, production was the least likely to lead to the top and therefore, presumably, the last functional area into which bright young things from the Harvard Business School would direct their pattering feet.

That situation has changed under the impetus of foreign competition and the powerful teaching of the quality and manufacturing gurus. As key industries discovered that their ability to market was being sabotaged by their inability to produce (a discovery rubbed in by Japanese producers of all manner of goods), so the production expert rose from Cinderella to Princess Charming. Salaries and status rose correspondingly; when companies are pouring belated billions into automation and improvement of both product and process, you can't entrust the investment to anything but the brightest and best. And they in turn can't give of their best unless, as in Japan, production and marketing work closer together than Laurel and Hardy.

That's the truth which GM Europe applied when it created the Omega executive car range, the first new model entrusted wholly to multi-disciplinary teams. All ten disciplines were employed on all thirteen Product Development Teams. Team members worked together in a carefully mapped process which emphasised speed less than the desired result: total transformation of the top-end image for Vauxhall and Opel. Throughout all phases, the multi-disciplinary mode prevailed. Whether the team concerned was working on the engine, or the doors and hardware, or the wiring harness, the design, product engineering, manufacturing engineering and production staff had colleagues from marketing, quality, sales, service, purchasing and finance.

The Product Development Team approach looks logical and sensible, and is: in the pioneering Omega sessions, the asking of apparently 'dumb' questions often had highly intelligent results. Many ideas sprang out of the interaction between disciplines, just as you'd expect. What you wouldn't expect, though, is that Omega got going in the late 1980s, a canyon of time after Japan had shown this particular way. Why had it taken so long for GM to follow such impeccable logic? For that matter, why was Omega the first range where, with equal logic, final approval rested, not in Detroit, but with local top executives?

Mainly, it's mistakes of management such as those unconscionable delays that have crippled the car-makers and have generated the mishaps of mechanicals. At one point, the recalls of US cars seemed to have reached epidemic proportions – and it was no coincidence that, while you could have called VW's Beetle ugly, noisy, uncomfortable, slow and inconvenient (and, if you were Ralph Nader, unsafe), you could not say, by industry standards in the Beetle's long day, that the machine was badly made.

In a later generation and higher price-bracket, much the same is true of the Volvo – an eyesore to many cognoscenti, and no great shakes in performance, either. But, as with the Beetle before it, the ugliness became endearing to buyers who valued the car's solidity, safety, reliability and quality. The marketing man, of course, won't let that escape. Reliability, he will say, is Volvo's gimmick – in other words, whatever a company does right is good marketing, and whatever it does wrong is because its marketing is bad.

The marketeers in their heyday not only pushed production men into the cold, but also ousted the salesman. The standard sneer against 'non-marketing-oriented' companies is that they have merely called the sales manager a marketing manager. This is more sensible than importing a costly and expensively educated marketing manager and downgrading the little matter of selling. Just as you cannot market anything you cannot make, so you cannot market a product you cannot sell.

Selling, like production, is one of the grubbier aspects of management. Instead of hitting machines that break down, you come up against people who say no, or maybe. The great marketing companies were all founded on nothing more elaborate than the hard sell – 3M, National Cash Register, Procter & Gamble, Coca-Cola, Shell, and IBM. IBM's acolytes would sing, of Thomas Watson Sr., 'He is the fairest, squarest man we know. Sincere and true, he has shown us how to play the game. And how to make the dough.' The further they drift (like the men in head-office eyries) from the hard base of making dough by selling, the more ineffective the companies become in the market-place.

'What business are we in?' may have helped the occupants of the eyries in brooding about the future and about the delicious directions that the company could or should take. But even that is dubious. Every single large company that diversified into computers had excellent reasons, based on realistic definitions of its business, for adding computer capacity. Yet every single one suffered untold grief as a result. They failed, not by misunderstanding what business they were in, but by not seeing what business computers were in – and at the start, overwhelmingly, that was the replacement of punch-card machines: and doing so, at that, in competition with the then almighty IBM.

The first real marketing question is this: 'How do we truly make our money?' The answer, even in the largest corporations, usually comes down to that one basic area, established since its time began, in which the company is the lord of the market: in IBM's case, catering for the data-processing needs of the large corporation and the corporation man (a simple proposition that was shattered in the 1980s by the small PC). Defending and extending this basic position must have the overwhelming priority. The next two marketing questions are: 'How can we improve the key products and their manufacture?' and 'How can we improve our selling?'

The major asset of any business is the expertise acquired over time in its fundamental activities, and that is defined, not by broad markets, but by specific products. The US railroaders would have made a mess of road or air transport because, lacking equipment and experience, they would have failed to understand unfamiliar technologies of selling or operation. The moral is not 'Look after your production and selling, and your marketing will look after itself', but simply that stuffing the company into a bag marked 'marketing concept' makes not a whit of difference to its myopia, arthritis, constipation – or any other of the diseases to which corporate flesh is heir.

The proof of this vital proposition is evident from the

performance of what seemed to be the most successfully market-oriented – or, in its own preferred phrase, customer-led – corporation of them all: IBM. Suggesting to an IBM executive that he was not a marketing man was like doubting whether Jack Nicklaus played golf. Successive managements had worked back from the sales orientation of old Tom Watson all the way down the line through production to R & D. A young executive started a project at the development stage, was joined by people from manufacture during development, and stayed with his baby right through its manufacture and marketing world-wide, and the development of its variants and improvements.

The customers round which IBM allegedly built its business, though, became progressively disenchanted. If anyone is perverse enough to want a recipe for failing their customers, the following treble dose should take them a long way towards that objective. First, fail 'to keep pace with significant change in the industry'. Second, become 'too bureaucratic and too preoccupied' with the company's 'own view of the world'. Third, be 'way too slow getting new things to the market'.

All three grievous faults have been ascribed to IBM, not by some jaundiced outsider, but by the new chief executive, Louis V. Gerstner, imported in 1993 to save the ailing behemoth. He was reporting to investors after a year in office. But IBM hadn't needed a new boss to diagnose these failings. Its management could have heard the same message many years before – from the customers themselves. IBM's efforts to turn back the industry's clock, its constipated processes, attempted dictation to customers and lags in product innovation were obvious, and increasingly resented.

In the pursuit of every dollar going, IBM had forgotten the essential paradox. You never succeed unless the company is accurately directed towards its markets and customers. But you can't achieve that sense of direction unless everything else in the company, everything that doesn't carry the marketing label, is as good as, or better than, the performance and attributes of the competition.

Sure, IBM lives by the marketing concept – and died by it.

The case of the PC Jr. and a whole series of subsequent failures, when products and performance fell far short of customer expectations, toppled the old IBM into the dustbin of the past. But in the main 'marketing concept' is simply shorthand for the concept of the whole corporation. Nothing less will do.

5
Big Business Blues

Everybody knows that the bigger the company, the sloppier its management, but everybody is wrong. The big company has the best managers, the best management, and generally the best technology, the best products, and the best production equipment – because the big company has the big money, and all these pleasures cost plenty. True, the large corporation can easily become constipated, tongue-tied, muscle-bound, spendthrift, and overweight, doing all it can, via these dis-advantages, to outweigh its assets. But the mammoth's strengths give it an invaluable asset: staying power.

Large corporations are in essence as durable as Old Man River. The whizzkid companies come and go, rise and fall, but even an often rudderless vessel such as US Steel goes rolling along forever, though it changes its name to USX along the way. It takes prodigies of mismanagement – usually in thorny forests such as mergers, into which many a man has disappeared without trace – to break a large company. ITT had to commit every folly in the conglomerate book to sink into disrepair and disrespect; yet there it was in 1993, still alive, if not exactly kicking. Net income of $913 million represented only 1.3% of its assets and a mere 4% of its enormous $22.7 billion of sales.

The received view, which looks at the failures and fiascos of the leviathan rather than its strengths, requires correcting by what an American writer nicknamed the 'Lestoil syndrome', after a once obscure New Jersey detergent firm. Expounding the Second Truth of Management, that all good management is merely an expression of one great idea, Lestoil broke out of obscurity by bottling the heavy-duty detergent which it sold to industry, and offering the heavenly liquid to housewives as well.

TV advertising, cautious at first, bolder as sales soared, quickly shifted Lestoil out of New Jersey and into the New York big-time. The highly salaried managers at Lestoil's massively larger competitors, Procter & Gamble and Lever Brothers, had (as is their wont) totally missed this opportunity, despite their massed brainpower. In the end, however, the mammoths reacted with multi-million-dollar force, swamping Lestoil in a sea of green bubbles. Hence the Lestoil Syndrome – and it happens all the time, and to anybody – even in a high-tech industry with unlimited growth prospects, even to the man who practically invented it: one Joe Engelberger.

Before he literally said 'Let's make a robot' in 1956, there was no robotics industry. By 1983, when Engelberger's creation, Unimation, had sold 6,800 robots world-wide, it was also, alas, chalking up a first-quarter loss of $558,000. At that point, Westinghouse Electric, for a mere $107 million, swallowed the lot, including the 'grand-daddy of American robotics' – the pioneering Engelberger. He lasted only a few months on a battlefield into which the US giants (as well as Westinghouse, there were GE, GM, Cincinnati Milacron, etc) had piled.

As a writer for *Management Today* soberly observed, after quoting a Cincinnati executive to the effect that 'Robotics is a very expensive club', it is 'safe to bet that the only members of the club will be the big corporations' by 1990. By then, of course, the club was dominated by the Japanese. And did Westinghouse reap rich harvests from its buy? If so, the fruits were lost in a long-running series of management errors: in 1993 the group lost $326 million, despite sales of $11.6

billion – and that was a thumping 31.2% of the shareholders' equity.

It's commonly been observed that more innovations by far come from small companies than from big corporations. It has been far less noted that the small company, like Unimation, generally loses, not just its smallness (that is inevitable, if its innovation succeeds), but its independence. That shouldn't be inevitable at all. The main safeguard against these events in the US was the trust-busting fervour which sustained the Justice Department – and stopped the giants from swallowing everything in sight. In the new era of corporate sexual permissiveness, though, anything goes – and many companies have therefore gone: companies that, in previous decades, would have survived and flourished.

Under the new dispensation, they often shrivel away, as when IBM, trying to build its capability for a global attack in telephone exchanges by purchasing the up-and-coming Rolm, swiftly turned the purchase into down-and-going. Rolm was one of a myriad smaller, new companies that, in the burgeoning world of microelectronics, have produced better products first and marketed them best. But that's where the writing appears on the wall: enter the Lestoil Syndrome. In the worst situations, the giants retaliate, the competition intensifies, the growth levels off and the stock falls.

Even a fantastic growth company like Tandem can suddenly look vulnerable. Only born in 1974, with the brilliant notion of building a computer that would never stop working, never go down, Tandem never grew by less than 90% in any year up to 1981. The next year, its expansion was positively feeble – a mere 50%. Even 1983's crawl (only 34%) looked like lightning compared to 1984's rate of less than a quarter. Since IBM and others were trying to scramble on to Tandem's slowing bandwagon, it's no wonder that the stock collapsed from $45 to about $16 in a mere eighteen months – and this, remember, was a company still growing at a pace which, by any standards save its own, was remarkable beyond the dreams of avarice.

Even that setback was nothing compared to what hit Tandem in the microprocessor age, when its Unique Selling

Proposition had ceased to sell. The shares slumped by 27.5% in 1993, completing a miserable decade for shareholders. Their investment's value had declined by 4.7% annually as Tandem lurched towards a 1993 loss of $518 million – substantially greater in relation to sales, assets and equity than that year's $8 billion deficit at IBM.

The smaller company has to steer between Scylla and Charybdis. On one side, failure looms. On the other, success may call into play the ancient management maxim: 'If you can't beat 'em, buy 'em.' This has its tragic aspects: little David hurls his stone against Goliath, who takes his bruises and then, with ridiculous ease, plucks up his adversary. But the tragedy is inherent in two facts. First, the Davids are worse managed than the giants, and this is hidden behind the smokescreen of their success. Second, an essential ingredient of the little guy's success is the somnolence of Goliath.

Outside every big, fat company there are sectors of the market waiting for a lean competitor to thrust his way in. No corporation, no matter how rich and superbly staffed, can pre-empt every possibility in the market or in technology; and the wealthier the company is, and the more massively entrenched in its chosen sectors, the harder it may be for its directors to react – for reasons of economics as well as pure inertia. That certainly helps to explain IBM's otherwise mysterious lags in everything from mini-computers to lap-tops.

Likewise, Gillette's initial failure in the stainless-steel razor-blade war wasn't simply its refusal to accept the fact that a little British company called Wilkinson Sword could provide serious competition. Gillette could compete technically – it made stainless-steel blades for the Swiss and Swedish markets before the word 'stainless' ever dropped into Wilkinson's consciousness, and Gillette even owned the patent for the critical FTFE coating of Wilkinson's wonderblades.

But Gillette had a huge world-wide production apparatus geared only to make carbon-steel blades, which, because they became blunt quicker, were bound to sell in larger quantities and at lovelier profits than stainless-steel blades. No wonder Gillette didn't want to know about the horrible things. But in management you can't (though executives do it constantly) shut your eyes and hope the competition will go away. Eventually Gillette was forced to compete, after losing significant slices of a seemingly impregnable market share in country after country.

The oil countries, like the oil companies before them, have been forced to learn similar hard lessons about the difficulty – actually, the impossibility – of having your cake and eating it: you can't monopolise the market and maintain high prices and profits without reducing sales. Any A-level economist could have told OPEC that its strategy would never work. True, many graduate economists, even some with Nobel Prizes, couldn't see that Milton Friedman, almost alone, was right: that either oil prices or oil sales were bound to fall – probably both, as duly happened.

Every time a fat monopolist, whether his name is Sheikh Yamani or Nelson Bunker Hunt, tries to exploit a dominant supply position in some market (Yamani of OPEC in oil, Hunt in silver), his Achilles heel is quickly exposed: that both demand and supply are elastic – that is, they can move in either direction, up or down. The days have long gone when the oil companies could fix world prices – in Europe and all points East – on a cosy formula linked to the free-market quote in (of all places) the Gulf of Mexico; the logic was only slightly stronger than fixing the price of beef in Chicago by that of yak's meat in Siberia.

Under this umbrella of artificially high prices crawled in the first cut-price independents; these tiny folk made handsome profits while charging much less. The big companies faced a horrid dilemma. Did they cut prices to cut out the independents, and sacrifice profits? Or did they maintain their profit margins and forget about the new competition? In the end, the issue was settled for them: the independents made such fast inroads that (thus getting the worst of both worlds) the majors lost market share and still had to cut prices. In the end, after much painful loss of profits, the Lestoil Syndrome came into play and the independents were bought up – at the traditional premium prices.

The harder a leviathan is hit by small-fry competition, the

more likely it is to undergo the whale-like upheaval from which its progress mostly springs. The leviathan can bask for decades at a time before some terrible shock (like the great lumps that Wilkinson carved out of Gillette) makes it shoot out of the water on a sudden career of high-speed performance – usually brief, but not in Gillette's case; in the decade to 1993 its investors gained by 29.4% annually, the tenth fastest rise in the *Fortune* 500. It's easier for giant companies, despite their inertia, to react to challenge than it is for the little challenger to meet the awakened giant's attack. For the challenger's deficiencies are the mirror of the champion's strengths.

The sudden-growth star normally has one or two thrusting and forceful personalities at the top – entrepreneurial types who lack interest in the routine of administration and organisation. Below these leaders are few, if any, middle executives able to plug the gaps. First, the needs of the company rapidly outgrow the capacities of the people on board at the start of the upward trajectory, when the company was much smaller. This calamity notoriously hit the Italian domestic-appliance makers, long after they had become indecently rich by flooding Europe with their refrigerators and washing-machines so efficiently that even the then mighty Philips was forced to surrender.

The rot reached so deep into the Italian industry that in 1984 its flagship company, Zanussi, awash in debts of $615 million, was forced to accept takeover by Electrolux, the Swedish giant. Its boss, Hans Werthen, had proved, by multiplying sales twenty times since 1967, that the fault lay more in the Italians' management than in their markets. Werthen, less fortunately, went on to prove that aggressive expansion by acquisition has grave disadvantages in anybody's hands. By 1991 Electrolux was struggling to earn a midget 1% on both sales and assets.

For all the attraction of the growth stars, people with high management talent tend to go where it is most recognised and best rewarded – and that generally means, not the up-and-coming growth company (which usually underpays in salary and bonus, and offers the much less certain reward of equity), but the heavyweight corporation. Any investor, or any takeover bidder, who buys a second-rank growth company for its management is flying blind. The management only looks good through the distorting glass of the boom-type profit record.

Some challengers do make it to the top – more in America, where risk capital is relatively abundant, than in Europe, where the established companies have a hammer-lock on the available financing. From Xerox and Polaroid onwards, there have been occasional stimulating examples of challengers turned champions, riding new technology that the giants wouldn't touch. Both these companies, however, lacked the staying power of 3M. In 1993, indeed, both relative newcomers were losing money, while 3M was earning a more than solid 9% on sales, 10.4% on assets and 19.4% on equity.

Eastman Kodak's figures, however, were far less flattering. Its reactions, although belated, to Polaroid's technological challenge galvanised Kodak into producing, in the Instamatic camera, its first great marketing innovation since a couple of concert pianists turned up with Kodachrome. Likewise, Gillette was stung by Wilkinson into marketing the Techmatic razor, its first improvement in basic wet-shaving technology since the royal days of King C. Gillette. But Kodak failed to develop an effective counter to the Japanese makers of colour film. In 1994 it contrived the amazing feat of losing $1.5 billion on $20 billion of sales with one of the best-known brands in the world.

All the same, how much technical and marketing advance (if any) would have taken place if Kodak (or Gillette, for that matter) had preserved their too-cosy monopolies? It's fascinating, too, to note that Polaroid and Xerox, as they and their markets matured, showed exactly the same inertia in the face of competitive challenge; and were likewise stimulated, after over-long delay, to dig into their pockets and their labs to seek the new wonders which are the attacked giant's best, indeed only, means of defence.

While neither company (more notably Polaroid) found the blockbuster it sought, their sales remained enormous.

Only inept direction, which Xerox tried to exorcise with Total Quality Management from the mid-1980s, prevented them from exploiting a benevolent circle. Because they are relatively well-managed and exceedingly rich, the leviathans, as noted, have historically attracted most of the new talent, which in theory should help to soup up their management horsepower and make them richer still.

But the managerial talent of larger companies differs from that of growth stars. Its quality is shown in the effectiveness of formal systems, in the recognisable ability of individuals deep down inside the organisation, in consistent performance over the years, and in this very power to regenerate. Royal Dutch-Shell is the biggest example that Europe can offer of this, as of everything else. Its managerial reputation was once so potent that *Time* magazine fulsomely lauded Shell's superiority over the American oil majors.

It often happens that the summit of pride for a corporation precedes a fall. When the profits stuck fast shortly thereafter and the McKinsey consultants were called in, Shell was revealed as another constipated, overweight bureaucracy that could only be cured by painful slimming at the managerial health farm. Recognition of its own defects is an excellent therapy for management. Shell led the oil majors into the giant-tanker era and prospered accordingly; as the 1990s began it led the global industry with $104 billion of sales on which it earned a healthy 4%.

Because it builds up so much blubber over the years, a large corporation is relatively easy to pare down; great lumps of fat can be sliced away without any visible effect on corporate efficiency. This is the lesson of Lord Weinstock's calculated surgery on taking hold of the General Electric Company. Its net capital rose in three years by only £4.5 million, while sales galloped up by £23.6 million and profits by £10.6 million.

As Weinstock wielded the knife, critics argued that the cutting would go too far, until the very heart of the old electrical giant would be chopped out. In fact, the amputation of superfluous offices, factories, and staffs left GEC so formidable that its two bigger rivals, English Electric and

AEI, couldn't stay in the game; both succumbed to GEC bids, while the bidder went on to prodigies of growth. From £1.4 billion in 1975, sales soared over threefold to £4.8 billion in 1984; earnings per share quadrupled as profits climbed to £940 million – a thumping 19.6% return on sales.

Eliminating a million of running sores is just as effective financially as creating a new business earning a million. Loss elimination, moreover, requires no capital, and may actually free it, if the culprit can be sold off; new businesses always involve investing new money, a job at which large firms are worse than they know. The potential weakness of the big corporation lies not only in the sluggishness and inefficiencies bred by long chains of command and entrenched bureaucracies, but in an inability to behave like the small company entrepreneur, no matter how it tries.

However, cutting is not the same thing as creating. For all the company's virtues, few people can point to a major new business that has emerged from GEC. In the computer industry, true, IBM can point to the AS-400 minicomputer and the PC as giant businesses built from scratch; but in both cases other companies, Digital and Apple respectively, had pointed the way. In laptops, true, most of the strong early running was made by a huge company; but that, significantly, was Japanese – Toshiba.

Big-company managers are far better at running a soundly based business that's been going for decades; the money that Honeywell, for instance, has milked out of thermostats over the years could have bought up every small gee-whizz company along Boston's Route 128 and still left change. Which, of course, encouraged Honeywell to buy one such company and become yet another failed giant in computery.

On this argument, big companies should give up the seldom successful effort to launch new businesses. If they discover bright, aggressive entrepreneurs in their midst, managements should encourage these rarities to go into business for themselves – and keep a slice of the equity for the good old company. Most of the offshoots, however, will fail. (Fear of failure within the big company is a prime cause of its entrepreneurial inertia; one key to making a personal

fortune in business is to lose inhibitions about going bankrupt.) Those breakaways who succeed, though, can always be
acquired in the big company's own good time. Cynical,
perhaps; but it's the better way.

Xerox provided clinching evidence of its own passage
from entrepreneurial creation to established corporation in
its first major diversification. It bought up Scientific Data
Systems, a little computer breakaway turned sometime
bonanza; and Xerox (behaving like an established giant all
the way) paid far too much ($900 million) for a company
that promptly lost much fine gold. SDS had been purchased
because the Xerox boss of the time saw, perfectly correctly,
that an office-equipment maker of the future would vitally
need computer capability.

Unfortunately, Xerox bought the wrong company, managed it wrongly and still ended in the wrong position –
without the computer strengths required in the present for
the office of the future. Still worse, the desperate effort to
dam the computer losses diverted management's attention
from the issue of exploiting the amazing inventions of its
Palo Alto Research Centre. Xerox consequently missed
entirely PARC's wonder-product, the personal computer,
whose potential far exceeded even the wealth created by
xerography.

In this market (and others), despite such unpromising
examples, Goliaths have kept on buying up Davids at prices
which only seem reasonable by comparison with the purchaser's own mighty assets. Thus the great GM forked out
$2.5 billion for Electronic Data Systems in pursuit of its
sudden desire to become to information processing what it
is to autos. Whether doomed to failure or destined to
succeed (it actually worked out well financially), the buy
represented only one thirtieth of GM's existing wealth. A top
executive put the best possible gloss on this particular deal to
Business Week: 'We're being more outward-directed, and
we've stopped thinking that we're going to invent everything
ourselves.'

You could put that differently: that GM's bosses were
under increasing pressure to concentrate on and refine what

they know – running large commercial bureaucracies – and to avoid activities of which they are ignorant. That quotation, paraphrased, comes precious near to the policy recommended above: admitting that 'we're no good at doing new things; we'll let somebody else do it, then buy them up.' Normally corporate mythology has dictated otherwise, as much at GM as anywhere else; to quote a vice-president from Du Pont, the entrepreneurial man who bucks the system is the man who makes it.

Asked to give an example, the Du Pont vice-president came up with a hero who started the company's antifreeze business – back in the 1930s. In more modern times, plagued by a lack of entrepreneurs, Du Pont pioneered a device designed to break the log-jams. Called by the fancy name of 'venture management', this set up businesses within the business. One manager got total responsibility for a new project. It was all his, to nurse to profitable fruition; all his, that is, subject to the normal limitations of corporate budgeting and policy restraints.

A few large companies realised the full extent of their disabilities in these respects, and went still further, by hiving off development projects from the main body of the corporation. The project team was separated not only geographically, but in life-style; their premises, isolated and simple, were known as 'skunk-works'; and only when they had achieved success (in theory, far faster than would have happened back at the glass-walled ranch) were they brought back out of the cold. In this way, the skunk-works were expected to crash or vault the big company's bureaucratic barriers.

There's the rub. The corporation's checks, changes, habitual slow, grudging reactions, and heavy overheads are exactly the forces that stifle entrepreneurial initiative. A new business may need new forms for its success; the old norms of a corporation may be deadly. For all Du Pont's depth of resources, hefty research spending, and sophisticated techniques such as venture analysis (computerised assessment of projects, renamed 'venture annihilation' by aggrieved managers), its flow of new riches has disappointed deeply.

Its trumpeted Corfam synthetic leather had to be folded for a pre-tax loss of $100 million, after a series of marketing and manufacturing errors. There may be lush things in Du Pont's cupboard – although one item on its old list of unmarketed new ventures was discouraging. This was an office copier that used ordinary paper. As a Du Pont man told *Time* magazine, 'We may just be too late. Perhaps we should have moved faster.' By the 1990s, the giant was totally overhauling its R & D, painfully conscious that $11 billion of expenditure – for all the good it produced – might as well have been sunk into a large black hole.

The tragedy of the new venture manager in the large corporation is what seems to be a strength – the fact that all the corporation's resources are behind the venture. The small men can't take four years to launch a product; they don't have the time, so they take four months. They can't install expensive engineering, because they haven't got the money – so they find a cheaper way to manufacture, which produces a cheaper price and so automatically builds in a marketing advantage.

If people like this save money, it's money they badly need. But if a corporation man is given a budget to invest, he spends it – for there is no personal gain in economising. The small entrepreneur runs hard because the bet is all or nothing. The corporate insiders – the 'intrapreneurs' – are on double or quits. If the project comes off, they are heroes. If it's a Corfam-coated failure, the miscreant probably stays put. In the rare cases of dismissal, there is usually some other job somewhere else.

Yet it is possible to buck the system – not from the bottom, but the top. When IBM chairman, Frank B. Cary, got riled beyond endurance by the fact that other people's personal computers were 'stealing the hearts and minds of my executives', he set in motion IBM's own PC project. The team was given little more than a year, instead of the usual three years, plus an override which bypassed IBM's elaborate systems and broke many of its shibboleths (like making as much as possible in-house).

The result was a triumph that has already passed into the

Hall of Business Fame. So has Sony's Walkman – although only one man in the company never wavered in the belief that the project was worth pursuing. Since that one man was Akio Morita, the president, the Walkman went ahead, with marvellous results. But a young engineer named Stephen Wozniak couldn't get the same response from David Packard or anybody else at Hewlett-Packard who possessed Morita's power of decision, thought and execution. Which is partly why Apple was born (when Wozniak teamed up with Steve Jobs).

Nevertheless, Hewlett-Packard by 1994 was running second to IBM in computers – a convincing demonstration that the big corporation can succeed, if it's really serious about innovating. It must, however, loosen the whole structure of checks and balances, reports and committees in which decisions are arduously taken and painfully executed. At the same time, the routine operations that go on for eternity are always a happy hunting-ground for improvement. A great deal of work inside an organisation serves only the organisation; it has no direct relevance outside, which is the only place where money is earned. All this work can be dumped without loss.

Large companies further compound the perennial problem of effective management of large numbers by over-hiring. For all the waves of cutbacks in managerial numbers, far too many able executives sleep peacefully within those ample bosoms. As a former ICI executive once wrote, 'If everyone in giant corporations of this nature' who was earning a large salary 'were lined up, and the even numbers dismissed, not only would those left behind cope more easily with their tasks, but those dismissed would have a major impact on industry.' (This was in a cosier era, when the dismissed could expect new jobs – as they can too rarely in 1994).

The paradox of too many competent executives when (according to the complaints of most chief executives) there are not enough to go round, is easily resolved. The extant executives are used for the wrong jobs or pointed towards the wrong objectives by the kind of big company top management that (to quote an actual case) maintained a separate sales force to sell its own commodity to its own subsidiaries, who (naturally) were not allowed to buy from any other source.

This management had imported bright, aggressive, market-minded newcomers to run the businesses closest to the market-place; but it offset the contribution from any of its ventures that survived pregnancy by losing all the money it could in older parts of the company. Great companies would crash into these barriers less often if they saw themselves as they really are: not as thrusting, entrepreneurial commercial go-getters, but as bureaucracies with a tendency to domination by *apparatchiks* – people who have grown old in a company's service and traditions.

The delightful chairman of one multi-national jewel once said, 'You can't turn a group like this upside down every eighteen months.' That is the authentic voice of the *apparatchik*: if a corporation urgently needs turning upside down, even eighteen months after the last upheaval, inversion it must have. It is the *apparatchik* who stops the big corporation, time and again, from cashing in on its innate superiority. It is the anti-*apparatchik* who, time and time again, proves that the corporation can be freed from its self-imposed chains.

6
The Question of Working Life

The workforce of the West has suffered incessant change and threat of change since the oil-price rises of 1973 shattered the dream of continuously rising prosperity and threw millions out of work. Hyper-inflation destroyed savings and devoured purchasing power. Automation utterly changed the basis of production, and reduced the number of jobs, in industry after industry. Recession clobbered bargaining power so severely that, right across the board, once-powerful unions found themselves in broad retreat.

Yet, with rare and special exceptions like the British miners' strike of 1984–85 (one of the greatest failures of militancy on record), industrial relations didn't worsen – they improved. It was hard even to remember that rebellion by the workers had alarmed managements all over Europe and North America as the 1970s began. That upsurge of unrest followed oddly on a decade in which, thanks to the blessings of behaviourial science, the worker's well-being had ostensibly received more nurture than ever before.

Inventions in employee relations ran from the joys of job enrichment to the rewards of productivity bargaining – and even to a new name for the discipline itself: human resources management. Yet the unions wanted still more for the steadily dwindling number of human resources in their care. Mysterious claims such as employee participation and co--ownership began to be heard alongside that simple, age-old need, more money.

By 1994, though, it was clear that even sharing the employer's own growth in capital wealth was not enough. The received wisdom had moved on to a different argument – that employees, like customers, deserved to be satisfied: indeed, that one satisfaction couldn't be achieved without the other. Moreover, employees couldn't be satisfied unless they contributed to the utmost of their ability, not as automata obeying orders, but as thinking men and women able to question and improve the way they worked.

Management thinkers had been arguing this case for years before. Under the lash of competition from better motivated and higher-skilled Japanese workers, Western companies, too, began to doubt the value of their own authoritarian attitudes. The lag is passing strange, given that the leaders of big business have long cast themselves as leading humanists. Most annual reports contain ritual tributes to the labour force ('Again the staff distinguished itself by its team effort, its enthusiasm, and its loyalty...').

Corporate heads are also fond of phrases such as 'Its able and dedicated employees continue to be the company's most valuable resource' or 'people are our most important product' or 'our most important asset'. Actually, people are often less important than physical assets – companies sometimes move whole operations to new towns, leaving their labour force in the lurch. Almost the entire New England textile industry shifted to the more pliable South; but its executives took care not to forget the up-to-date machines, either then or when they moved back to a now chastened North.

Even if people can't be replaced collectively, they are always disposable individually, especially in America, where swift 'downsizing' (i.e. reduction of workforces by involuntary lay-offs) is hailed as the competitive asset of 'flexibility'. Against this background, too few managements paid their labour forces enough attention until trouble actually broke out. Applied to machines, the same procedure causes instant chaos. But the labour force has not in general been regularly maintained. It is treated as an asset, possibly, but as a fixed asset that only requires attention when the wages plumbing goes wrong, or the pay boiler blows up in a strike, or the whole company springs a financial leak.

Most managements let their reactions to the emergency be dictated by external forces – the unions, the government, the law. In the Thatcher-Reagan years, companies gratefully accepted government's retreat from labour relations, although the withdrawal really amounted to intervention on the employers' side. Unions were faced down by President Reagan when the air-traffic controllers struck and by Mrs Thatcher, more spectacularly, when the miners inanely opposed pit cuts. But too few employers have turned the unions' weakness into lasting strength for the organisation.

Look at corporate America's relations with its labour force over recent years, and in comparison Jekyll and Hyde are Tweedledum and Tweedledee. For instance, 'quality of working life' or 'QWL', was warmly espoused by, among others, Westinghouse, TRW, Northrop, General Electric, Honeywell and General Motors; blue-chips as ever were, all converted, apparently, to the gospel of quality circles and other forms of worker participation.

Consider, however, this equally impressive list of top American corporations: the same General Motors, Ford, Chrysler, Timken, Armour, General Tire and a squadron of airlines. All these were among companies pressurising the unions not for participation, but for capitulation – giving up previously won conditions and wage levels under the threat of economic duress. Some give-backs are amazing; for instance, the meat-packers won a three-year wage freeze from their brow-beaten union.

Then consider the unheard-of scale of lost jobs. At Mobil, General Electric, USX, Union Carbide, Exxon, Ford, Amoco, Bethlehem Steel, Navistar and Du Pont, the losses over the 1981–91 decade ranged from 44,235 to 138,900. It takes an awful lot of quality of working life to make up for such quantities. So what was the true mood of American management? The strong arm or the soft touch? In reality, the name of the game was the same: to reduce labour's share of added value either by restricting wages or by raising output – or preferably both.

But the give-backs and cutbacks give the lie to any idea that US management has been suffused with new humanitarian – or even Japanese – principles. The pressure was not from the heart, but the pocketbook. Westinghouse, for instance, was, as John Thackray wrote in *Management Today*, 'a company badly in need of some magic after disastrous acquisitions, coupled with a crippling $1,000 million loss from fixed-price uranium contracts which were taken on as part of its nuclear reactor sales'. It badly needed to raise 'value added per employee' by 6% annually through a 'productivity-enhanc-ing programme', heavily involving quality circles – those Japanese devices (now made obsolete by total quality) in which groups of workers seek a joint solution to productivity problems.

William F. Schleicher, editor of the National Productivity Report, was among several observers far from convinced by the efforts of the 1980s: 'Management is using smoke words – "productivity", "quality of working life" – when really more than half the time the problem lies upstairs in the manage-ment suites' innumerable paper-pushers, the excessive layers of management. When production scheduling is poor, or purchasing doesn't have the right components for manu-facturing, management tries to cover up, saying quality circles will solve the problem.'

When the need for better profits comes in at the door, too, avant-garde ideas about permissive, progressive management tend to fly out of the window – anywhere in the world. Thus Sandoz, the chemical giant, seemed highly progressive in the 1970s. It shocked the formal, conservative Swiss by banning the use of titles in-company. Flexible working hours, infor-mal dress, attitude surveys, participation in decisions – you name it, Sandoz had it.

But enter the slower growth and harder profits of the later 1970s; enter, too, a new managing director; and re-enter nineteenth-century virtues, along with twentieth-century pressure for performance. Top Sandoz managers had their bonuses linked strictly to results: a euphemistically titled 'overhead value-analysis programme' really meant a McKinsey cost-cutting exercise that lost 15% of HQ staff their jobs. The chief cutter, Dr Marc Moret, noted that his ability to 'eliminate nearly 1,000 jobs without damaging consequences seems to indicate the cuts were justified' – and that neatly sums up what happens to people when performance, as ultimately it has to be, gets put before participation.

Boards seem to regard the care and maintenance of the labour force as an inferior function. In America, the personnel chief has as much chance of becoming president of the US as president of the company. In Britain, few 'human resources directors', as they now prefer to be called, are true directors – that is, on the main board. Status matters less if the chief executive makes labour relations his responsibility and knows how to manage them. Few do, and most wouldn't want to. The deterrent is that human beings in the mass are hard to handle; they are unpredictable, obstinate, demanding, intractable, and the wretches answer back.

Boards have preferred to mull over multi-million-pound investment projects, negotiate large and comforting mergers and their own pay deals (also large and comforting), and compose optimistic three- or five-year plans, rather than getting involved with the messy events on the factory or shop or office floor. This is a fatal error, precisely because manpower is not in reality an asset. It is more like a supply of raw material, changing but essential – the most important supply that a corporation consumes.

Because this is so, the workforce representatives are a company's most important suppliers, which makes it all the sillier in unionised companies that boards of directors have so little contact with union leaders, either at national or factory levels. In large tracts of America, the necessity for unwholesome contact can be avoided by keeping the plants free of union contamination. This usually involves either locating factories in the equivalent of the Australian outback – far from civilisation – or continually keeping a jump ahead of whatever the unions might demand.

The same gymnastic trick has been tried by American

subsidiaries in Britain, and it works; moreover, it works for the right reasons, even if done for the wrong ones. It demands that management think how to bribe the worker. It means switching from passive management of labour to active concern with its desires, treatment, and satisfaction. There is, of course, no reason why such active concern can't be combined with recognising unions. Most Japanese firms located in Britain combine the two (though they generally take the sensible precaution of recognising only one union, not the usual British plethora).

Even at the simplest level of forestalling strikes, no managerial effort can produce a better return on investment. After all, if the workers don't turn up, no other resource, except the stocks, has any current value. Yet managements are constantly surprised, even hurt, when their own folly makes the labour force march out. At one British engineering works, where the loyalty of the men and the company's prestige were both taken for granted, the management was so shattered by a walkout that it called in consultants. They found that a complex pay claim had been submitted two years before – so complex that the management, unable to understand it, had never replied.

The late, great A. J. Liebling tried in vain to persuade the American public that there are always two sides to any strike, that a deadlock requires an obdurate management as well as an obstinate union. The public, however, starts from the idea that the union is the protagonist, presumably because the strikers have to take the first active step by leaving the premises and posting pickets. Very few strikes are ever studied to discover who really is to blame; and the cause is often some abject management failure.

The public, or much of it, at least seemed to have grasped this truth when the railway signalmen launched a series of one-day strikes against their newly created employer, Railtrack, in the summer of 1994. Not only did the strikers have a plainly reasonable claim; but the company conducted itself with manifest incompetence, withdrawing an offer that had apparently been tabled, issuing confused and confusing statements, and showing all the antics of puppets on a string

– with the latter held by a government obsessed with keeping down wage settlements.

It took this major piece of mismanagement to resurrect the old spectre of militant public-sector unionism, laid to rest finally, most people thought, by Thatcherite policy, and with wonderful results. Yet in reality no economic miracle has followed the unmanning of the unions. True, unmanning in another sense – the reduction of workforces – has produced apparently encouraging rises in productivity. The encouragement ebbs away, however, when you note that it's been won from static production.

Nor do smaller and more docile workforces in themselves take industry towards Japanese levels of working and contented co-operation – which are far more important in keeping down Japanese costs than lower basic rates of pay. The relative all-quietness on the Western labour front since the start of the 1980s plainly doesn't indicate any great rise in worker contentment. As to whether seething discontent lies beneath an untroubled surface, if you really want to know people's feelings, you have to ask them – which usually means buying an employee attitude survey.

Having workers wrestle with the questionnaire (which a significant proportion never complete) is worthwhile, although the results will invariably look disappointing; that is, if you believe a 100% satisfied workforce to be obtainable. At Rank Xerox, for example, the results in its various national operations typically range from 46% satisfaction to 77%. But that reflects variations between countries rather than between individual companies. British workers are simply very hard to please; the norm is only 56% – that is, nearly half the British labour force is dissatisfied.

Often, workers distrust executives even more than executives distrust workers. The distrust can always be overcome by intelligent and honest management: the fact that distrust survives suggests that management falls well short on both adjectives. The ideal workers, from management's point of view, do what they are told without argument; never make mistakes; are punctual, clean, and tidy; produce maximum effort on a consistently rising scale; accept any working arrangements their superiors ordain; and never demand more pay than the firm can afford (i.e. the minimum that the management thinks it can get away with).

The blue- or white-collar paragon is expected to live a working life far more virtuous than that of the average executive – for that individual argues, makes mistakes, sometimes slacks, always expects big annual increments (larger than a blue-collar man usually even demands as total salary), and, though mostly clean and tidy, is often unpunctual. Yet the executive, cosseted with fringe benefits to the limit of the law, looks forward to substantial advances in real wealth year after year on the long road to a heavily pensioned retirement.

All men and women want the security of stable and predictable earnings, with a rising standard of living over the years, but in the conventional corporate context the 'workers' don't want any part of management's job. 'Industrial democracy' and 'worker's participation' sound well on a militant unionist's lips or on the brochure for an expensive management seminar. But it's hard enough to achieve democracy in any group of executives (what you might call executive participation) in most companies; letting other employees into the act is exceedingly difficult at the macro-level.

At the coal-face, though, great advances can be made. Self-managed work-groups, giving the members considerable power over what they do and how, have been highly successful in several companies. Total Quality Management likewise hinges on semi-autonomous groups tackling problems, often on their own initiatives, and always with all the means they require to produce their own solutions. But only a small percentage of employees are involved in these advances. The bulk of the workforce remains where it has always been: at the receiving end of a command-and-control culture.

Those executives at the middle level put up with being frozen out of the big decisions because they feel that they belong. Only in rare circumstances, and in carefully paternal companies, does the British or American worker share the same faith. In West Germany and Japan, historically the world's most strike-free industrialised economies, belonging is built into the social system, and paternalism cements the structure. Although the recipe is difficult to follow without the same social ingredients, that is the only way of making 'the most important asset' feel important.

But paternalism is no panacea. Real paternalism doesn't mean that the parents knows best. Like everybody else, parents are wrong half the time. The real need is to find managers who can look at the treatment of labour from labour's angle as well as their own. But this is not only hard work; it offends against the Third Truth of Management – no manager ever devotes effort to proving himself or herself wrong. Instead, companies prefer top-down injection of the newest medicine for satisfying the unsatisfied worker – 'job enrichment', say, or 'empowerment'.

The first was a marvellous 1960s piece of word-coining. Who can resist being 'enriched'? It means asking the workers about their work and finding ways to make workers' jobs more interesting and their performance more effective – the enrichers are peddling goods that sensible managements have always kept in stock. The annals of enrichment are unsurprisingly full of ripe successes. There was huge improvement in performance at one US factory that completely altered procedures to give more initiative to the workers – one old sweat promptly recalled that 'this was how the job used to be years ago'.

The old method had been abandoned to improve productivity, and now engines were being reversed for exactly the same reason and with exactly the same result. Empowerment, as that example indicates, is an extension of enrichment. The workers are encouraged to take the law into their own hands, even if they're still on an assembly line, rather than a flexible manufacturing cell, which is a basic self-managed group. At its simplest level, empowerment expects the worker to halt production if defects appear: a familiar practice in Japan since the 1950s.

Enrichment and empowerment generally raise performance, as do all changes that grab the interest of workers – installing piped music or (preferably) taking it out; painting the walls red, white, and mauve; returning them to plain green; enriching jobs or taking out the skill element by mechanisation; making the lighting brighter or changing its colour. Typically, the improvement in performance lasts for a limited period and then trails off; the workers regress towards their mean. They respond to the stimulus of somebody taking an interest, and backslide if the stimulus is allowed to wear off.

Executives lose interest too. Detroit Edison in the mid-1950s reorganised 1,000 employees in the accounting office, proving that job enrichment worked – but the office has been reorganised several times since and everybody has forgotten about it. Similarly, workers whose operations are studied in an unchanged operation habitually raise their performance (unless the study is designed to cut their pay per job in a piecework system, in which case they naturally lower their speeds). But foolish managers operate on the assumption that labour forces respond only to the one stimulus of money: hence the constant tinkering with schemes for payment-by-results.

Many of these schemes enshrine a hopelessly wrong principle – that you should pay people more to work sensibly, which means, of course, that up to now you have been paying them to work stupidly. As a former president of Honeywell once observed, 'It takes a very good factory management to make incentives work well. It takes outstanding supervision and if you have that, you don't need incentives.' Many years later, the same company's Newhouse plant in Scotland was a model demonstration of the newer approach – totally committed to total quality, which had produced large payoffs; but also totally committed to the policy that people didn't get paid for their excellent quality contributions: because, naturally, those were part of the job.

Total Quality Management à la Honeywell would never have achieved its momentum in the West without the Japanese example. Many observers have begun to point out, however, that common-sense strictures must be applied to naive beliefs that Japanese methods (whether in detail, like continuous quality improvement, or at large, like the whole paternalistic system) are the solution to Western anxieties. The main lessons that the Japanese have to offer aren't the very few too deeply rooted in their culture to be transplanted, but those which can be learnt by looking at any business or plant in the West that follows good labour practices.

A good Japanese company like Canon will have the following critical elements in its personnel policy: (1) carefully controlled numbers, (2) good, progressive pay, (3) good jobs, (4) excellent training, (5) promotion by assessed merit, (6) continuous and effective motivation programmes, (7) constant communication, (8) highly accessible management, (9) social equality within the company, (10) growth and constant change in products and processes . . . and so on.

These are standard elements (or should be) in any company, East or West, that takes its labour relations seriously. But even they won't guarantee peace, quiet and uninterrupted, bounteous production. Like fighting wars, managing people is full of disappointments – logical policies may not have logical results when you are dealing with human psychology. But illogic doesn't have to reign.

Management must, following in the footsteps of the best Japanese and their like, give the labour force a guaranteed acceptable level of earnings; consult fully with its people in changing equipment and methods or anything else, but with management retaining the obligation to lead; create a long-range manpower plan designed to provide steady employment; plan opportunities for promotion and good rises even for the unpromoted; give constant training throughout a man or woman's career; and equalise fringe benefits between all grades of employee.

None of this, however, is done because the good management expects good results to fall as manna from heaven as a direct consequence of good labour policies. It won't. The good company employs people humanely, generously, and thoughtfully because doing so is right and anything else is wrong – in principle, in practice and, almost certainly, in its outcome.

BOOK II:
MONEY GAMES

Introduction:
One Thing Doesn't Change

Management in the 1990s is in the throes of substantial, far-reaching change in most areas. Even Mammon has not been exempt from the revisionism of the gurus. Robert Waterman argues in his 1994 book, *The Frontiers of Excellence*, that profit-hungry leaders should heed a paradoxical message: 'Don't put profits first!'. He cites research into 1977–88 by John P. Kotter and James L. Heskett: it showed that companies which valued employees, customers and shareholders equally far outperformed those which put shareholders first.

Among the major companies studied, the first group grew four times faster in revenue, almost eight times better in job creation, came an amazing 756 times ahead in growth of net income – and gave their shareholders twelve times as much capital appreciation. Without question, on this evidence, profit should take a back seat while companies concentrate on the non-financial performance measures from which financial returns flow so bounteously. So much for theory. What about practice?

Consider these isolated but not unconnected events. In June 1994 an out-of-court settlement lowered the curtain on the case of Terry Smith. He had lost his job as head analyst with Phillips & Drew over a perfectly respectable book pointing out that sins of creative accountancy were being nakedly and unashamedly committed by some very large British companies. His employer, owned by a perfectly respectable Swiss bank, UBS, was the very same house that withdrew another analyst's note warning readers to avoid a poisoned chalice – the Robert Maxwell offer of shares in Mirror Group Newspapers.

Next in July 1994, the Department of Trade and Industry published its inspectors' report on the purchase of Atlantic Computers by the defunct British & Commonwealth. The latter's demise had been readily achieved by paying £400 million for a computer-leasing business which eventually generated losses of £550 million. According to the inspectors, Atlantic had reported £127.6 million of profit in 1983–88, a period when, if prudent (i.e. proper) accounting policies had been followed, Atlantic couldn't have reported 'any significant profits'.

The Atlantic revelations came amid a veritable glut of other cases in which directors of major firms were roundly accused of reporting non-existent profits. In another financial scandal, the drugs and surgical equipment maker Fisons had discovered years of systematic over-reporting of profits through 'trade-loading' – bunching sales into the last period of the financial year at exaggerated profit margins. In hotels, Queens Moat Houses had achieved similar results by taking in end-year profits that wouldn't be made (if ever) until the following year.

At another 'perfectly respectable' company, a famous US multi-national, December regularly sees anxious stuffing of unearned revenue (for instance, from licensing agreements that wouldn't come into effect until the next year) into the accounts. 'What this company needs,' said one executive, with grimly unconscious humour, 'is twelve Decembers a year.' Over in America, General Electric was still licking its wounds of humiliation after discovering that its Wall Street business, Kidder Peabody, had conjured $350 million of profits out of nowhere at all.

Robert Waterman is whistling in the dark. Three forces have combined to intensify the pressure on managers to report the highest possible profits that accounting conventions will allow. The first is the spread of pay for performance – the increasing role of bonus payments and stock options, etc in the executive pay packet. That's coupled with the adoption, at stock exchange insistence, of quarterly or half-yearly financial reports that intensify short-term pressures. Finally, Terry Smith is only one member of a legion of financial analysts whose power in the land has greatly enlarged; mostly, their appetite is slaked only by high and rising figures for earnings per share.

Winning their approval is one major object of an old industry with a new name – 'investor relations' or 'IR'. Everybody involved – corporate managers, auditors, analysts, their institutional employers and the IR practitioners – has a vested interest in putting profits and the share price first and foremost. The Terry Smith case is easily understood. His former Swiss employers come from a closed and secretive world where the sins of bankers (and they have been plentiful) are buried deep.

Such men have a fellow feeling for the offended businessmen, like Robert Maxwell (pre-death and disgrace) and the Grand Metropolitan directors, led by Sir Allen Sheppard, who objected to Smith's writings. Their motives are the ones of real interest. Maxwell, being the greatest and greasiest crook in financial history, couldn't afford any hint of informed criticism. The whole crazy Maxwell structure was resting on foundations as imaginary as Atlantic's profits, supported only by published accounts of the flimsiest value; the slightest breath of hot wind could have blown the house down.

The exposure of Grand Met's expert (or over-expert) accounting, though, wasn't going to undermine a multi-branded multi-national. The company's branded strength and strategic flexibility had convinced investors, and were the main reason for buying the shares. Of course, when a powerful chief executive all of a sudden learns that his beloved accounting techniques have been cited as bad examples by the head researcher of a top securities house, handles are liable to be flown off. Yet what excuse is there for using even one accountancy method, let alone several, in order to present a cosmetically better bottom line and balance sheet?

If the cosmetics produce a higher tax liability, creative accounting chews up shareholder value. But even if the tax implications are skirted with equal ingenuity, the company has a tiger by the tail. It can only revert to more conservative practices in a year sufficiently bountiful for the reported figures to take the strain – or one so awful that another few millions lost make no difference. Unusual accounting practices sustained over several years have this nasty habit of one day blowing up in the perpetrator's face.

The investment analysts, you might think, are there to expose these shenanigans, and sometimes they do, without suffering the penalties of Smith or the Maxwell whistle-blower (who also had to change employers). Analysts, though, have a foot in both camps; their services are directed towards advising investment clients on what to buy or sell, but their powerful employers badly want the business of the large corporations who are the subjects of the analysis. The conflict of interest is self-evident, and there's no doubt which interest is going to win.

The same statement is true of the 'permanent conflict' of interest within the corporation between long-term, Waterman-style management and the financially driven short term. The phrase in quotation marks is that of Bernard Fournier, the managing director of Rank Xerox, which, along with the parent Xerox Corporation has devoted a decade of intense effort to battling back against Japanese competitors with successful long-term programmes built around Total Quality. But this is an American corporation, driven by financial results – which has sometimes made it 'very difficult to protect quality investments'.

Cutbacks in non-financial programmes produce quick financial benefits, so 'A few companies stopped the quality drive, and the [quality] indicators went right down'. However much today's top managers preach non-financial virtues, in other words, they still practise in the same way as yesterday's money-grubbers. Earnings per share and price per share are the goals and the goads. When the chips are down, it's only the chips that count – even if some are counterfeit. That's one aspect of naked management that can only change for the better, but which has hardly changed at all.

7
How Profits Get Plucked

If management had a god, it would be Mammon – symbolised by a column of profits. Even in the deepest British backwaters, the most stagnant Midwest hinterland, the darkest Ruhr iron foundry, possibly even the most paternalistic sweatshop in Osaka, every executive knows that profit is the name of the game, the objective and the measure of managerial performance. But what is a profit?

In common-or-garden life, the answer sounds easy: profit is the difference between what something costs and what you sell it for. Common-or-garden ideas, however, become complex and slippery in the higher (or lower) reaches of business management. True, profit is the difference between costs and revenues, but what are costs and what are revenues?

Quite commonly, after a losing fight against takeover, or against financial collapse, profit forecasts and actual reported, audited profits turn out to bear no more relation to the truth than a sci-fi fantasy. The discrepancies aren't minor; at the fugitive Asil Nadir's Polly Peck they added up to £300 million, which seems a hard sum to mislay. The essential point thus illustrated is that conventional accounting does not produce the one accurate figure by which managers are supposed to live.

True, strange things happen in the heat and dust of battle. But odd things also occur in time of peace. The largest manufacturer of them all, General Motors, in 1988 plucked an estimated $1.8 billion out of thin air through some creative accountancy changes. This saved the colossus from reporting a miserable 8.6% return on equity for that year. But the clever accountants couldn't prevent GM from crashing into billions of losses in the early 1990s as its sins of commission and omission came home to roost.

Just as pride goeth before a fall, so has cosmetic surgery on the profits often preceded a collapse. For instance, the first spots of sickness at Lockheed broke out in 1968, when it added 50% to alleged profits by a switch in accounting for overheads on the government contracts which provided all but a tenth of its takings. Even then, Lockheed's performance was distinctly earth-bound, which added fiercer point to the vital question: 'Had Lockheed actually made that extra 50% or hadn't it?'

Even if the previous method understated 'true' profits, could the Lockheed management take credit, in reputation or in pocketing bonuses and salary increases, for extra profits that had been 'earned' by its accountants? Lockheed's example is made more glaring by the Nemesis that lay in wait; but other managers all over the world constantly recook the books by which they are judged.

Thus Texas Instruments, clobbered with $660 million of home-computer losses, managed to keep its corporate deficit to a relatively modest $145 million by the neat device of putting all the tax benefits in its 1983 accounts – even though they weren't all being used that year. Then consider the findings of security analyst Thornton O'Glove, quoted in *Fortune* magazine on the case of Union Carbide. One year the company 'lengthened depreciation periods for machinery and equipment, and started taking the benefits of investment tax credits into accounting profits in the year they arose instead of spreading the credits over time. Both changes increased reported earnings.'

O'Glove thinks the new procedures contributed 18% of Union Carbide's earnings per share in the first year and

15%, 28%, and 26% in the following three years. Then there's Allied Bancshares, whose treasurer had a neat explanation for its special reserves: 'When you are bumping along with such good earnings, you don't get any benefit by showing extraordinary increases. Some years we could have reported extremely higher earnings than we did.' As they piled up the reserves, the outside accountants, Peat Marwick Mitchell, began raising questions. ' "Golly, folks," they told us, "as clean as y'all are looking, this is getting a little ridiculous!" '

The breasts of such managements were no doubt clean, their motives pure. But either before revision or after, the accounts must have portrayed an untrue picture of their lovely corporate finances. Bearing out the point about finagling going before a fall, not only did Lockheed run into financial setback shortly after its fine exhibition of dynamic accounting – Union Carbide was unable to raise its earnings per share over an entire decade.

Perhaps the creation of invisible profits is a sign, registered in the conscious or subconscious of executives, that the real profits are drying up. For there is a real profit, just as there is reality behind the notion of capital employed. However, conventional profit is outstretched for elasticity only by conventional capital employed; and expressing one of these prize uncertainties as a ratio of the other mystery – dividing the profit by the capital to get a pretty percentage – cannot measure anything at all; that is, while the true ratio must be a vital indication of the true health of a business, what, as Pontius Pilate asked, is truth? What is profit?

The question has become even more insistent in the light of the late Richard Nixon's most important contribution to economics – and maybe to world history: the international monetary system in which currencies, instead of being tied to a fixed dollar, are free to float against each other. This poses a truly insoluble problem to accountants and to managers trying to use accounts as a management tool – for movements in exchange rates over which nobody has any control, and for which nobody is to blame, can make an almighty difference to profits.

Except, of course, that they don't. If a company has an affiliate in Britain earning £10 million on £100 million of capital, that is worth $24 million if the pound is selling at $2.40 (as it was in Mrs Thatcher's finest hour). If the pound drops to $1.20 (as it did), and the affiliate turns in an unchanged performance, the numbers change dramatically; and a $12 million profit represents a disastrous 50% decline. Moreover, the assets in dollar terms are theoretically worth 50% less.

Some managements were trapped in an exquisitely painful version of *Catch-22*. Their American overlords demanded that they make their financial targets in dollars – even if the dollar fell against their home currency. Thus (to use British figures again) an affiliate boss who had committed himself to a £10 million profit at $1.80 ($18 million) was expected to produce $18 million come hell, high water or a $1.20 exchange rate. On the other hand, if the pound had risen to, say, $2, he would still have been expected to hit the original £10 million target – and the extra $2 million would have gone into the profit column, no doubt to self-congratulation all round.

Businesses and heads of corporations don't earn profits; they earn money. Profit is an abstraction from the true, underlying movement of cash in and cash out. Any small businessman who has had trouble meeting the payroll knows the painful principle: without enough cash, you drown. Larger businessmen have learned the same lesson in the same brutal way; the mighty Chrysler in the US very nearly ran out of hard currency; so did Rolls-Royce; so did a one-time textile star whose chairman recalled to stockholders, 'We were unable to pay the interest on the loan stock, or the wages on the Friday night, and already several cheques had bounced.'

A big company's cheques can rebound just as high as those of a little shopkeeper. But many top executives, even in suave and sophisticated organisations, have been slow to master the truth that what counts at the end of the day is the cash in the kitty – not the abstractions in the books. The object of honest managers is to fit the abstraction to the reality as nearly as they may. Any managers who toy with procedures to invent a higher profit must search their souls long and harshly. Will the change paint a truer likeness, or will it obscure the truth?

For certain high-tech companies, the dilemma is acute. They need, and badly, lofty stock-market ratings to attract the capital for which they slaver, so they have high incentive to report high profits. Yet their spending on research and development has an unpleasant way of devouring any cash left over from financing equally voracious long-term manufacturing projects.

How such stars treat R & D, and how they value stocks and work in progress, determines their 'profits' far more than what they actually manage to sell. When the managers of Rolls-Royce, as one executive later put it, 'were having trouble showing a profit', the directors adopted a new magic formula. They assessed 'the value of R & D recoverable from sales resulting from existing aero-engine orders'. This lusty sum was not charged against the income for the year in the accounts (though it was paid out of that income). The money spent was instead counted as an asset, and Rolls (hey, presto) duly showed a profit.

This handy device has been employed by utterly respectable companies with the noblest intentions. But the money to be made from future engine sales was not the question that should have bugged the engineers of Rolls. The real issue was whether they could earn enough bread from existing business. The answer was crystal clear from its own books several years before the Rolls-Royce calamity. The company couldn't, and didn't, earn nearly enough.

Unable to cover its dividend, let alone all its R & D spending, from profits, the company raised £17.4 million from its poor benighted stockholders one year. In effect, they thus paid for their own dividends, which was kind of them. Rolls went on having trouble 'showing a profit' because there was little or none to show. It was bad books, as much as the RB-211 engine for the Lockheed Tristar, that ran Rolls out of cash, unhorsed the chairman and unravelled the company.

If published accounts, with a little easy disentangling, can reveal hard reality to outsiders, there is no excuse for insiders missing the point. The harsher the truth, however, the happier executives are to hide it from everybody – especially themselves. The lives and ambitions of the Rolls-Royce men were bound up with building 'the best aero-engines in the world'. As the chairman put it, 'We don't care whether you propel 'em with squibs or with elastic bands. We'll be up in front whatever the method.' To admit that they could not be up front at a profit would have negated their whole existence.

A misinformed executive is a doomed one. Witness one brave boss of a small British company. He went after export business on the heroic scale at prices that covered only component costs and direct labour – and failed to take any account of increased overheads and direct expenses. 'Why didn't somebody tell me this before?' demanded the poor fellow, as they led him away to liquidation.

The first fact of life that any manager needs to know is the likely cash effect of decisions: what must be paid out, how that spending will be financed – including what income the firm will receive – and when. Cash-flow accounting excludes notional expenditures (items, such as depreciation, that don't represent physical cash leaving the premises) and also deletes notional income (such as the money that will be earned when, please God, somebody buys the inventory). It includes all real spending (such as R & D) and is only interested in real receipts (the safe arrival of somebody else's cash).

True, if company accounts were written only in this hardheaded way, a different distortion would follow. For instance, if the inventory is about to be snapped up by a screaming public, just counting its cost, without taking in any added value, must understate the lucky company's profitability. There was one building contractor who only took in profits when his bills were settled – and accountants thought him dangerously eccentric. As a matter of fact, he was, but not for the reasons advanced by his critics.

As later events revealed, the arrival of profits in his accounts didn't take place until long after the work had been completed (especially since this particular financial genius garnered his profits not from the original contract, but from the claims for extra work). This was fine, so long as business continued to be good; but when, one far from fine day, it turned down, the grim reality of his trading experience was concealed by the profits being taken into the books from long years before. The first the world (and maybe the genius) knew of all this was when the company suddenly and comprehensively went bust – still showing a profit.

But are such distortions any more severe, or dangerous, than the folderols of conventional profit or loss accounting? That is a subject on which Saul Steinberg, the now ancient whizz-kid of computer leasing, who built a still greater fortune by switching into insurance and out of leasing computers before the latter business died on him, had an interesting education. His teacher was Robert Maxwell in the days when the latter's fame rested solely on Pergamon Press.

As the boy genius who invented Leasco by dazzling financial manoeuvres, Steinberg must have had a good and twitching nose for a balance sheet. Yet he accepted Pergamon's declared profits and forecast, and compounded his folly by buying shares in the open market – an escapade which eventually forced Leasco to write off some ten million sorely needed pounds. Yet the balance sheet told the story, even on a casual, but curious glance; in the year of a reported £2 million profit, Pergamon's cash ran downhill by £2 million.

That £4 million slalom should have led Steinberg to ask some tough prior questions. As it was, later researches – much too late for Leasco – turned that £2 million profit into only £495,000; and that was before taking account of stupendous losses on the company's doomed effort to imitate the *Encyclopaedia Britannica*. This was an early demonstration of Maxwell's addiction to the Goebbels theory of truth; returning from a world tour, he claimed vast sales of his encyclopaedia when not a single set had been sold.

Books illustrate beautifully why a profit need not be a profit. The highest point at which the publisher can value a book is his own selling price. This assumes that the books will

all be sold. If they are not, the publisher has taken credit for
an unearned profit, and future losses lie literally in store.
Books can be valued at cost (which assumes, less hazardously,
that sales will at least reach the break-even point) and then
written down yearly. Or they can be valued as pulp (virtually
nil), which accurately mirrors the cash position, at the
expense of favourably distorting profits in future years.

Of the two extreme positions – stating current year's
profits at the highest or lowest possible level – the latter must
be most desirable, less misleading to the honest publisher.
Reality, however, lies somewhere in-between. Always select
the most conservative accounting portrayal which is consistent with previous years and with the inexorable reality of
cash flow in and out of the business – and which puts off
paying tax as long as possible.

Precisely when the cash reality shows up is less important
than the knowledge that, one day, show up it will. One small
company reported large monthly losses although its bank
balance was mounting sky-high. The explanation lay in ultra-
conservative accounts (subscription revenue was coming in,
but being phased over a whole year); and the prognosis was
rudely healthy. The reverse situation – a business combining
high, wide, and handsome profits with a rapidly rotting cash
position – more often than not leads but to the grave.

With financial half-truths (or downright untruths) the
outcome is the same as with boxers; the bigger they are, the
harder they fall. Yet sometimes the 'truth' produces absurd-
ities on the capital side of return on capital employed. The
return (or the profit) is whatever executives choose to make
it within a latitude wide enough to cover many sins. But the
similar yo-yo characteristics of capital employed operate
differently. For instance, should you value property at cost or
present-day worth? Because of the general inflation of
property values, revaluation of a store chain could easily
double the capital employed. This is a more 'realistic' and
conservative figure – yet, if you do revalue, the return on
capital will halve.

Assuming (extravagantly) that profits are truly calculated,
which is the more accurate return? The conservative one

may be more misleading; it puts forward, as a realistic alternative (it seldom is), the proposition that the properties could be sold off en bloc at market value. You could argue that whenever the property worth of a business rises above its value as a going concern, the business should be folded and the property leased. What's the point of sweating to make a profit if you can earn the same in easy rent? Alas, on this criterion, half the businesses in the world would be forced to close.

There are sometimes potent reasons for revaluing your assets, and rapidly. When the British government announced that it would switch to a return-on-capital basis for working out its price for milk, the dairy chains reached for higher valuations as one man. That was entirely understandable. But the nonsense of accounts, in which disappearing or appearing tricks can be worked with profits and everything else, was never more fully revealed, and over many years at that, as when Anglo-Saxon accountants bent their brains to the question of inflation.

For decades, the impact of inflation had been blithely ignored, even though it was perfectly obvious that conventional accounting, based on historic (i.e. actual) cost, over-stated profits – not because a pound earned after 10% inflation was worth 10% less (though it was), but because the replacement cost of assets became higher than the original cost. It's the book-publishing argument all over again. If you use inventory in making a product, do you charge the price it really cost in pounds – or the price it will cost you to replace it?

The answer became of more than academic importance when inflation advanced into double digits. Companies which were showing profits might actually – were actually – failing to make a true surplus large enough to cover their dividends, quite apart from any other purposes. Worse still, they were paying taxes on profits that were non-existent, crumpled by hyper-inflation. So the greatest brains in accountancy set to work on 'current cost accounting' – a revision of the rules that, by reflecting the ravages of inflation, would give a more accurate, more honest picture of these profits.

This admirable effort, though, hit several snags. One of the most prominent is that companies gain, as well as lose, by inflation. Replacement costs rise, sure. But repayment costs fall, too: that is, a company that borrows £100 million in 1985 won't repay 100 million 1985 pounds in 1995. It will pay back those 100 million smackers less whatever the intervening amount of inflation has been. The financial picture wouldn't be accurate and honest without taking that profit into account – except that it's a profit that has never been pocketed.

The conundrums of inflation accounting were predictably (I cay say that safely, because I predicted it) still unresolved when hyper-inflation subsided, leaving the accounting profession, on both sides of the Atlantic, still unable to agree on the cure for a disease that had largely disappeared. But every attempt to make accounts more real (as many accountants joyfully pointed out) only made them more fictitious. In the real world, anyway, real managements and real corporate finance men were perfectly happy with fictitious operations of their own – for real reasons: for example, the beleaguered banks.

You would expect these institutions, keepers of corporations' money, to be the keepers of their financial consciences as well. But under the pressure of their own misjudgments, the big US banks adopted practices that roused a New York accounting professor, Abraham Briloff, to a high pitch of indignation: 'the essential process of gamesmanship with and within accounting still prevails', he thundered.

'One would have assumed', Briloff continued, 'based on ordinary, logical reasoning, that the loss would inexorably have to be recognised when a bank picks up a property worth $1 million in exchange for a loan on its books of $10 million. And one might have expected a certain inexorability with respect to bank accounting when the banks were compelled to swap a $100 million New York City bond for a new bond worth $60 or $70 million.' In fact, to Briloff's wrath, the banks didn't adjust their accounts at all.

Profits that really have crumbled, it seems, can stay intact just as magically as profits that never existed at all can be conjured out of thin paper. A favoured wheeze for companies losing money on favourite ventures, borrowing a leaf from the aerospace accountants, is to call it 'development spending' and capitalise it (i.e. overstate profits by that amount). Lord Thomson, busy dissipating some of the profits of North American monopoly newspapers and broadcasting, in the doomed effort to turn *The Times* into a goldmine, called his staggering losses (made for sixteen consecutive years) 'development' and treated them as such.

The accounting treatment made the drain no less, however, as was demonstrated when the disgusted Thomsonians finally decamped – and had to write off some £30 million. Their loss was Rupert Murdoch's gain: the Thomsons' *Sunday Times*, worth many times its purchase price, helped wonderfully to sustain his fortunes when over-borrowing threatened collapse. It took much financial wizardry, and dazzling juggling of banks and bankers, for Murdoch to escape intact; but in the end what saved him was his operational genius as a media tycoon.

Financial gimmickry has nothing to do with operating a business; the company director is only playing with numbers. The trouble is that not only investors and financial writers get mesmerised by the number game; so do the directors themselves. And when the profits in the case finally rot away, it is too late for the mesmerised director to wake up.

8
The Accountancy Dodge

Whenever a company fails, or a management wakes up covered in financial mud, one relevant question seldom gets asked: 'What were the accountants up to?' Every failed management was advised, hectored, and helped by its own accountants, its auditors' accountants, possibly those of its favourite money-lender. Accountants are highly trained professionals in the management and recording of financial transactions. Yet collapse and calamity reveal them blithely or blindly accepting figures that would set alarm bells ringing in a half-trained mind.

This is nothing new, no product of the notorious excesses of the greedy 1980s. Long ago, a whole series of disasters in the US, from the Penn Central crash to the Continental Illinois crunch, raised unquenchable doubts about the efficiency of audits – given such sights as the lack of resemblance between reality and the published reports of the befuddled railroad, not to mention the beleaguered banks.

The Penn Central affair was only one of several contemporary horrors – like National Student Marketing, Equity Funding and Stirling Homes; names mostly long forgotten despite stupendous frauds and/or misrepresentations: forgotten to be replaced only by the next catastrophe, like the abrupt collapse of confidence at savings and loan growth star (or ex-star), Financial Corporation of America.

Here the regulators, stepping in where the auditing accountants had apparently feared to tread, decided that a $31 million second-quarter profit was in reality somewhat different: a $107 million loss. Such a sequence, such a size of disasters, questions the accountant's usefulness as a source of management information, as auditor of the accounts, and even as a reliable keeper of the financial score. But that should be no surprise. The accountant is playing an elaborate game, whose purpose is not to tell the truth (for truth is a chimera), but to stay within the rules.

The rules in turn are not designed to make managers more efficient, or to inconvenience crooks, or even to keep companies solvent. They are there simply to allow the game itself to proceed. That explains how accountants so unctuously wash their hands of blame or dirt when disaster strikes – even so vast a disaster as the collapse of the Bank of Credit and Commerce International. They can always try to prove (and have been forced to try by a wave of legal actions) that they played their game according to their rules. Unfortunately, management is a different game entirely – that of producing more resources than the ones you started out with.

It's not the accountant's fault, moreover, if the executives they work for suffer from the widespread malaise of good old financial ignorance. Most executives, like most people, but more oddly, do not truly understand money in a personal sense (they handle their own financial affairs unintelligently) or in their business capacity. That's certainly true in Europe, and truer than you might think in an America where top executives feather their own nests with avaricious acumen. It was in the US that big-business managers (even unto the sharp-eyed hawks employed by money-lender Walter E. Heller and the cautious corporate owls of American Express) tripped over in their eagerness to become the victims of Billie Sol Estes, filler of phantom harvest silos, and Tino de Angelis, filler of phantom salad-oil tanks.

The problem is not even that managers lack the accountants' technical education in money – although that, too, can produce strange effects. One respected chairman of a family company complained bitterly when told that he couldn't finance a pet project. 'What,' he grumbled, stabbing at the company's lovely new balance sheet, 'about all those reserves?' Nobody had told him that reserves in accounting terms merely exist to make the left-hand side of the balance sheet equal the right-hand side. More often than not, however, guilty executives (assuming that they are also honest) are more innocent than unlettered.

A grim story about one crashed company reveals the distinction. One of its too-late rescuers put the corporate figures in a new presentation. The recast showed, sadly but convincingly, that the outfit could never make a profit, no matter what. He duly presented his findings to his fellow directors. 'Your figures are wrong,' answered one. 'But they are your figures,' said the outsider. 'Well,' remarked the inside man, 'that's an interesting way of looking at it.'

Financial genius, fortunately, is not required of the business manager. But managers, the uncrashed as well as the crashed, often possess the reverse of genius – blind refusal to see inconvenient financial facts or, if confronted with the revolting truth, to admit its significance. The results of their innocence (which in the case of artists in the company-promotion racket may not be so innocent) are written all over their overdrafts.

The essence of money in management is, first, that cash in must exceed cash out. This Fourth Truth of Management is the Law of the Barrow – known to every sweatshop on Seventh Avenue or barrow boy in Petticoat Lane. A cash deficiency is not solved by borrowing money from stockholders, from equally innocent financiers, or from far too friendly neighbourhood bankers. Debt merely postpones the day of reckoning: sooner or later (and the sooner the better) there must be a cash surplus, and the more you borrow, the bigger that eventual surplus has to be. But like any small businessman sprinting for trouble, a great many top executives incur immense expense, and allow subordinates to pile up still more extravagance, without more than a misty idea of the monetary consequences.

One management consultant learned the Law of the Barrow by starting four businesses of his own. He saw two flourish, while two shrivelled up. With a bookkeeper as chastity belt, he had watched over the cash of the two ripe successes like a jealous husband. In the two sour failures, the cash was left to look after itself. Yet in larger companies directors often pay no attention to the amount of existing cash or its future availability (to make sure that they don't run out of the stuff).

The accountants and auditors will make sure that their client does discover these two indispensable facts. Accountants, since they are often called in as undertakers, know more than anybody about the life-or-death importance of cash. But as auditors they have often certified accounts, referring to events well past, though they don't know (and can't be expected to know) whether or not at the moment of approval cash is pouring out in great lukewarm gouts.

The bigger the company, the more academic an audit becomes. The auditors for Royal Dutch-Shell presumably earn every pound, guilder, and dollar of their magnificent fees. But they can't do much more, in a company that gets through $99 billion of business each year, than approve the performance of Shell's own internal accountants, advise the directors on knotty points of tax law, do the odd spot-check to see that nobody has run away with bits of the company – and collect those enormous fees.

The notion that auditors are at arm's length from directors is, in any case (as everybody should know), a blatant fairy-tale of accountancy and management. The stockholders in theory appoint the auditors – but in annual general meetings that are under the thumb of the directors and their captive proxies. Finance directors and auditors are in close and cosy contact. Even suppose an auditor does smell an accounting rat; he won't dream (except in nightmares) of making a public row. He will try to persuade the director to change his malodorous figures; or, more commonly, the director will persuade the auditor that the inventory in Nicaragua really

105

has doubled in value overnight. In the end the auditor almost always has to accept the business judgment of the directors.

Sometimes, alas, it's not the board's judgment that auditors must accept, but its lies. The most conspicuous and unpleasant evidence of this was the revelation of bribery and corruption – 'illegal payments' in the vernacular – at the end of the 1970s. The corporate miscreants, from Lockheed downwards (downwards being *le mot juste*), employed what John Thackray, writing in *Management Today*, called 'varied and ingenious gimmicks' that 'were all but impossible for outside auditors to detect'.

According to one study, 'independent auditors were repeatedly stymied by corporate clients that entered the amount of the illegal or improper payment on their books, but misrepresented its real nature or purpose; or by hidden Swiss bank accounts; or by phoney duplicate books, etc.' The ingenuity at Schering-Plough involved eight different formulae in seven different countries – and over $810,000 in questionable payments. Reports Thackray: 'These disbursements were variously listed as commissions, professional service fees, or cash discounts on sales, general office expenses, travel and entertainment, and grants and consultancies, or a representation expense.'

Not only are accountants not lie-detectors – they aren't businessmen. (As one accountancy firm proved by going into a wine company, noting correctly that it was wildly overstocked with one of Bordeaux's greatest years and instructing its customer to sell off those marvellous wines – later worth much fine gold – at cost price.) In the end, the accountant adjusts his fiction to the executive's version of the facts. Dishonesty need not enter his or her head. Accountants know perfectly well that firms which gain a reputation for being uncooperative don't get audit work – and audit work is their basic source of income, to which accountants are not wholly indifferent. The key is that they are free within the rules of their game to choose whichever version of the same truth they like.

That's still the case, even though auditors should have

been put on their guard, not to mention their mettle, by the increasing likelihood of facing lawsuits in the event of real or suspected dereliction of duty. As one writer was moved to observe, 'There isn't a major auditing firm that has escaped public SEC censure or a barrage of costly suits in recent years' – costly being the word; when the offended parties sued Arthur Andersen, alleging duff audits of John De Lorean's car firm, the price-tag was £350 million (though, as the author wryly noted, 'in such cases it is the corporate clients and ultimately the shareholders who foot the bill, by paying, in the fee structure, for more costly indemnity insurance').

The tale of two truths is an intrinsic part of 'turnaround jobs', of the company-revival game. New management moves into a deadbeat, loss-laden company and turns it round – as Lee Iacocca famously did with Chrysler (turned round once before by an earlier management, as it happens); or as a host of professional turnaround men have done with the legions of battered businesses created by the storms of the 1980s. But the key is more easily turned than appearances suggest. If the past conduct of the company has been paralytic, doing better is no terrifying test of the new men. The accountant, moreover, can help to make a turnaround man look more beautiful than he is.

The technique is to examine the corporate patient coldly from top to bottom. Every loss that could or should be taken is written back into the accounts, thus flatly contradicting the previous accountants' version of events. If the sick business has only rudimentary financial controls, every cupboard will be full of old bones; simply installing a sensible system ensures that no more skeletons will accumulate in the subsequent year. That year, the first of the new management, inevitably shows an inspiring improvement because of the absence of the previous year's bumper write-offs. This only heightens the optical-illusion effect which arises in all turn-arounds, even if the accountants lean over backwards not to gild the new man's lily.

Penn Central is a case in point. Compared to the financial chasm of 1973, when earnings per share reached an abysmal

negative figure of $119.33, almost any subsequent manage-
ment performance would have looked good; and a number
like that of 1982 (a positive $3.02) must seem like a miracle.
Innocents (the turnaround executives, as well as investors)
often look at the before-and-after figures and beam broadly:
but what about the absolute figures? What about the real
strengths of the company? In 1983, Penn Central reverted to
type – losing forty-eight cents a share – yet management
could still claim that the much-changed company was performing vastly better than ten years before (for what that was
worth).

Turnarounds should always be compared, not with the bad
old days, but with present standards of good performance.
Even a phrase like 'present standards of good performance',
however, leaves an executive in the helping hands of accounting conventions. The profit that an executive shows is 'after
depreciation'. Many British executives believe that the with-
ering-away of depreciating assets is real. You can, of course,
go too far the other way. Back in 1926 (which shows that the
more things change the more they are the same), Arm-
strongs, the famous British defence contractor, showed a
profit 'conjured out of optimistic depreciation figures' when
on its way to the slaughterers.

The distinction is between profit and cash flow. If you buy
a machine for £1 million and it has to be scrapped after ten
years, it makes evident sense to knock off 10% each year; but
in the process a fiction is created – that the company has
made £100,000 less money in the first year, £90,000 less the
next, and so on. In fact, the directors get their hands on
the 'depreciation' money, to do with what they will, and
the company pays less tax. The real depreciation, and its
real financial impact, takes place only when the thing is
scrapped.

The reverse analogy is that of a man who buys a house,
reckons it will be worth twice as much in ten years' time (7%
per annum compounded), and credits his income with the
7% appreciation each year. Clearly ridiculous. But the
shareholder has no way of knowing whether the directors
have allowed too much for depreciation or too little. Some

accountants used to argue, before hyperinflation set in, that in the US the amounts written off in depreciation over the years were excessive. In other words, higher profits should have been reported to stockholders – and higher dividends could have been handed out.

The boot, however, then moved swiftly on to the other foot. In 1979, *Business Week* worked out that, five years before, American companies had so far failed to allow for inflation in their depreciation policies that they paid 63% tax on their profits – and then paid out all but 1% of the remainder to their stockholders as dividend. That year, two-thirds of US companies were still using FIFO accounting (First In, First Out) for use of inventory: that is, they chose the method which maximised their tax and minimised their provision for the inflation of their replacement costs.

Thanks to such self-defeating stupidity, the companies of America, so *Business Week* concluded, paid $17 billion more tax on 1978 profits than they should have done. They also gave shareholders two-thirds of the residue – much of it money which was vitally needed to repair the damage caused by the years of under-investment laid bare by Japanese competition. But tax laws have encouraged the stockholder to shun dividends, anyway. The net result, as Peter Drucker once pointed out, was to put more and more easy money into the hands of fat, old, established corporations and their executives – who, by every test, are least adept at using the stuff.

The inferior use of capital by big companies is self-evident even from the accountants' figures. In 1969, the median return on invested capital of the 500 largest US companies was 11.3%; in 1983 the figure was still only 10.8%; in 1993, acclaimed as a whale of a year for profits, it was 9.3%. Given that invested capital, as noted in an earlier chapter, is a flattering base, it's clear that, even in a period of greatly reduced inflation, many companies had little or nothing left over with which to create new resources for expansion.

The annals are full of cases of giants which have failed to earn enough to cover the interest charges on big long-term borrowings. One director in such a fix explained that a business of colossal size, doubling every seven years, can't hope to generate all its capital internally. But if the cost of capital exceeds the rate of return, a manager can't hope to generate any income at all from investing the new money.

Directors don't deal in concepts like the marginal cost of capital. So they gladly borrow long-term money at going rates of interest when they have existing businesses earning below that mark – unless they have the fortune to find and listen to an accountant who spots their folly. Far better to close or sell the corporate drags to finance the new and hopefully more rewarding ideas. Yet most executives, because of their fond attachment to what they manage rather than to its results, insist on retaining interests or products that run the gamut from poor profitability to aching loss, without understanding that even a low-profit business is a tax on the company's good apples.

Even more amazing, great companies purchase others for prices which appear to demand the financially impossible. Thus, to justify the $7.3 billion price-tag on Continental Oil, the purchaser, Du Pont, would have had to achieve an average 28% on equity for two whole decades; and that necessity compared with an actual return of only 22% recorded by Conoco in a period of stupefyingly high oil prices – which nobody expected to recur.

In cases of great merger misfortune, such as Dunlop's union with Pirelli, which promptly ran into horrendous Italian losses, the accountants may kindly arrange to have the losses put outside the company's accounts altogether. That, however, doesn't truly dispose of the losses, which were real enough to burden Dunlop with £50 million of write-offs, starting it on the path of mounting debt and declining effectiveness that led to virtual bankruptcy and actual take-over.

Financial figures are not the be-all and end-all of a business. Far from it – accurate money statistics are valuable only as a universal way of portraying physical reality. Profit is the result, not the objective, of efficient management; it is the outcome of selling, pricing, producing, distributing, and organising effectively. If the figures are terrible, it is always because the directors have failed in more tangible areas than the books. The latter, as an index of performance, do, however, serve as weapons to control, as guides to making physical efficiency less inefficient – provided you have the will.

One tasty little financial graph produced inside a big company showed a line plunging down right off the graph paper; it was a chart of the downward variance from budgeted losses. In situations like this, accounting has ceased to have any relevance to management. Control means taking action when the instruments give their warning. It's no good sitting helplessly in mission control, like many accountants and their bosses, while the company spins off forever into financial outer space.

9
The Inflationary Singalong

Nobody has taken a tougher line against inflation down the years than the big-business executive. Nobody deplores high wage claims with greater fervour – or greater self-interest – since nobody else faces these monstrous demands. Nobody has applauded right-wing, anti-inflation politicians louder or backed their parties, Republican in the US, Conservative in Britain, more willingly or with more cash. And nobody was more baffled when in the 1970s, and then again in the late 1980s, as the right tried to damp down inflation, sales fell, profits crumpled, orders melted away, stock prices slid, and money got hard to find and ruinous to borrow.

Corporate man never paused to note that, of all bene-ficiaries of moderate inflation, nobody had out-benefited the corporate boss. Every executive knows that the ultimate proof of corporate success is growth (a few suspect that profitable growth, while tougher, is far more meaningful). The blue-chip that doubles sales in seven years, assuming that some profit cream goes with the jam, can reckon to earn the thanks of shareholders, the warmth of stockbrokers, and unreasonable options for the brains in the boardroom. For most leviathans, more dazzling progress looks pure pie-in-the-sky; to double every five years, a £2 billion monster must find £300 million of extra sales in the first year alone.

Short of acquisition, there is little hope of reaching this nirvana – and acquisition is not true growth. Of itself, a £2,000 million company's ability to pay £300 million for somebody else's sales says nothing about the purchaser's managerial quality. Even a self-generated (or 'organic') growth target of only 10% a year must be a definite stretch; at least, most corporations can't seem to reach that mark without the benefit of inorganic acquisitions.

Remember those figures, quoted in the first two chapters, showing the poor performance of the *Fortune* 500 over the 1973–83 decade? In the 1960s, in an era of rampant pursuit of growth, only 38% of the 500 doubled earnings per share, measured in inflated dollars. While that decade saw intense and accelerating inflation rates, those figures were laughably low compared to what lay ahead after oil prices exploded in 1973; yet the proportion of the 500 doubling this vital statistic in the decade to 1983 was still a mere 43%.

Far, far worse, in the decade to 1993, the proportion of doublers slumped to 26%. Over three decades, the great majority of the large companies, despite organic growth, despite wide diversification by product and geography, despite a raft of acquisitions, not only failed to keep pace with inflation – they fell behind it to a huge and alarming degree. True, 54% of the companies had shareholders who doubled their money between 1983 and 1993, thanks to the rampant Wall Street of the early 1990s. But that, of course, again meant a massive lag behind inflation for capital worth in the stockholders' hands.

On the record, real and strong growth should dangle in front of shareholders' eyes like a vision of the earthly paradise. True, 150 of the *Management Today* 250 doubled real earnings per share in the ten years to 1990. That was much more like the standard required, but said more about the rotten performance in the first year of that decade than about the excellence in-between.

In many companies, real growth – of the physical variety – has been all but invisible. Physical output as an indicator means nothing in a large diversified company, and that definition fits almost every significant firm. But unit sales of vehicles in the big car companies do mean something, and they have grown very slowly; GM sold only a fifth more cars from its US factories in a booming 1993 than a decade previously. But prices have powered up to an average $18,497 over the period, producing a much sharper rise in dollar sales.

In US industry generally, looking at one five-year period, *Business Week* noted that 'historical-cost sales for the average large company have grown at an annual rate of 10% for the past five years – but there has been no growth on an inflation-adjusted basis'. In 1993, even though profits for the *Fortune* 500 rose by 17%, sales were virtually static – and no doubt price rises, as much as containment of costs, explain the discrepancy. Company directors only fail to see that general inflation makes their money growth much easier because they share a common delusion of people throughout the world.

Next to depression (which nobody believed in, except John Kenneth Galbraith and Eliot Janeway, until the oil-price shocks), inflation is the dirtiest word in economic jargon. Enormous ingenuity has gone into discussion of cost-push and wage-pull, of spirals and equilibrium levels. However, economic expansion is a good thing for nations, companies, and individuals alike – right? Now, the faster a market or an economy expands, the more demand will press against supply and the more prices are likely to rise. The only big exception is when (as in the US after Eisenhower or Carter) a yawning reservoir of spare capacity is waiting to be filled. Once that has been done (as under Johnson), prices gallop away; politicians reach itchily for the economic reins; and the complaining voice of the housewife is heard in the land.

Consumers, like executives, have been brainwashed. They think of money as a constant measure when (as they constantly complain) the measure constantly changes its length. If the value of money is falling, it means little to say that prices (or sales or profits) are rising by that same sinking criterion. The man whose £75,000 house sells for £150,000 seven years later claims that he has doubled his money –

though he should know that, because of the inflation that pushed up the price of the house, his £150,000 is worth nothing like twice the £75,000 of seven years back.

Managements know just as surely that a £75 million profit today is not worth thrice the £25 million of 1984; but that won't stop executives from boasting that profits have trebled, or from being applauded for their splendour. The executive has also personally exploited the hidden truth about inflation. It isn't what you can buy with your pounds or dollars that counts, but what you can buy with your time. Expressed in these terms, most prices have fallen substantially – and much more for the executive than for lesser hired hands.

That's true by definition; otherwise living standards couldn't have risen over the years. The reason why the British worker can afford to buy a better car today, even with a much higher price-tag, is because it represents less of his annual pay than a worse car ten years ago. That goes for nearly everything else. How much the average executive salary has risen is a matter for debate, but the higher the rank, the more likely it is to have risen more rapidly than anybody else's; and that doesn't count increased fringe benefits, capital appreciation on the home, a share in inflationary stock markets, and all the other goodnesses of the good executive life.

That's not the end of the executive's blessings. If inflation reflects rising demand, sales must be rising, and rising sales (other things being equal) mean rising profits. New plant put in at today's lower capital costs, too, will earn profits at tomorrow's higher prices. Typically, however, executives do not rejoice over this fact: instead, they fret because the plant will have to be replaced at higher costs.

But this may also work to the executive's joy. It implies that depreciation rates are too low, in which case current profits (on which the stock price and management bonuses depend) are being exaggerated to the benefit of the board. Even if depreciation rates are raised to the right level to compensate for inflation (and nobody knows what that is), the higher depreciation (if the Revenue can be conned into accepting it) will result in lower taxes.

Most corporations, and most executives in their private capacity, are heavy borrowers, often over long terms at fixed interest. This too has a lovely result – or would have, if executives could curb their weird insistence on investing the money raised at rates of return below the cost of capital. The real cost of the interest payments declines as inflation rolls onward; and the final repayment is worth much less in real terms than the original loan. So the opportunities for exploiting inflation are always there. If executives have failed in an inflationary past to cope with its problems, the reason may lie in their own weakness.

That weakness won't help them in what is (maybe temporarily) a non-inflationary run in the 1990s. The executive is pulled in opposite directions by self-interest and by conditioning, which includes the belief that corporate actions should be in the public interest. Self-interest dictates that directors should charge the highest price that the traffic will bear. The public interest dictates (or is thought to) that prices should never rise at all; but since rise they must, should do so by the merest smidgen. So administered pricing creeps onward and upward like lichen.

Prices are not treated as they should be, as the most decisive element in the marketing and economic mix. They become a fixed base to which inflationary increments are added from time to time. The cost-plus mentality takes over. Firms fix their prices by costs plus a percentage, and accept increases in costs as some God-given plague to be passed on to the consumer if at all possible; if not, the costs get handed over to the shareholder in massacred profits, slashed dividends, and tumbled stock prices.

In bad times, company after company blames miserable profits on unprecedented rises in wages and other costs. In the 1970s, the rises really were unprecedented; but exceptional cost pressures were not so unreservedly to blame as companies liked to maintain. Take some of the worst US losers in the period 1978–82: steel (profits down 11%), automotive (17%), tyre and rubber (17%). Excessive wage costs, the results of previous inflationary settlements, took much of the blame; but that was by no means all.

The truth is that these excesses were the responsibility of exactly the same managements which perpetrated such admitted howlers as the fatal lag behind Japan in steel technology, the poor quality and productivity levels in US auto plants, the failure to follow the radial revolution soon or fast enough in tyres. Even without world recession, even without world inflation, these and many other gratuitous follies would have cost these companies dear. As it was, inflation simply disguised the full extent of the folly – thus, the auto sector's profits, after allowing for inflation, would have been down, not 17%, but a thumping 29%.

The worst embarrassment that a company can contrive is to get caught in its own private deflationary spiral in an inflationary era; and it happens, more often than not, because managers put expansion first and profits well behind. This folly has severely stained the once pure growth records of the chemical companies of West Germany. They too blamed wage pressures, though labour costs matter much less in chemical plants than in car factories. Price weakness was a far more serious cause; and much of it resulted from their own errors of capacity planning and pricing policy, which have gone on blighting chemical profits, on both sides of the Atlantic, with only intermittent relief, ever since 1970.

An American chemical executive, coming into Europe from the lush green home pastures, where companies know a pretty price when they see it, complained, 'There is awful and unjustified price weakness in Europe.' The Europeans cut prices to keep the Americans at bay; a self-defeating gesture, since the Americans, being richer, could better afford to give away their goods. Not that the Americans are blameless.

To take one instance, every executive in synthetic fibres knew that the amount of nylon-making plant being planned would eventually flood every nook and cranny of the market. But knowledge never stops a determined expansionist. American executives went on buying their way into European nylon at prices that became still more ruinous, as the backwash of the world surplus hit their cosseted home market.

117

The airlines have recurrently showed with equal thoroughness how to create your own private deflation by over-ordering jumbo jets, just as they over-ordered 707s earlier in the jet era. If capacity had only been balanced with demand, prices could have been slashed and yet profits would still have risen. A glut absolutely guarantees that prices will slump at the same time as operating costs soar, because of the heartbreakingly low use of capacity. At this point, executives customarily institute sweeping cost-reduction programmes, laying off employees on all sides, without reflecting that the costs being cut must have been inexcusably fat before.

Inefficient use of labour is endemic in industry. Whether the men down tools for tea breaks, as in Britain, or stand guard around the Coke machine, as in the US, or get sick with suspicious regularity, as in Germany, or are kept in full employment when they can't lift a finger, as in Japan, the results are the same. Their companies don't reap the full harvest of their new equipment; and they don't get maximum protection against the impact of inflation on their wage bill.

Take just one example among a myriad: there was a plant in the British paper industry which faced almost every threat a management could wish not to face – including recession and ferocious price competition from the much better placed Scandinavians. It was producing 80,000 tons of paper a year with 1,500 people when the management finally gave up the ghost. The plant was taken over by an American company, which proceeded to manufacture 150,000 tons a year – with 400 employees.

Companies waste more than men; they also throw away expensive material. It's estimated that American and European manufacturers may waste as much as 25% of raw materials in the production processes. Since the general spend on these goodies ranges from 30% to 80% of turnover, that's no mean waste. But executives look through the wrong end of the telescope. Budgeting first in terms of sales, and setting targets in terms of profits, they pay too little attention to costs. Even when stringency and crisis force them to carve away at everything in sight, they first choose the soft targets, such as advertising budgets, rather than the hard target, which is the corporate incompetence.

Excessive costs arise, not only from maladministration, but from bad equilibrium. The deliberate creation of excess capacity is only one example. Another is making too many products and offering the excessive lines at tempting prices that are bound to yield amazing losses. If their cost accounting is weak enough, the executives may not even know that the losses exist (in disaster after disaster, the undertaker's diagnosis is the same: 'inaccurate costing and lack of financial information').

But higher prices will weed out losing lines that can be dropped forever, preserving only those for which the customers are prepared to pay – and the results can be delectable. One new British management, anxious to escape from big unprofitable contracts in an underdeveloped country, but also anxious to keep face, elevated its tender (twice) to a level that looked certain to lose. It got the job (and might even make a profit).

In mythology, the executive is a rapacious creature who charges as much as he can as soon as he can. But the robber-baron spirit of John D. Rockefeller seldom rides in the great corporation. Its executives charge prices that are too low (i.e. unprofitable, and less than the traffic will bear) for too long – and then make bad worse by offering discounts on the listed price. The sales side, in particular, has to be heaved away from a natural lust for low prices: no commission-crazy salesman ever willingly accepts any price change that might, by any stretch of his imagination, make his selling task harder.

But price increases and discounts often have only marginal effects on demand; and the price increases, or saved discounts, then flow through as pure, pretty, and undiluted profit. A former boss of Mars in Britain agonised for months over whether to raise the Mars bar price by a penny – the hardest decision he ever faced. He never regretted the plunge for one sweet minute.

Those who argue that inflation is a destructive economic force are bound to oppose maximising returns by maximising prices; and many managers likewise miss the management logic. 'You can't charge that much,' was one sales manager's anguished cry. 'It cost so little to produce.' (His cry could be echoed in many industries today with perfect justice; even in cars, the direct cost of assembling a Ford Taurus in Detroit in 1994 was $840 – a mere 5% of the cost to the customer).

Anti-inflationists ignore the economic damage of under-pricing. For years Jaguar managers laboured under the delusion that their spiffing cars had to be cheap, starting at under £2,000 in the UK home market. This outlandish value for money produced a vociferous pile-up of unsatisfied, waiting customers – many of them Americans, who wait for nothing. The lost income robbed the company of the resources needed to raise its production capacity to something near the level of demand.

As a result of Jaguar's self-denial, BMW, whose prices have never been restrained by scruples, stole the market. It was soon making more cars in a day than Jaguar did in a week, and the gap has widened since. Executives, however, find it just as hard as governments to leave the correction of prices to the forces of the market. The pressure of governments anxious about inflation has greatly reinforced businessmen's own fear of public reaction, their own instinctive sympathy with the irrational feeling that there is a 'fair' price that results in a 'reasonable' return.

Words like 'fair' and 'reasonable' are purely emotive. For instance, in the second quarter of 1994, Ford earned an after-tax profit of $945 apiece on its cars. Chrysler earned $1,360 – 44% more. Did this mean that Ford's prices were fairer? Or that its products were better value? Or does it mean that Chrysler was managed more effectively? Then take super-markets. One year Kwik Save had a return on sales of 5.1%, getting on for double the Tesco figure. Does this mean that Kwik Save's prices should have been lower? In fact, its success was founded on undercutting – the higher margins resulted not from higher prices but from lower costs.

That's the key to successful exploitation of inflationary and non-inflationary times alike: to make higher profits than the other fellow at lower expense. Companies which have offered progressively higher quality at relatively low prices are considered leading fire-fighters against inflation. In point of fact, nearly everybody's price levels have risen steeply over the years; the moral is that, even at higher price-tags, the successful company's goods are well within the customer's vital willingness to pay – and its return on capital will be much higher than that of competitors which are less effective in offering the market perceived value for money.

The company that gets inflation on its side will rush past those who are content to be its victims. After all, when all prices are rising, it's easier to put up your own without anybody noticing. So long as inflation is publicly execrated more than deflation (a process that is, incidentally, very much nastier), wise directors may have to hide the fact that they charge the optimum price – not simply the price that covers the movements of costs and the competition. But even if a management manages badly in pricing and everything else, inflation, with luck, will partially conceal its failure, upgrading executives who would otherwise be done down professionally – and (far more painful) in their own pockets.

10
Why Mergers Make Mayhem

Business history is festooned with amalgamations. The mightiest manufacturers in the US and Britain – General Motors and Imperial Chemical Industries – were created by merger artists. The colossus of Europe, Royal Dutch-Shell, arose from another bout of corporate love-fever. But merger as a fine art didn't appear until the 1960s, when it got elevated to the upper reaches of the management stratosphere, stamped with the seductive, scientific-sounding word, 'synergy'.

Ostensibly, this meant a magic process in which two and two made more than four. More properly translated, synergy means that the deal makes no financial sense, but (please, God) something will come out of it in the end. Most mergers are created in such pious hope; their guiding drive is less financial or industrial logic, but, in various forms, the urge to aggrandise.

Yet a merger is nothing but a straight financial investment. One company pays cash, or shares (i.e. the right to participate in future cash earnings), or some hybrid security for another company's cash potential. The manoeuvre is no more sophisticated fundamentally than an investor's phone call to his broker – except that only a consummate sucker would pay a broker twenty times earnings for stocks selling in the market at a multiple of fifteen.

Industrial companies, however, play the sucker all the time, none more so than Britain's Midland Bank, which paid $820 million, or three times the market price, for only 57% of the Crocker National Bank – and then sat impotently by while this awful West Coast purchase lost so much money ($178 million in a mere six months) that it eventually had to be abandoned altogether. The more cunning conglomerates, in their formative years, at least avoided this trap. Their key deals were schemed to elevate earnings per share, never mind whether the morsel was worth eating for any other reason.

As time wore on, though, conglomerate executives usually grew careless; contrary to their own myths, they began to pick up the bad habit of buying companies for ransoms that diluted their earnings. This bad habit became contagious in the 1980s, when overpaying with over-borrowed money drove even shrewd and concentrated businessmen like Rupert Murdoch uncomfortably close to the jaws of death; and when, in the same media business, Warner merged with Time on terms that ruled out profits for years ahead.

Conglomerates, at their naked best, pursue only the financial goals of mergers, because money is their obsession, life-blood, and governing lust. Others merge regardless of cost because, for all their pretensions, financial maximisation – or getting truly richer – is not their object. Maximisation is the name of their corporate game, true; but maximising the corporation, not its effectiveness or its share price, is the mainspring.

In Europe, especially in Britain, this urge for bigness was reinforced from time to time by politicians who believed that economies of scale (i.e. the unreliable idea, exploded forever in the 1980s, that bigger equals cheaper) were required weapons for fighting the good fight against US economic imperialists. Many ill-starred European mergers were put together under this strange banner – including Pirelli-Dunlop (tyres), Agfa-Gevaert (film) and VFW-Fokker (planes). All were dissolved after failure at every level:

strategic, tactical, financial and human.

The conventional wisdom has consequently reversed. Europeans have begun to learn, as did the anti-heroes of so many American mergers, that the opposite of synergy is dissipation: that two and two can make less than four, and that sometimes they don't add up at all. These awakenings have still left most boardrooms dreaming of glory. Bids and deals pre-empt more top management time than any other pastime – and to minimal effect. Every study has shown that polygamous companies grow no faster, in terms of earnings per share, than firms that stay resolutely single.

Fortune magazine once quoted merger expert Michael Seely of Investors Access Corp. to the effect that 'in the past decade only one-third of all mergers have enriched the acquirer's shareholders, one-third have been awash, and one-third have ended up costing investors money – sometimes lots of it.' As that indicates, marvellous benefits are desperately hard to buy, and grotesque losses too easy to pick up; and common sense tells why.

Managers can only buy three kinds of company – good, middling, or bad – and in only one of two circumstances – contested or uncontested (i.e. rape or seduction). The perfect combination seems to be the seduction of a truly beautiful company; but the seducer must usually overpay, since beauties are seldom bargains. He may overpay still more in cases of opposed rape, which commonly results in an auction. As Hanson Trust and other raptors showed many times, the companies to buy are the raped, bad ones – the only ones likely to be cheap in relation to their assets (if any are left), the only ones whose potential (if any) is sure to be under-exploited.

Even here lies no certainty; bad eggs make poor omelettes. Inescapable logic stacks the odds against the purchaser – good companies come dear, bad companies are bad. The Fifth Truth of Management also applies: however high its level, management capability is always less than the organisation needs. The junior partner (or mergee) seldom brings in super-competence. After all, the hotter its management, the less its reason for merging. So the merged marvel has a broader management span, but even less management capacity in relation to need.

Worse still, the over-stretched management has the new, self-inflicted, and often chronic anxieties that come only with managing mergers. And human beings, when faced with more problems than they can handle (like rats in a psychologist's maze) do nothing. Hence the familiar unconsummated merger – two companies that sleep together in name only. When Pan Am merged with National Airlines in 1980, for instance, the big idea was that the international passengers would no longer be lost to Pan Am when arriving in the States; nor would Pan Am be forced to take its passengers from the US interior off other lines before flying them to foreign parts. It sounded like a great idea.

The acquisition proved so troublesome, though, that Pan Am's management didn't get round to merging the National schedules into its own, the rationale of the whole deal, until the middle of 1982 – by which time terrible damage had been done to the combined (or rather uncombined) airlines' reputation and to Pan Am's finances. Having lost money ever since the merger, it was financially grounded – and then the great pioneer of airline travel was hacked into pieces.

Mergers supposedly made in heaven are friendly by definition; and maybe they are doomed to relative failure. The senior partner, being amicable, can't pick up the mergee for anything less than a pretty price, which rules out any remote hope of financial bonanza. The pervading friendliness, too, means that nobody gets sacked, and no activity beloved of the mergee's managers gets dropped. So much for synergy.

After a hostile takeover, unhealthy inhibitions are fewer. The opposing board of directors may even be forced to walk the plank without ceremony – and that, while crude, is not the worst way of making merger sense. You can't make an omelette, or sense of a merger, without breaking eggs, and the longer the egg-breaking is delayed, the fewer the benefits will be. But there's a catch. If the acquiring management knows nothing about the business concerned, it's not in much of a position to judge the performance of the managers or to step into their shoes if that performance is deemed unsatisfactory.

By no coincidence, four of the seven worst mergers found by *Fortune* were of this know-nothing nature: two oil companies (Sohio and Atlantic Richfield) buying into copper, etc, and torpedoing their earnings per share by 23% and 19% respectively; another oil company (Exxon) buying into electrical equipment and utterly wasting $1.24 billion in the process; yet another oil group (Mobil) purchasing the company which, among other undesirable things, owned the Montgomery Ward stores – a deal which knocked 39% off one year's earnings before the bad buy was put on the block.

Since mergers do bring problems that can't be solved without time, trouble, and sorrow, buyers should be doubly careful about price. But most bidders are doubly cavalier. They follow the advice of art dealer Lord Duveen to earlier American millionaires: 'If you're buying the priceless, you're getting it cheap.' For priceless, read desirable, and you have the formula for merger after merger. One avid finance director admitted that his latest buy had cost several millions too much. He explained that the overcharge had kept his dearest corporate enemy from picking the plum.

'We are paying far too much [it was over £15 million],' said a property man on another occasion, 'but it fits into the pattern of our future development.' If the second half of that statement was true, then the first half was false – and vice versa. In effect, the stockholders bet their money (or have it bet for them, willy-nilly) on the chief executive's judgment. He may be warped by vanity, or if a battle is on, by simple hatred of being beaten. 'It became a personal matter' for one company chairman, 'and he had to raise the bid twice before he finally won, the last time even against the advice of our financial advisers.'

An expensive merger always exacts a heavy toll on the bidder's management, and mergers may expose the ghastly secret that the bidder has no management at all. The mighty Pennsylvania Railroad was popularly considered to be a whizz at running railroads, and at piling up money in side ventures.

When it wed the New York Central, the Pennsy's Stuart T. Saunders said that the railroad was getting 'a new type of manager'. (He added, a little more realistically, 'Our programmes have pulled us back from the brink of disaster ... but they have not rescued us from the financial danger zone.')

Industrial logic was rapidly overtaken by the reality of two struggling managements that had to divert their inadequate energies to new struggles – many with each other, some with diversified nonsenses, most with the terrible illogic of trying to fit two distinct rail networks into one. By themselves, possibly, neither line would have gone bankrupt; together, they were doomed.

The Leyland Motor Company was famed for lean, keen, efficient management when it united with the British Motor Corporation. Since BMC had mislaid one-fifth of its market share since formation (by another merger), its capacities for mismanagement were regarded with some awe. Leyland's high repute outlasted the merger by only a few months. The senior partner revealed many of the mergee's faults – in marketing, middle management, under-investment, one-man decision-making, ageing product lines, and a vacuum instead of labour relations. As the British Leyland Motor Corporation, and then as plain BL, it therefore neatly completed the good work on market share – reducing it in all by a staggering half.

It takes a very bright executive to make a merger into a success; and a very bright executive often is too bright to try. The duller executive cannot see the problem (or solve it). When one large oil company starts paying billions for unrelated businesses the others plunge in pell-mell; then despite the terrible errors committed in this phase, they switch back to oil buys – also for billions, of course. Similarly, insurance companies and building societies vied with each other to purchase estate agents, and with them licenses to lose barely believable sums of money.

Fashion continues to call the tune. Once upon a time food firms, almost as one, diversified away from food, because of its slow growth. Their efforts to find faster expansion elsewhere met with notoriously scant success. Then, again in almost perfect unison, they returned to base, guzzling other food companies with every sign of voracious appetite. The only matter on which the gorging giants seemed to disagree was whether to go for the big bite (like Nestlé with its $3 billion swallow of Carnation) or the strategic nibble. Even nibbles weigh in heavy on the financial scales. It cost Unilever, for example, £355 million to buy Brooke Bond; but that was only 2.7% of the purchaser's sales.

The tiny size of over-priced acquisitions against the bidder's own elephantine proportions is no excuse, as ICI found. A buying spree huge in numbers rather than bullion preceded the losses which made the giant vulnerable to predators and break-up: which the management pre-emptively then inflicted on itself. A series of bad small buys rapidly reduces the chances of improving the return on a mass of capital – which is the prime object of acquisitions, or would be in an ideal world.

In real life, power is a more compulsive force, conscious or unconscious. Just as too few executives will genuinely delegate authority (for that robs them of their power and manhood), so few throw away chances to add new realms. And history and their contemporaries will applaud them for their power-drives. The titan J. P. Morgan, a wheeler-dealer manipulator of Maxwellian proportions in his time, won eternal fame for his bloated, stock-watered creations, never mind that lesser figures had to make the monstrosities pay.

In these unaltered days, there are even cases of companies buying others they simply can't afford. With $2 billion of retail sales in lumber and building supplies, an American company named Wickes looked able enough to pay $193 million for the Gamble-Skogmo department and speciality stores. The catch was that the purchased company had a billion in debt, which weighed down the buyer, especially in a recession, like a lead balloon. After losing $400 million in fifteen months, Wickes had to go into Chapter 11 bankruptcy.

At that, Wickes survived, achieving some strange kind of glory by becoming the largest US business to emerge from bankruptcy, thanks to the heroic efforts of one Sanford Sigoloff (though even he dropped over a billion dollars of sales in the survival process). Baldwin-United, on the other hand, cooked its own goose permanently by borrowing $1 billion it couldn't conceivably finance to buy the biggest home-mortgage insurance company in the States. In the catastrophe that followed (a $673 million loss in 1983), Baldwin's own sales in single-premium deferred annuities (and maybe the savings of subscribers to them) were destroyed; so was $44 million of Merrill Lynch money, as the mighty brokers were obliged to repay customers for their Baldwin losses.

The only case for agglomerating is often a perverse one: that the bigger a company gets, the more over-burden, deadwood, or rubbish it accumulates for some future hero to cut away, elevating the profits and price/earnings ratio simultaneously, to the joy of all mankind. At Sara Lee, previously Consolidated Foods, some sixty businesses (out of 125) were sold off during a period in which net income, far from falling, rose by 70% in five years. At Burmah Oil, net capital employed shrunk by no less than 30% in nine years as its disastrous diversifications were off-loaded, with the inevitable result that return on assets rose as the latter's quantity fell; profits soared by 709%.

A good conglomerator can provide textbook theory in how to merge, if merge you must. The only merger object is to enhance the capital value of the company; and the best buyers have always thought and bought big. A £200 million company rarely has any good excuse for a £2 million buy. The deal can't have any noticeable impact on earnings; and small companies fit uncomfortably into big pockets. Unilever paid several millions (less than 1% of its own capital) for a plastics growth company. The new business was unrelated to the rest of its oversized group; and the latter's weight soon crushed the golden goose's entrepreneurial character – and its eggs.

Big guns shouldn't be deployed on too narrow a front. The conglomerates, of course, overplayed the logic of buying big; thus George Walker, eager to bust into the really big time by buying Grand Metropolitan's betting shops, virtually busted

Brent Walker. It is easy but irrelevant to conclude that property men don't know how to run betting, an activity that is easily mismanaged. Walker's mistake wasn't made so much in the management as in the original decision to buy.

The weakness of most mergers is not that ignorant managers enter unfamiliar businesses; it is that the price was wrong, regardless. If the price is right, the synergy and the management can very possibly look after themselves. If not, it will take years to close the gap by the workings of 'industrial logic'. This overworked phrase is usually no more than posthumous justification. Cadbury and Schweppes, two generally healthy companies, one in chocolate, one in soft drinks, had very little in common; only the 'industrially logical' lust to create a food combine capable of spitting in the eyes of General Foods, General Mills and Nestlé.

Neither Cadbury nor Schweppes competed seriously with any of the three (except for Nestlé and Cadbury in chocolate). Their deal mixed up what used to be the high-premium, high-cachet business of Schweppes with a low-margin, low-growth bulk operation in confectionery. Either Schweppes paid dear to get into chocolate, or Cadbury paid expensively to move into soft drinks. None of the major competitors lost a wink of sleep as a result. By 1992, General Foods had been eaten by Philip Morris, to form a business eight times as large as the Brits, who were now concentrating on beverages. In this smaller pool, they were a bigger fish (seventh in the world, whereas twenty-five food firms still outranked them).

The corporate slumber lost through mergers is mostly within the merged company as managers try to put together what logically could always have been left asunder. Take Philip Morris, once the shining text for marketing professors because of its achievements with Miller High Life beer – raised from also-ran to number two by high-powered promotion. Riding high on this success, Miller paid $520 million for Seven-Up in 1978; half a dozen years later, Seven-Up had still to turn a profit as the cola giants continued to turn the screws.

That wouldn't have seemed so ghastly had Miller still been

doing its stuff; but the High Life brand peaked and, as it thereafter slid down the slope, so did earnings – and so did the value of a brand new $450 million Ohio brewery. The 'disasters' moved a couple of *Business Week* writers to comment that Philip Morris would have been better off to purchase its own shares than to buy into beverages – alcoholic or non-alcoholic. Undeterred, the tobacco giant turned its destinies over to its acquired food executives, and promptly ran into the cigarette price disaster that wrecked the share price and cost the CEO his job.

It's industrially logical to buy a business that takes you into an entirely new market. Aha! But it's also 'logical' to buy one in exactly the same market – hopefully killing two birds for the price of one. This is the only form of synergy actually proved to work, in the negative sense of closing down one of two factories or two distribution forces (note that the magic doesn't lie in the expansion of the mergee's business by the buyer's magic touch).

The predators at their peak form are much better at this negative synergy. In the game only for the money, they sell off everything surplus or movable on sight. One conglomerate executive even had a man standing by in Germany waiting to chop off a loss-making limb the instant the take-over was complete. This demonstrated absolutely sound tactics. Since deeper human motives than financial sense are always involved in mergers, you must start fast to make the best of what (more often than not) will be a bad deal.

The first step (better taken by far before consummation) is to find out exactly what the package contains. In the worst circumstances, that discovery may end all further interest. Assuming that you do still want any part of the company, then decide what you want and don't want in assets and in managers. Mergees always have some seniors who shiver the spine, and some juniors worth their weight in silver dollars. Casting the former out (as generously as possible) and promoting the latter (at high speed) is the proper routine.

As for unprofitable operations, close them, all of them, especially those where, according to the anguished cries of the incumbents, prosperity is just around the corner. These pets mostly go on eating profits forever. Where the mergee's operations, brand names, distribution, and so on can be swallowed into the bigger company without any loss of business, do it, right now. When skeletons rattle out of cupboards, take the losses and write-offs at once.

When executions have to be carried out, sooner is always better than later. Don't leave sentenced operations waiting interminably in death row. Of course, a merged company is no different in these respects than an unmerged one – executives are always putting off the evil day, especially an evil day that they themselves have created.

11
The Over-Compensated Executive

Most executives are badly paid, not in the sense that they get too little (many get far too much), but because they are paid in the wrong ways. Their take seldom has any true relation to their personal success or to the company's. Come rain or shine, their dinner pail stays full. The resulting gross discrepancies are more apparent in the US than in Britain, though the British are doing their unlevel best to catch up. But even in America linking an executive's efforts to his immediate rewards is more pretence than effectiveness.

The soul may be rejoiced by seeing that in 1992, at a time when average chief executive 'compensation' in *Business Week*'s survey soared by a hardly defensible 56%, the CEO of IBM suffered a pay cut; his shareholders had lost 31% of their investment in 1990–92. But the pay cut wasn't enormous (17%); and, at $1.3 million of compensation in 1992 and $9.6 million over the whole period, John F. Akers was a long way off the breadline. The boss of Ford Motor, having presided over an enormous loss of $5 billion, was punished with a mere 18% rise to $2.6 million, poor guy.

Another oddity is the way multi-millionaires tie their rewards to profits. Before the war, Sir Allen Clark, the founder of Plessey, gave himself a contract for a nice slice of the net. After the war, as one of the new breed of electronics tycoon, when the company profits and his own fortune in shares were vastly swollen, he continued to grab so huge a take that average salaries for his directors were the highest in the land – entirely because of the greedy old boy's quarter-of-a-million cut.

Henry Ford II, while still in charge of the family fief, was another whose pay was geared to performance (one lousy year, his company income slumped all the way from $600,000 to $515,000). Thomas Watson Jr. of IBM was no different when in the chair and the driving-seat. Even though their fortunes yo-yo around in the stock market in one day by greater amounts, magnates go through the solemn charade of pretending that their annual recompense in some way affects their performance as profit earners.

Nor are family scions averse to fat salaries. At Anheuser-Busch, for instance, Adolf A. Busch III earned nearly a million bucks as long ago as 1983; in 1990–92, he pocketed $15 million. Eponymous heroes also head companies like McDonnell Douglas, W.R. Grace, Wrigley, Tyson Foods, Hilton Hotels, and Marriott Hotels. Despite the enormous personal and family worth which the names represent, all but one of their bosses took home at least $1 million in 1992; while J. Peter Grace, whose company is a by-word for undistinguished performance, pocketed $19 million in 1990–92.

The Houghton family of Corning Glass has a collective worth in the hundreds of millions; Dan Houghton, the incumbent CEO, increased said millions with $8 million of 'total compensation' in 1990–92. There are very few examples of family restraint, although the reigning Wrigley did take a 4% cut in salary and bonus in 1992; however, since he still earned $699,000 and received another $1.5 million in 'long-term' rewards, this was some way short of the supreme sacrifice.

Indeed, compared to his peers, Bill Gates of Microsoft looks positively saintly. He paid himself a piffling $285,000 in 1992. You could argue that any salary is bound to look feeble against a personal fortune, created by his founding shares in the software empire (of which he still owns 30%), that has passed $7 billion. After all, that fortune is the equivalent, at modest rates of investment return, of $1 million *a day*. But as a general rule riches don't seem to restrain greed – and neither does responsibility.

You could argue that this is not only right and proper, but axiomatic: that what mostly determines any top executive's pay is the size of the organisation in which he works. A law invented or discovered by the nineteenth-century Italian economist Pareto explains practically everything about business. (Roughly speaking, it says that 20% of customers account for 80% of turnover, 20% of components account for 80% of cost, and so forth.)

His law shows that all organisations build a pay pyramid. The broader the base, the higher the summit of the pyramid. I learned about Pareto's law on pay from research inside the personnel department of Rolls-Royce. Maybe this work had some connection with the pay rise which the chairman got in 1969, shortly before his company completed its crash: one of the many weird illustrations in history of the poor correlation between pay and performance.

The mythology is that superior US corporate performance is greatly stimulated by stock options, cash-incentive awards, and the like. But studies done before these goodies became all but universal revealed, among the top 100 US companies, no distinction in results between managements that granted themselves every financial stimulus under the sun and those tiny few that bumbled along on straight salary – except that, by performing no better than the straight-salary managers, the carrot-danglers got much richer.

The argument about whether or not these financial inducements are effective has thus become entirely academic, because no man or woman in their right minds will work for a company where the loot is less. The stock option is in truth a device to enable a manager – generally a hired hand, not somebody who owns the company – to get rich; really rich, easily and without risk. Rising up the ranks of a great American corporation can lift a man to dizzy heights of wealth; and it isn't even necessary to run the corporation successfully.

If that sounds too good (or bad) to be true, it isn't: *Business*

Week once listed seven executives whose stockholders saw their investments decline in value over a three-year period by amounts ranging from 9.8% to 67.2%. Collectively, the sorry seven hauled in $20.8 million of pay and other emoluments for the third year – making an average of $3 million per failed manager. In 1990–92 the UAL boss Stephen Wolf earned $17 million while his airline's shareholders saw their investment decline by 26%.

If a man is actually successful, like Thomas Frist Jr., the hero who overbuilt Hospital Corporation of America, and then took it private, the take becomes truly phenomenal – in this case, $129 million. True, the investors in the buyout saw their $300 million of equity swell to $2.83 billion after a slimmed-down company returned to the Stock Market. But the Frists owned 11% of that equity, meaning a family profit of $278 million. How much financial incentive does a man require – or, for that matter, deserve?

Frist argues in much the same vein ('This is an unusual situation, where a home run was hit and everyone was a winner') as William S. Anderson, who turned round a dilapidated NCR, and one year received $14.5 million for his pains. Anderson protested that (a) he deserved it, (b) it wasn't really one year's reward, but a decade's, and (c) because of the compulsory six months' wait before selling, under US law, he might never see the full $12 million of stock options which accounted for the bulk of his booty. He could well end up, Anderson opined, with a mere $9 million.

In fact, Anderson earned more straight pay than John R. Opel of IBM, in one of that company's palmiest years, and was entitled to five and a half times Opel's total remuneration. IBM had eleven times NCR's sales and nineteen times its profits. Equally odd, the president of super-chipmaker Intel, Andrew S. Grove, got a million dollars more than Opel; yet IBM had a large stockholding in Grove's firm. By 1990–92, however, IBM had contrived to end this anomaly; its failed and failing CEO got $1.6 million more than the soaringly successful Grove.

The anomalies are legion. Over the same three years, Tony O'Reilly of Heinz received $115 million, or 6.7 times the next highest take in food processing. Of eighteen food-processing companies listed in *Business Week*'s pay comparisons, Heinz came a poor fourteenth in return to shareholders and sixth (out of nineteen) in return on equity. That last figure looks almost reasonable – until you note that O'Reilly earned over double the compensation of all the CEOs whose ROE was higher over the period. How much would the Heinz chief have taken home if he'd been really successful?

All these funny figures prove only one thing – that who earns what in the US has become a matter not of who did best for the company, but whose hand delved deepest into the honey-pot. The American situation has always been bizarre. By 1968, fully seventy-three of the 100 largest companies had both stock options and incentive awards; another seven had incentive awards only; seventeen had stock options only; and three languished in the outer darkness of straight old-fashioned pay. Fewer than two-fifths of the goodie-stuffed seventy-three bettered either the median performance of *Fortune*'s 500 largest companies for ten-year growth in earnings per share, or the median for profitability that particular year.

The seven companies with incentives, but without stock options, did barely better. The less directly a management's pay was tied to the company's profit performance, surprisingly, the worthier the performance became. Stock-option companies with no incentive awards did very well on growth – 88% were above the median, and 59% beat the median for profitability. All three of the benighted straight-pay companies, however, outdid the ten-year median growth rate; and two of these three were abnormally profitable.

Some of the possible conclusions are too obvious to be true. For instance, growth-hungry investors would have been rash to charge into companies with generous option schemes before discovering which came first – the options or the performance. Often the executives, finding themselves on to a good thing, smartly arrange to share the bonanza. But incentive awards, unanswerably, seem to have no discernible incentive effect. The reason lies in the logic (or illogic) of incentive schemes.

Honeywell, in the days when it employed greedy, hot computer salesmen as well as the average executive, found that 30% of pay had to come from incentives before 'other guys get the driving go of the fellows in the Brooks Brothers' suits' – but what would the other 70% be paid for? Occupying the office space? The various schemes based on appraisal look like a solution: work out an executive's objectives with the person concerned, then relate pay to success in hitting the target.

But here, too, there is logical trouble: the manager gets much of the total pay for not meeting the objectives. You pay the incumbents for failing, and reward them with more if they do what they were hired to do in the first place. A manager is hired, and should be paid, to do a job that includes meeting a set of objectives and producing profits that can be reported to shareholders without sackcloth and ashes. If the appointees excel themselves, they are enriched anyway in a sensible company. If they fail, through a fault of their own, you may not want them at any price.

Incentive schemes have other snags, notably making sure that profit-linked bonuses really do reflect managerial merit. Head office can contain a bundle of superannuated dodos whose main contribution is, by all means in their power, to prevent the divisional directors from earning large profits. If the latter triumph against the odds, guess who collects the largest bonuses. And how do you distinguish between an executive who shuts off a £10 million loss and the luckier colleague, who, given the company's plum division, raises its profits by £5 million?

Until you near the pay stratosphere, what's more, you can rarely cut an executive's salary. A married man earning £40,000 a year can't take much of a slash – not so long as he has a wife, three children, and a mortgage to support. The incentive system tends to be all rewards and no penalties; that being so, it doesn't work. Systems of genuine incentives do exist; however, few boards of directors would dream of imposing this kind of straitjacket on themselves.

Pay in a deadly serious scheme starts from a base high enough to cover ordinary living expenses and no more. Part of pay above that level is linked to profit performance; part is tied to share performance (which executives can fiddle less easily than the profit figures); part is tied to performance on non-financial criteria, such as quality and innovation. The share-linked element, moreover, carries a downside risk. The money is either in deferred earnings, or in shares held in trust. If the shares fall, so does the money in the executive's hope chest.

Contrast this with the typical salary position in a large company. Pay is determined by rank and rises gratifyingly year by year with time and seniority. With it, up and up goes the pension entitlement. The executive knows at the beginning of the year what he or she will earn over the next twelve months, which will be more than juniors get – and as much as peers. Given a choice between this security and the razzle-dazzle uncertainty of true incentives, ninety-nine executives out of 100 will plump for security.

As for the 100th, he or she won't stay long in a big company anyway. For all their talk about the entrepreneur, about risk-taking, and about the golden lure of profits, the majority of executives are staid by talent and temperament. Their instinctive, silent reasoning must be, 'Why expose myself and my family to financial risk, when secure employment depends on making my superiors feel secure about me?' Against this background, pay systems in all companies – including stock-option schemes and incentive plans – gravitate, or degenerate, towards bureaucratic stability.

Executives have great difficulty in recognising this desire for financial peace and quiet in themselves. Whenever right-wing politicians cut taxes on top incomes, a supposedly clinching argument (much beloved by both Reaganites and Thatcherites) is that reducing the tax bite gives executives greater incentive to take risks, win orders, and generally sweat harder. The unexciting record of most big British companies after this notion was first applied dismayed the incentive advocates not at all.

Obviously, the cuts were too small. Reduce top taxes still further, and British management would really show what it was made of. Their make-up, alas, proved to contain a substantial amount of greed. The top directors of sixty of Britain's largest companies paid themselves nearly 25% more in 1993. *The Guardian* reported that 'salary rates for the ten best-paid jobs' among these large companies 'have galloped ahead by anywhere between 58% and 4,833%'. Half a dozen executives topped a million pounds in total income – and none of their companies had exceptional years.

In reality, tax rates seem to have little effect on effort. For many years, the Swedish economy, just as highly taxed as the British was, grew faster. True, Sweden's super-performance is a thing of the past. But exactly the same point about high taxation can be made about Japan. Nor could the old tax argument explain away the yawning gulfs between the performances of different managements whose members all pay much the same tax rates. Still, you can't blame executives for arguing that they would work harder or better if taxed less, even though they lie.

What they really want (and who doesn't?) is to pay less tax. High taxes, again, were blamed for the lush fringe benefits with which many British executives were cosseted before an aroused Mrs Thatcher swung an axe at them: the chauf-feured cars; the personal Rolls or Jaguar; the house and gardeners; expensive public schools for the children; the executive dining-room, butler, and wine-cellar; the trips to South Africa in the winter; the flats in Mayfair or Belgravia; and so on.

We don't actually like having all these presents, ran the argument – the tax system forces them on us. Before the war, however, and before taxes became so penal, British com-panies had their grouse moors and their private trains, as well as today's popular treats. A survey by Shell once established that most of its executives pined for the life of a country gentleman – and among older British chief execu-tives today country sports are far and away the most popular pastime.

The British company traditionally provided its leaders with life as their more leisured grandfathers might have known it; and if most American executives live lower off the hog, at company expense, that too is more a matter of social tradition than of the tax system. The tradition has always been broken by egregiously greedy men like F. Ross Johnson, the former R.J.R. Nabisco boss, with his fleet of corporate aircraft, huge personal expenses and sporting entertainments; or the late Steve Ross of Time Warner, whose corporate spending feats were equally legendary.

Not that Americans of less conspicuous consuming habits hate using company money for their own creature comforts. That soaring skyscraper in Wall Street, Park Avenue, or Westchester County, that chairman's office festooned with rare art and furniture, that private jet, may be good for the corporate prestige. But they also do no harm to the executive's own ego. The Germans are more frank; they admit that the depth of floor carpet matters almost as much as the size of a German director's salary.

The stock option has become roughly the same thing in the US – part of the furniture, which executives expect to find there, but which doesn't motivate them recognisably. If fortune shines on the company, they pocket the profits. If the stock slumps to the floor, that's the way the cookie crumbles – there are stock options in the most moribund of America's corporate giants. And every year there are fewer top executives who could echo one virtuous vice-chairman:

'I pay my own golf club dues. I pay my own Clipper Club membership. We have no company country club. We don't have a company plane. There's no financial planning done for me or other executives. I fill out my own tax returns.'

The statement shouldn't of course, be extraordinary; that's the way things should be. Nothing in the work or achievement of the average American CEO explains the leap in income from $190,383 in 1960 to $3.8 million in 1992, a leap of 1,922%. In the process, the CEOs advanced inexorably from 40.5 times the pay of the average worker to an amazing 157 times. Even engineers only managed to multiply their pay sixfold during the sensational surge of the CEOs – which accelerated markedly in the 1980s. The positive economic impact of this greed, naturally, was imperceptible; and that's no surprise.

Over a certain level, pay always loses its importance. This

is the weakness of commission systems. Once a salesman has earned what he reckons to be adequate, he is much less interested in earning more for the company. That level of adequacy varies between individuals and between cultures; in the US the cut-off point is very high. But even one of the world's all-time selling champions, H. Ross Perot, stopped selling computers after reaching the ceiling imposed by IBM. (With his own software company, he made more money in less time – on paper – than any man in history; then lost more in less time – on paper – than anybody, when his stock-market bubble deflated; then finally and truly cleaned up to a billion-dollar tune after General Motors bought his company in 1984.)

The general theory of remuneration is to pay people their market value, pay them still more as their responsibility and contribution rise, and not to keep expensive deadwood around the premises. Only executives who are themselves incompetent keep on at £50,000 a year people whose services are worth half; only a misguided management congratulates itself on getting senior executives for £100,000 a year when the going rate is £200,000. For some reason, the proprietorial company finds this lesson hard to master. One multi-millionaire took exception to paying his new managing director, in a billion-pound company, more than a marketing whizzkid would get elsewhere.

The fact that labourers may not know their hire value is no excuse for paying them less. In Britain, where people are traditionally even more secretive about money than sex, executive reticence helped to keep pay before tax far below European levels. By 1983, the Swiss and the Germans had worked up to 100% more than their British executive counterparts; and both countries had caught up with, if not surpassed, American standards for upper middle managers. An executive pay-lag is one sickness that no country can afford in the new global age of truly international and interchangeable executives.

Giving some pay, somehow, in the form of shares is one right and proper antidote; but not because it will produce superior corporate performance (it probably won't), and certainly not because a capital stake will make the manager more forcefully independent. Cravens who won't argue with a superior because they are afraid of losing their jobs won't argue any more readily because they have a stock option. Executives should be deeply invested in their company's shares for two different reasons: first, people who devote much of their lives to capitalist concerns deserve capital; second, they also deserve to share the sorrows as well as the joys of the shareholders – when shares go down, it should hurt, and preferably more than it hurts the latter.

But the corporate bureaucracy is most unlikely to reward its executives unfairly; and the unfairness is certain to get less and less the nearer the executive gets to the top. For top executives are in the happy position of fixing, or helping to fix, their own pay. That's the explanation of the afore-mentioned surge during the amazing explosion of US executive fortune in the early 1980s. When the golden parachutes and so forth floated gently down to earth, many and miraculous were the results.

There was nothing miraculous, though, about the results for many of the companies concerned. Steve Ross's creation, Time Warner, paid two executives the stupendous sum of $42.9 million, in the years immediately after paying the creator $34.2 million; from 1990 to 1992, investors gained not a single nickel. In those three years, it was quite difficult for investors to lose money. There were a few major US companies where 20% or more of their wealth disappeared; but only three of the CEOs responsible (among them, IBM's unfortunate Akers) suffered a decline in personal pay.

In Britain, Fisons' profits collapsed in circumstances little short of scandal; the brief tenure of chief executive Cedric Scroggs was capped with a payment of £750,000. At another troubled company, British Aerospace, John Cahill left after another brief spell, this time as chairman, with no less than £3.2 million – and that was after generously waiving £1.5 million of his actual entitlement. Removing Ernest Mario from Glaxo as its shareholders suffered non-growing pains cost the company £4 million – and all these payments flowed from decisions made, not by the investors, but by their supposed guardians on the board.

The internecine bliss of said guardians was perfectly summed up by a great *New Yorker* boardroom cartoon. In it the table is surrounded by smiling faces and the chairman is saying, 'Gentlemen, I think we can congratulate ourselves on voting these large increases in salary, thus ensuring to the corporation our continuing loyal services'. Or not, as the case may be.

BOOK III
BOARD GAMES

Introduction:
The Boardroom Revolution

The boardroom, as the following chapters describe it, remains the ultimate bastion of naked management. In the power game, the top people hold all the aces. True, Pehr Gyllhenhammar, the architect of Volvo and one of Europe's most powerful managers, saw his treasured plan for merging with Renault defeated by a rebellion of the upper echelons. But that revolt was masterminded by Volvo's second-in-command; who, no doubt, is now very much in total command – which is where chief executives dearly love to be.

But their dominance is being undermined by a universal and insidious force: the network. Paradoxically, the information technology which seems to offer senior management greater control is actually going to place increased power and freedom in the hands of their juniors. It's a cliché of management theory that information is power. But the network makes it far more difficult for top management to monopolise information – and thus makes it much easier for the former worms to turn.

Much the same thing happened with the advent of the telephone. Seniors expected the new weapon to increase their control; instead, it encouraged juniors to answer back in ways that eyeball-to-eyeball contact would have made impossible. The network is still only used by a minority, say a third, of companies even in the most advanced country, the United States. But its use is spreading like a fire storm. By the millennium every PC that can usefully be tied into a network will be – and that will change the top-down structure of corporate management for keeps.

The debate over information technology is over. It's been swinging between two negative poles – necessary evil or 'without-which-nothing'. Most of top management still belongs firmly to the first school. It recognises that computers are essential, but objects to almost everything about them – above all their costs and disappointments. The enthusiasts, in contrast, are deep into a future where so much competitive activity will hinge around IT that, to quote one expert, 'non-players will be shut right out of the game'.

The game is management itself. IT is not a threat to the boardroom, but a promise, an opportunity to manage the business system in ways that were simply not available to previous generations. 'Without-which-nothing' places the emphasis on the wrong strategy: 'with-which-anything' replaces the defensive with the positive – and it's in the executive suites where the vital attacking battles will be won or lost. Boardroom players have to generate an overall competitive strategy which the information technology can serve, and possibly modify. But once that task is complete, the system will usurp boardroom powers.

In the words of MIT's Chris Kemerer, the IT specialists will work with the business units to discover the objective and 'work their way up through the policies, procedures and technologies that will be necessary to arrive at the particular goal'. So organised and integrated a process won't easily be challenged, even by the most obtuse seniors. The process may force unpleasant rethinking on them – like one man at Bankers Trust who objected (but vainly) when its 'technology champion' showed that goals could not be met unless foreign exchange was separated from money transfer.

Self-evidently, the IT revolution is aligned with the revolutionary trend in management, which is to devolve genuine authority to clearly identified and viable units - and never mind what going horizontal implies for existing vertical architectures. The 'real solution', according to author Jessica Keyes, 'is to simply bite the bullet and invest on realigning the organisation into a structure that is most effective [and in] wrapping a technology architecture around the process'. If the boardroom's *modus operandi* is ineffective in these terms, it's the boardroom that will have to change.

The mainframe computer, sealed off from the corporation at large, was the boardroom's toy. But its solo day is done. At a recent seminar, one IT manager, defending his centralised system, belittled the value of PCs; he was promptly savaged by two of his network-loving peers. Of course, networking has its drawbacks; but they are enormously outweighed by the advantages, which doesn't only mean the great and growing initial cost differentials. More: the move 'offers new opportunities for innovation that weren't present before', writes Keyes. The mainframe still has its uses, irreplaceable for many companies; but whatever their business, they will lose competitive advantage by sticking to the mainframe alone.

By the same token, IT makes major strategic gains available – and once top management has agreed to go for those gains, profound change in the way they manage the company has been mandated. For example, sharing IT powers, letting computer speak to computer across corporate borders, offers both sides significant economies and business advantages. Once the networks are linked, however, chief executives are locked into partnership with key people who don't work for them; those who do, moreover, relate, not to the ultimate boss, but to their associates, inside and outside the firm.

It would, of course, be perverse to integrate systems with customers, supplier or other partners and to allow a disintegrated system to persist within the organisation. The technical and economic challenges involved are enormous. Du Pont, for instance, is to spend $200 million over five years to create a uniform information network over eighty businesses and fifty countries. Such networks will encourage much flatter organisations, which in turn will necessitate integrated systems for control and collaboration.

The massive re-engineering needed to provide integration will involve what one consultant calls 'wrenching and difficult' organisational changes. In some ways, the wrench will empower those who already have power. For instance, the Frito-Lay snack food company's executive information system spotted sales declines in the central US. Tracking through the system, the CEO narrowed the problem down to Texas, then to one sales division, then to one store chain. Within months, a white-corn version of Tostitos was attacking the local competition that had caused the trouble.

Top management can thus use what Keyes calls 'info-marketing' for a whole range of investigations, from 'tracking a competitor's moves to tracking your own company's progress in bringing a product to market'. None of that can be done without IT. But neither can it be done without setting up information highways and byways along which anybody can travel. The analysis of international and external data as a guide to better decisions will help the boardroom; but the same data, and the same ability to analyse, will inevitably percolate much further down the corporation.

If this were only a means of empowering lower management (and through them the ranks lower still), the boardroom Mafia could maintain its power and privileges without losing much except internal effectiveness. But with its whole competitive edge at stake, that loss is just what the company can't afford. The analogy is with Otis; its elevator customers benefit, not only from a database that contains all information about repair calls, but from continuous electronic monitoring that summons engineers before the user even knows there's something wrong.

Similarly, the network gives all managers access to all the information they require about customers and suppliers, internal and external; plus the ability to monitor what's going wrong and right; plus feedback on the reactions and actions which follow from the monitoring. Eventually, all boards will be presiding over a 'techno-business' – a company with so developed an IT capacity that the latter can stand as a profit centre in its own right, even serving third parties.

Two extant examples are Federal Express, with Mrs Fields, the cookie business, following close behind – and these two cases inadvertently make a crucial point.

Neither company has been spared serious problems despite innovative use of IT. The brilliant employment of hardware and software is a necessary condition of success; but as the surviving conservatives in the boardroom say, you can't manage with a computer. What the diehards forget, though, is that today you can't manage competitively without, not just a computer, but a whole network of them. The grand old order described in the following chapters is being destroyed from within by little new electronic devices.

12
Managing by Minion

The modern principle of decentralisation makes enchanting sense. Simply split the corporate leviathan into big lumps of homogenous activities, then break down the homogenous lumps into individual morsels. Each lump and morsel has its responsible boss, and all bosses have another boss upon their backs to bite 'em. Gone, or kicked upstairs, are the functional directors of production, marketing, engineering, or what have you – jobs so loosely defined that nobody could tell when they were mangled. In their place stand the divisional executive and his subsidiary executives and their subsidiary executives, each in charge of a distinct business.

If the arrayed subordinates all perform according to plan, the chief executive and the summit sidekicks have little to do, except pat backs, collect pay, plan the future and wait for a rich retirement. With all this going for it, the decentralised company should have soared into new orbits. It hasn't; decentralisation has often meant deterioration. Du Pont is the daddy of all decentralised and financially motivated managements. In the 1960s, its sales growth lagged behind that of other chemical giants. Its earnings per share growth was negative – a decline of 1.79% a year.

In 1993, the giant could look back on a grisly decade;

earnings per share shrank by 6.4% annually. Admittedly, the years of travail were bothersome for the entire chemical industry, beset by soaring feedstock costs initially and then by sinking prices (produced in part by its own addiction to over-expansion). All the same, Du Pont's stockholders had cause to complain; the return on their equity in 1993 was a paltry 4.9% – and, on assets, that shrank to 1.5%, thanks to a barely visible 1.7% margin on sales.

Yet Du Pont had decentralised down to the last digit long before; British rivals even used to gibe that Du Pont's board members were just a bunch of chemical bankers. Difficulty in recovering adequate loot from decentralised divisions is not, however, confined to the bankers of Du Pont. Some companies even started to wonder whether they should reverse engines. 'Recentralisation is the word now,' said an American executive gloomily at one stage. 'But I haven't met anybody who's actually done it.'

He never did. By 1994 decentralisation had achieved a new and stronger lease of life. The spread of computer networks held out the promise of running large, even global corporations with a sublime combination; total control and information at the centre and meaningful independence and freedom at the periphery. In terms of electronic and managerial technology, the combination should work. The problem, in the present and future as in the past, lies with the practice.

The decentralisation theory has no fatal flaws in itself. It just doesn't generally fit the real-life way in which companies work. The conglomerates fell foul of the reality. Some of them (some by accident) collected quite good companies in their stamp albums. But decentralisation was their supposed essence. The conglomerator sat at the centre of the spider's web, while, all around, the new acquisitions, separated by distance, organisation, and the different natures of their trades, spun away.

Very few big black spiders, however, could leave well enough alone for long – and the lust to interfere became still more irresistible when 'well enough' turned to terrible. At ITT, for example, the bright young men at HQ dreamed up the idea of dominating the business of contract cleaning for offices. So out went the ITT raiding parties to big city after big city, buying up the market-leading cleaners and making their deliriously happy family proprietors suddenly cash-rich.

But the bright young men saw that their new properties were under-managed. So they sent out other bright young men to tell the former proprietors how to run their businesses. The ex-bosses liked that so little that, one after the other, they left, taking their best contracts with them. ITT found itself competing against the very people whose companies it had bought – and competing, what's worse, at a terrible disadvantage in local knowledge and industry know-how. At that point, intervention became essential: but, of course, useless.

Another conglomerate, Litton Industries, seemed to discover perfect decentralisation. It kept the head office small; broke big units down to optimal, more manageable size; exerted strict financial control by fast, frequent, and elaborate reports, including weekly cash statements; placed able sharpies in charge of operations; and promoted them swiftly when they succeeded. And the top duo, the late Charles B. (Tex) Thornton and Roy Ash, held strategy sessions at which, with the unit managers and the latter's group bosses, they belaboured the questions at the core of any business – where it was going and how it was going to get there.

One of the many Litton executives spun off into other careers has reminisced, though, that the strategy sessions were actually futile. Why? Because Ash and Thornton simply didn't know enough about the businesses to ask the right questions – not that this stopped them from trying. And so at Litton the system failed, not because of act of God or national economic crisis, but because of miscalculations and plain mismanagement in two of the new decentralised joys, ship-building and office machinery.

No structural device (and 'strategy sessions' are only gadgets) exists by which the head office can both manage and not manage. A clear choice has to be made, one way or the other – and you don't have to guess which way the head-office manager will jump: into interference, with both feet. Managing directors or presidents are possessed by ambition, power-drive, and vanity; they have climbed many miles, over long years, to reach the top. Once arrived, they seldom breathe in, dock their highly polished shoes on the desk, and drop any desire to manage actively. The motivations that propelled their rise are just as powerful once they have risen.

The decentralised corporation, with its profit centres, its corporate plans, and its group executives, becomes a labyrinthine mechanism to let the head-office heads play at being executives – for in the end they cannot manage. Decentralisation, even in quite small companies, is not a theory, but an inevitability. Some executive, somewhere down the line, is in personal contact with reality – the customer who won't buy, the product that won't work, the machines that won't produce, the employees who feel alienated from the company that provides their livings.

The longer the rope between that executive and the summit, and the more the people on Everest seek to know and influence what is happening in the far foothills, let alone the valleys, the more the company becomes an expensive device for generating unused information. But modish decentralisation rode over this truth, in the opposite direction. Turn everybody, it said, even the salesperson, into an executive. Push responsibility further and further down the corporation ladder. Substitute individual initiative for central initiative. Achieve coordination through a common corporate philosophy plus common controls and common corporate systems.

This, note, isn't just the fashionable theory of collegial, devolved management purveyed by every worthwhile guru in the 1990s. Rather, it's been the refrain of thinking management and management thinkers for decades. That kind of company is the never-never land of business. Advocates of such wonderlands should consider a letter written in blood by one employee of an American group alleged to be a rare example of successful big-time management of diversity. Like most corporate frames, this one crumbles slightly if growth is assessed after deducting inflationary increments, or profita-

154

bility by knocking off near-monopoly markets in the US. But still, it was, relatively speaking, a good company and a lesson to Europeans – or was it?

The letter from its humble son, well down the scale, out on one of the European limbs, read: 'We have a very able sales manager who in turn reports to New York, but he is not able to see us very often. I have been told that I must be responsible for everything to sell my product – marketing, sales forecast, advertising, mailing campaigns, etc – everything to enable me to sell my product better. I am completely inexperienced in how to do this.'

Every day some decentralised employee, like this victim, is told, in effect and sometimes in so many words, 'This is your business and your responsibility. It's all yours – off you go and run it.' But the person may not have the resources to run the department or the true independence that alone makes sense of the policy. The more important the operation, the more hotly superiors breathe down the subordinate neck. The less important, the more likely the underling is to be strung up in that salesman's position – left alone, to hang himself, or to be hung by some offended superior.

The organisation chart won't reveal that somewhere in darkest Germany, Stygian England, or murky France is a sales manager whose boss is 3,000 miles away in Manhattan, and whose own subordinates have all but forgotten what he looks like. That boss on Park Avenue is too remote and too busy with his own bureaucratic spawning of words and figures to understand the local business. Even if there is enough time to explain the business to him, is there really any point? The Sixth Truth of Management lays down that there are only two possibilities: either executives are competent to run the business or they are not.

In the first instance, leave them alone. In the second, move them. In neither case should another executive try to run the business through the subordinate by remote control. Often the besetting preoccupation and sin of the distant superior is to demonstrate that he really is superior. The inferiors in turn become too preoccupied with the pressures from on high to avoid stupidities themselves – such as giving impossible responsibilities to unprepared salesmen.

When the victims fail, the calamity is demonstrably not their fault; it's that of decentralisation carried to its usual centralised excess. The whole idea stemmed from the exact observation that businesses have grown beyond the scale and scope of the centre's ability to command. But responsibility, other things being unequal, can be pushed too far down. The Peter Principle seeks to prove that eventually executives are promoted beyond their abilities. Incompetents are manufactured more often from above, by demoting responsibility below the critical point – the level at which the organisation allows it to be carried.

Many large groups have committed the sins of centralisation and decentralisation at once; they condemn their lesser executives to fail by this sure-fire method, while the abler executives waste oceans of time, initiative, and energy in preparing and discussing plans and reports and budgets for the allegedly detached centre. Every westbound transatlantic flight transports the boss or sub-boss of some European subsidiary of an American multi-national to Des Moines, or New York, or Pittsburgh. Briefcases bulging, the passengers are on their way for the monthly or quarterly confrontation with their superiors.

A supplement, less common in the 1990s (fortunately) than it used to be, is for the parent's senior management to go on a grand procession, like the Doges of medieval Venice, around their satrapies; and nobody stops to query all this travel (which is easier and more enjoyable than work). The reality of multi-national decentralisation, especially in companies with more or less homogenous product lines, can only be experienced truly from within.

In Dow Chemical, for example, the downstream manufacturing operations had for years been regarded only as outlets for the group's base product, ethylene – of which it was the world's most efficient producer. Unfortunately, the huge over-capacity of the recessionary 1980s made this less and less of an asset. The strategy of adding businesses (any businesses) that used the ethylene came to look increasingly absurd.

Actually, it always had been, since the added businesses weren't evaluated at all on their intrinsic merits (if any). The decentralised subsidiaries round the world had been nothing more than centrally dominated funnels for production. Now, under enormous pressure for more profits, they were expected to change emphasis – and how. Businesses were to be market-led, not product-pushed; so the subsidiary managers duly and dutifully started to try and develop their own national markets.

Then they met the unpleasant realities: the unanswered memos to head office about market and product questions to which HQ knew the answer; the US management hoarding information and experience that was vital to the development plans which Europe was desperately trying to form and implement; the European management which regarded with suspicion and often obstructiveness the efforts of national managements to maximise their returns from national markets.

And, of course, there was another problem; years of subservience had left the local managements themselves gravely short of experience at being what they were now supposed to be – real businessmen. Yet such multi-nationals always had the perfect set-up to decentralise truly, if they wanted to. The local business was geographically remote and clearly marked out by national frontiers, often by national market characteristics. Its management, too, was largely separated by nationality and language. And the overseas businesses, mostly starved neither for capital nor marketable products, were substantial economic powers in their own rights and own lands.

Under that dispensation, the parent's only vital functions were to watch and count its money, to coordinate (i.e. stop any one subsidiary from slaughtering the others), to soup up its baby's growth by providing any riches that the locals requested from the central cornucopia, and to change the management if it failed. But the overwhelming tendency was to absorb the national company into the parent, until decisions in Scotland, France, and the Midwest were homogenised into one bland whole.

That self-evident fault became a deliberately sought virtue (without the blandness, naturally) as 'global' corporations evolved from the late 1980s onwards. Ford Motor reorganised in 1994 so that all new model programmes would be global, masterminded from one centre, but applying across the world. IBM, in yet another desperate attempt to retain its across-the-board, centrally led structure, set up customer groups (banking, automotive, etc) whose writ would run world-wide.

Matrix management, which gave people three bosses (by nation, function, and product) went into retreat as managements tried to correct its mostly dismal results, even inside national boundaries. The giveaway signs are unmistakable. Watch for evidence that the centre is forcing the supposedly decentralised operations to share common functions – not the essentially central control functions, like finance and law, but the inessential. Rather, it's essential for the good health of the affiliate that functions such as marketing stay where they belong – close to the market.

The results when they don't are visible from a *Harvard Business Review* study by Carolyn Y. Woo. She looked at leaders with high market shares but low returns on capital – in contradiction to conventional wisdom (and misplaced common sense) which holds that high goes with high. Among various other masterpieces of mismanagement (like having heavier costs and higher prices), over half the low-return leaders shared more than four-fifths of the marketing programmes with other lines of the corporation's business, as against sharing 39% for the leaders whose returns were what they should be: high.

Over a quarter of the marketing channels were shared by two-thirds of the low-return laggards; again, significantly more than for the high-returners. What the successful entrepreneur almost invariably does – give carefully defined, separate businesses their own distinct marketing resources (meaning the armaments they need to sell effectively) – should apply as a general rule; and often this simple act of separation has been the key to magnificent turnarounds.

Muddle up the marketing, or anything else, and you muck

up the management. One of the key moments in IBM's post-war history, maybe the single most important step in creating the most successful multi-national of them all, was the decision to stop making the entire product line in every foreign plant. Instead, each would concentrate on its own products – shared with nobody else. As Sir Edwin Nixon, the UK chairman of the time, recalled, 'It was one of those management decisions which are absolutely right in retrospect, but which are quite difficult at the time' – 'quite difficult' being, no doubt a British, stiff-upper-lip euphemism for great pain.

Sometimes it's necessary, in the interests of a grander strategy, to coalesce rather than separate. Following much the same grand plan as IBM – that is, making collective sense of Europe, seeing it as a whole, rather than as separate territories – Ford Motor turned its back on what had apparently been a triumphant tradition. Once, Henry Ford II's British pied-à-terre was brashly independent, with a large minority of British stockholders, a self-consciously tough Irish boss, and a creaking but tolerably successful product line. But now the Americans from Dearborn descended on Dagenham. The minority stockholders were bought out, hundreds of millions were poured in to re-equip the plants and revitalise the products, and American executives arrived in droves.

At first their control lodged in a popular watering-place for American executives, Brussels. Then the outfit, Ford of Europe, was removed to the same lush Americanised executive block as Ford of Britain, which came under the direct managerial control of the Americans, for ill as well as good. The first, but not the last, ill was the choice of an American-style replacement for its top-of-the-market Zephyr-Zodiac range – long-bonneted, wide-wheelbased, gas-guzzling. It flopped, losing 90% of its market.

One British director of the time believes, rightly or wrongly, that Ford's mismarketing was compounded by production faults, in part because the local executives had no real faith in a project that wasn't truly and wholly theirs. But in what must have been a tough learning process for both the

Americans and the Europeans, the successful coordination of the European apparatus continued, until at one point the profits from Britain and Germany, with their supporting plants in Holland and Spain, were sustaining the whole Ford empire.

With so much at stake, nobody could seriously pretend that the Ford managers in Britain are still the captains of the subsidiary's soul and fate – as they should be, in theory. Apart from anything else, there has been constant turnover at the top; at one point, Ford had four managing directors in six years. The adoption of a European-wide policy for Ford, with production of European-wide models sourced as the European management decreed, took priority; yet with an unwelcome and surprising dénouement.

General Motors counter-attacked with such force in Europe that two top Ford men in swift succession disappeared from their posts in 1984. That didn't stop the rot. By allowing its European leaders to lead, and backing them with consistent investment, GM turned the tables. Now GM Europe was feeding its loss-making parent, while Ford of Europe's losses were adding to the parental stress. While GM's Jack Smith was propelled by his European success to the top of the whole corporation, Ford's Euro-summit, a publicly confessed management quagmire, lurched from one leader to another.

The difficult trick in global business is to apply the still relevant Sixth Truth of Management. In the simplest situation, if the locals say they know best what to produce, they should be left to prove it, and to pay the price if they fail. After all, if they can't be trusted on that, how can they be trusted with anything else, except the key to the executive washroom? It's a difficult trick, however, to achieve local autonomy and (just as important) the feeling of local autonomy while imposing transnational unity.

If you don't achieve that combination (as Ford has found the hard way), product failures will follow in this country or that. Cars are a special management problem in one respect, of course – as trains used to, they turn almost any adult into a schoolboy. At Volkswagen, stuck in continuing crisis in

1993, the top executives still thought it a splendid idea to spend a couple of days driving their new models around an exotic site 'like ordinary customers'. But even if the products are less compulsive playthings, the urge to fiddle is omnipresent – partly because the chief executive likes to take personal credit for any successes (the failures he leaves to others).

Effective decentralisation, however, means no fiddling and no meddling, except when mismanagement occurs. True, by then damage has been done. No matter how elaborate the early-warning system, the centre, even in the computer age, can be nastily surprised. In one typical Litton case, its Hull factory in England was expensively geared up to manufacture typewriters that it could neither produce properly nor sell; this became evident from reports only when the company was already locked into disaster. The mistake was not lack of reports; it was the original, strategic decision, in which the Litton bosses had 'participated', to use their word.

In most big corporations, top executives participate all the time; that is, they hold endless meetings to second-guess the executives who are supposed to be in charge. Once you decentralise, you become more investor than director. You should act like a sane one. It's interesting how old saws of stock-market investment apply to decentralised direction – 'Cut your losses, but let your profits run', or 'Reinforce success, and never invest in failure'.

One old-line board, that of English Electric, ignored both wise saws. It was notorious for inability to influence its largest subsidiary, Marconi, which had decentralised itself right out of the head-office orbit. When the offshoot's ideas and those of another part of the empire overlapped, both projects sometimes, ludicrously, went ahead. Both even developed their own computers. The correct answer, since the child went around the track much faster than the parent, was to back baby. But this would have meant downgrading the doomed computer business over which the main board actually enjoyed ('enjoy' being *le mot juste*) day-to-day control.

As the better managements of the 1980s realised, only when senior managers change their entire life-styles, abdicate the interfering habits of a managing lifetime, and substitute the fair but demanding standards of a hungry investor, can decentralisation be more than a myth – and often an expensive one. The relatively cheap and marvellously productive results of true decentralisation, though, have been demonstrated by enough companies since the oil-price shocks to provide proof as abiding as proof ever can be in management.

Time and again, the recipe's the same. Decimate head-office numbers; make the person in charge at the decentralised unit into a real chief executive; impose fast-acting information systems, and use them to squeeze out the top performance which, anyway, for the sake of their own remuneration and ambition, the appointees will want to achieve. Set down like that, the formula sounds little different from that which, say, Harold S. Geneen used to peddle fallaciously as ITT's supreme contribution to the art of higher management. The difference lies, though, in that head office and how its inhabitants behave.

Actually, it's a tougher trick to act as guide and goad, enhancing rather than reducing motivation and management performance, than it is to play the mastermind at the expense of your minions. For that's what the centralising head office in the half-decentralised company makes of its managers: minions. And they manage like it.

13
The Boardroom Mafia

Boards of directors have an aura of sanctity roughly akin to that of the College of Cardinals. The law sees them as they see themselves – guardians of the shareholders' rights and the company's long-term future. A pungent *New Yorker* comment, at the height of the Valachi revelations about the Mafia, is more accurate. The cartoon showed a board chairman snarling at his youngest and brashest director: 'Perkins, will you stop calling this company Cosa Nostra.'

Perkins was perfectly right. Since senior executives in most corporations are both the dominant directors and the controlling executives, the business all too readily becomes Our Thing. The board elects itself, reshuffles itself, congratulates itself. The directors are supposed to call the executives to account – and possibly did in ancient times, when the general manager of the business was a lackey, like the doorkeeper.

Today the general manager is either chairman of the board, or chief executive, or both. His first loyalty is not to the board as such, and certainly not to the unseen shareholders, but to an amorphous body of no legal standing, the upper management. The Mafia-like aspect of top management cosiness raises the large and well-aired questions about

163

the relationship between shareholders, directors, and companies that the Cadbury Committee sought to resolve in Britain. One question, at least as important, seldom gets any air: the relationship between the management Mafia and the efficient conduct of the business.

This issue is most transparent in companies (meaning almost all companies in Britain) where the executive-dominated, all-supreme board is at its zenith, and where a band of non-executive gentlemen (almost never gentlewomen) are supposed to exert some kind of influence over the assembled bunch of executives. You might think that in corporate America, the Mafia is under better control. As IBM slid towards disaster, it had only three current executives on the eighteen-strong board. Eight non-execs were businessmen from other industries, and the several retirees included a former IBM chairman, which is fairly standard US practice.

British companies, in the local tradition, often favour out-of-work politicians. The American system looks more sensible, safer, and less Sicilian; but, as usual in American organisations, first glances do not reveal last truths. The outcome, on both sides of the Atlantic, is remarkably close, despite the apparent contrasts. The most obvious of these differences is the position of the *capo*, the boss. In Britain's corporate families, the chairman is still often chief executive and managing director, despite the Cadbury strictures on the point. Surrounded only by his disciple-deputies, he (hardly ever she) enjoys double strength.

In the US, the chairman's job of presiding over the company used to be distinct from directing its operations. Thus major corporations commonly had both a chairman and president (plus a raft of more or less powerful committees, which needn't be chaired by either potentate). But ever since the title 'chief executive officer' became current, it has stuck firmly to the man (again, rarely woman) in the chair. The corporation may or may not have a COO (chief operating officer) to ease the burden; but the CEO is The Man.

Managers have the word of none other than Harold S. Geneen, the supreme architect of ITT, writing in his book

Managing, that the two-hat touch is wrong. Geneen should know – as he confesses, he 'wore both hats in my day, and it felt great'. The question, though, is whether it felt great for the company – and that, in the light of some of Geneen's other admissions, is far from certain. The infamous disaster in Canada, where $320 million was lost on a wood-cellulose plant, to which Geneen became personally and unstoppably committed, is one example.

According to *Business Week*'s review of his book, 'The resulting $320 million loss, he concedes, probably could have been averted if someone had just gone to Canada and looked at the trees – which, it turned out, grew to no more than an uneconomical three inches in diameter.' Keeping the chief executive in his place – one rung down – has its economic virtues. Or rather, the lonely summit has its uneconomic vices. First, nearly all the *capo*'s boardroom colleagues owe their careers to him and are used to his command. They are thus less likely to challenge his policies – no matter how terrible – and when the emperor's clothes fade away, it takes them far too long to see him bare.

Second, the chair's formal and ceremonial obligations eat up hours. Any portly fellow can cut the ribbons and show around the visiting firemen. Running the company requires talent and time. Like everybody else, the *capo* has only twenty-four hours a day. After sleep, ceremonial and publicity distractions, he's lucky to find more than twenty minutes to attend to a reasonably important division – and this assumes that he is well-organised. He is far more likely to devour available time with trivia that suddenly grab his emotions. Somebody should stop him, true – but who?

Certainly the stop won't be supplied by cronies who owe their non-executive places to the overlord's grace and favour. Hugh Parker, who built the McKinsey practice in London, has pointed out that the CEO's job is to extract good performance from his subordinates, while the chairman squeezes the CEO. But if the latter doubles as chairman, is he going to put pressure on himself? The board can't do it collectively. Executive directors whom the chairman is pressuring in his managing-director role will stay squashed. And non-executives won't rock the boat until it's sprung a large and obvious leak.

One major company had a mighty *capo* who loved flying kites – making and half-believing outrageous propositions. In the cold light of day, he leaked stories about how his fellow directors (none of whom would say boo unless ordered) had rebuffed him. The technique is that of the Dickensian lawyer who was always willing to agree but whose unseen partner (actually entirely somnolent) would have none of it.

Within the Mafia, too, a form of *omerta* applies: the code of honour lays down nothing but good about the *capo* until he is dead – or gone. After departure, the stories of the great man's weaknesses, foibles, and gross errors flood out. Not even Khrushchev telling tales on Stalin exceeds the relish of a successor executive recounting the sins of a predecessor (in which the successors were as deeply implicated as any Khrushchev). For proof, hearken to Hicks B. Waldron, the man charged with turning round the fallen marketing star, Avon Products, delivering himself of a few well-chosen words about the true marketing skills of the predecessor regime:

'They didn't have an understanding of any of the normal levers of marketing: like pricing and product positioning, segmented advertising. Although these were things everyone else knew, they didn't.' Just to rub in the incompetence of the old inhabitants of his new Kremlin, Waldron added that, 'There was a lack of professional management skills and a lack of attention to what was going on in the outside world.' Yet, as John Thackray observed in *Management Today*, there's a little problem here – the fact 'that Waldron and most of his team are somewhat implicated in the mistakes of the past. Waldron was an Avon director for a period of three years before he became chairman.'

It's evidently fair to ask what he, let alone the rest of the surviving management, had been up to all that time, while Avon's earnings were sliding by a full third. The more collective the leadership, though, the more collective the clinging. The code is only broken when the leadership structure itself is cracking under extreme pressure; its breach is a sign of corporate disintegration and the first stage in the battle for power. The pressure has to be intense.

Executives will dance the gopak for the boss, submitting to all manner of indignities – waiting for the master's squawk-box permission before going home; public rebuke; being kept waiting all day outside closed doors (a Robert Maxwell speciality); compulsorily submitting signed but undated letters of resignation; even (in one case) writing out copies of the chairman's thoughts – and still they won't protest. Their submission is an inevitable part of the system when a Stalin has emerged.

The business can then become more His Thing than Our Thing – but only if he too obeys the unwritten law. He must preserve the continuity of the corporation, by which is meant the senior executive roles within it. The upper management's desire to perpetuate itself collectively isn't easily distinguished from devotion to the company; the directors' rewards and their powers rest on preserving and defending those of the corporation. If the *capo* threatens the survival of the management family, therefore, he is as doomed as the late, bullet-riddled Mafioso Albert Anastasia.

That even a mighty *capo* can overstep the bounds was demonstrated by Harry J. Gray: a chieftain who, after his feats of super-management in raising United Technologies to $15 billion of sales, must have seemed invulnerable to anything – save age. With his retirement looming up, though, the sixty-five-year-old Gray decided that even the years should not stand in his way; nor would the company president, his heir-apparent.

In ridding himself of the latter, however, Gray so offended the rest of the corporate Mafia that they talked openly about ousting the *capo* himself. Given his outrageous high-handedness, the fact that boardroom verbiage took long to coalesce into action indicates how powerful a hold the *capo* and the code have inside the Mafia; two months after the ejection of the heir-apparent, there was the board expressing its confidence in Gray – and there was *Business Week* reporting the following picture of clear-headed determination among the lesser lights: '55% are conservative, 20% haven't made up their minds, and 25% say the king must go'.

Gray's successor (the same was true after the late Dr Armand Hammer, another famed dispatcher of heirs-apparent, left Occidental Petroleum) hasn't wielded the same unchallenged suzerainty. Both Shell and ICI, which had dominant one-man control pre-war, adopted explicitly collective management – Shell with a bevy of managing directors, ICI with an array of executive directors, none possessing direct power over operations. A rigid written code actually sought to ensure that the ICI chairman would never exercise the powers of chief executive, and ICI's directors once resolutely opposed a McKinsey suggestion that somebody else on the board should.

For a glimpse of the self-protective, self-perpetuating instinct at work, take this passage by a former chairman of ICI (the capital letters are his): '... in a Company as complex as ICI, it is extremely difficult for anyone, however able, to come in as Chairman and be an effective head of the Company. Inevitably, his lack of knowledge of the Company's affairs would mean the appointment of a Managing Director, who himself would have to be so well-informed of the Company's business that it would be just as well to make him Chairman and have done with it.' This neatly glossed over the fact that ICI had no intention of having a managing director in any shape or form.

It is almost as if the management Mafia, after bruising and unsettling experiences of a one-man past, had collectively breathed 'Never again'. Only in the 1980s, under the pressure of the worst trading conditions the company had ever experienced, did the ICI Mafia take its courage in both hands and entrust the chairmanship to an iconoclastic, executive-minded eccentric, John Harvey-Jones. With scant respect for the past, Harvey-Jones tried to close down the mammoth Millbank office (known to corporate jokers as Millstone House) and took the HQ weight off divisional necks.

Under this stimulus ICI even found the gumption to exit from two huge businesses – polyethylene and bulk polyester – which it had originally launched on the world. First in became first out: the result of putting first things (like effective business management) first. Yet Harvey-Jones's brief reign had ruffled more feathers than even he knew. After he retired, and was writing two books, his erstwhile colleagues exercised their contractual veto over any mention of themselves by name. Whatever it was they feared, the incident shows the management Mafia striking back.

Yet Harvey-Jones was proud of having made true collective management work. That's never a picnic at the best of times. The company tends to move at the pace of the slowest director. But this drawback is less unpalatable to some corporations than the insecurity of a *capo*-dominated regime – especially in times when *capos* (just as in the real Mafia) have been getting worse at their jobs: hence the spate of forced departures from companies as large as General Motors, IBM and British Petroleum.

Repeated American experiments with 'a president's office', with three or more persons forming a multiple chief executive, reflect this lust for collective security. It springs from the sheer difficulty, in the system, of developing the super-manager necessary to run, single-handed, corporations on this scale; although that's no greater than the difficulty of making one of these troikas run, or (still harder) cajoling harmonious music out of a managerial quartet.

Try as it may, the cult of personality cannot hide the fact that the typical top executive is interchangeable and disposable. There is nothing wrong with this absence of idols. Business management in the super-company is not an individual matter; it really should be a collective process. It must operate on the assumptions that somebody other than the leader may make the best contribution; that everybody's ideas are open to criticism, especially the boss's; and that the leader is not a giant among pygmies, but a first among equals.

In West Germany the chief executive is actually known as 'the spokesman of the management board' – though anybody who thinks that this phrase circumscribed the authority of a super-manager like Eberhard von Kuenheim, the man who built BMW's success, doesn't know West Germany: some German equals are much more equal than others. Similarly, anybody who thinks that the definitely dominant, giant-among-pygmies power of a Japanese president means dictatorial management doesn't know Japan.

In both countries, the appearances are deceptive; the reality, in the best companies, combines clear and decisive leadership from the top with strong contributions all the way down. The Japanese even have a system, the famous *ringi*, for ensuring that every involved department and every involved manager, is fully involved before a decision is taken. That doesn't safeguard against mistakes – minor, middling or calamitous: witness Yamaha's attempt to catch Honda napping in the domestic motorbike market.

The result was a bloodbath of over-production and price-slashing. The whole bizarre episode culminated in the near-destruction of the Yamaha parent's finances and the swift expulsion of the motorbike boss into outer darkness. For in Japan, as in West Germany (where two VW chief executives in succession were ousted), the supreme responsibility carries with it the supreme sacrifice in the event of failure, absolute or relative. The US, in contrast, has all too many examples of CEOs clinging to power, with the full support of the management Mafia, despite long erosion of earnings, or calamitous acquisitions, or both.

Executives won't take actions that are inimical to their own interests; they will always be tempted by decisions that directly benefit them, never mind the corporation. When one company proposed to merge fully with its own foreign subsidiary, a minor consequence was that the parent directors would no longer sit on the Paris company's board. At the meeting that discussed the merger, five and a half hours out of six went on this issue. One director protested that if he lost his regular lunches in Paris, 'It will be the beginning of Communism in this company.'

On the Continent the system of dual boards (with the supervisors appointing the executives) is meant to purify this impure relationship. But the German supervisory board is mostly as feeble as the annual general meeting in Britain or America. The supervisors meet infrequently; nearly all promotions and appointments are from within the existing management; and the upper management of big and typical German companies forms as heavy, impregnable, and self-respecting a body of men as an American professional football line-up.

By the nature of things, the upper tier of a two-tier board is seldom more than a gold-handled rubber-stamp. The Americans, technically ingenious as ever, have a two-in-one-tier system. The chairman, supported by the non-executive numerical majority on the board, is supposed to safeguard the long-term interests of the corporation (meaning, to establish corporate policy) as well as to cherish the stock-holder. Separate committees, chaired by someone outside executive management, grip the purse-strings – including the fixing of the directors' pay and perquisites.

That used to be the most Cosa Nostra-like activity of the British boardroom, though now 'compensation committees' on American lines have become general. In past, committee-less days one powerful boss, true, maintained that a small non-executive knot on his board likewise ensured that executive fingers didn't wander into the money box. Since the non-executives included his father-in-law, he may have been right. But the US system is plainly right in seeking to recognise and regularise the fact that a company's executive officers develop a vested interest in their own actions and their own status.

The American board is in theory designed to guarantee that the vested interests don't jeopardise the interests of the company as a whole. Except that (as the grotesque pay long lavished on CEOs show) it doesn't work that way. In the first place, the chairman is usually a charter member of the Mafia. At least he knows and understands the business and the men who run it (which isn't necessarily true of non-executive chairmen). But poachers seldom turn gamekeeper. The chairman/CEO won't challenge the entire basis of the upper management's operations and plans – after all, he was the genius who formed them.

Nor are non-executives, however expert in their own rackets, in much of a position to question the wisdom and integrity of the managerial élite, represented on the board by its senior group. Realism dictates that non-executive directors – as the City of London's one-time ornamental bank and insurance company boards found out – are in the hands of the top executives from whom all information comes. Any moderately astute executive can fend off a non-executive outsider (half of the latter's questions are likely to be silly, and the outsider never knows which half).

This assumes, anyway, that the senior company executive, serving as a non-executive on another board, wants to make life uncomfortable for the other boss who (very likely) asked him to join. The invitee isn't a fool. He has a board of his own, with the same situation, and he doesn't want to be uncomfortable, either. Consequently, the you-scratch-my-back-and-I'll-scratch-yours philosophy gets built into the corporate system, or 'you-serve-on-my-board-and-I'll-serve-on-yours'. A wider, clubby management conspiracy gets superimposed on the narrower one of the company.

Managers only get blackballed from the club and cast into outer darkness for gross transgressions against the rules – and even then it takes time, and too much of it. Chrysler once had a boss who (like most Chrysler bosses post-war) wasn't very successful at running Chrysler and got involved in scandal about his own business transactions with the company; it was a long wait before he was expelled. But really bad behaviour is not the problem; that's because appalling misconduct will eventually break up the management Mafia, which (again like its criminal counterpart) can sometimes be exceedingly inefficient.

The real trouble lies in the self-perpetuation of the mediocre, of executives who are never brilliant and never atrocious, but whose use of the assets is less effective than the dumbest stockholder could manage for him- or herself. There is no easy escape. The company is the upper management, and the upper management is the company, for so long as executives maintain an acceptable level of competence (or incompetence). Pressure rarely comes from inside because of the rare emergence of individuals outstanding enough to apply it. It can only come from outside because of a change or incipient change in ownership – mostly in the form of a takeover bid; in other words, from the injection of insecurity.

Human beings clustered in any group will always seek security, and that is the enemy of dynamic business management. Fairy Blackstick in Thackeray's *The Rose and the Ring* wished the princelings 'a little misfortune' as her christening present. It made them into excellent rulers. A little insecurity might do wonders for managements everywhere, for the idea that business life is short and nasty is an illusion sponsored by the Hollywood dream factory; most senior executives, though they talk and even think differently, sleep safe enough in their nests.

Anybody who doubts that should consider two exhibits. First, to quote *Forbes* magazine, 'Some of the nation's finest businessmen were on the board at Continental Illinois. What were they doing for their fees?' The eleven worthies presumably sat there pocketing their $15,000 apiece without raising Cain while the bank slid into the losses, primarily on overly aggressive energy loans, that necessitated the biggest financial rescue in US banking history: $7.5 billion.

Second, an august witness for the prosecution states that 'among the boards of directors of *Fortune* 500 companies, I estimate that 95% are not fully doing what they are legally, morally and ethically supposed to do. And they couldn't, even if they wanted to.' How come? Partly because 'management does 90% to 95% of the talking. Outside board members, who are not part of the management, sit there and listen; then they go to lunch, and then go home and open the envelopes that contain their fees.'

The writer is Harold S. Geneen, who should know whereof he speaks. As boss of ITT, his will was law. As a non-executive director thereafter, he is widely credited with having stymied efforts by his overburdened successors to lighten their load by selling some of Geneen's own bad buys. Had Geneen not been the ex-executive corporate Godfather, of course, nobody would have taken the blindest bit of notice of him.

Poacher turned would-be gamekeeper, Geneen in his retirement now wanted to remove all management members, including the chief executive, from the board, which would have an 'independent management auditor' at its disposal to 'check policies and performance' in the same way as financial figures are already checked (though, given the high failure rate of the latter checks, this proposal shows a truly touching faith).

The ITT ex-Czar hoped that all this would result in 'an informed board of outsiders, led by one of its members as chairman', with a 'quality and intensity of board meetings at a level not seen for many years'. Oh yeah? The fact is that no company can be managed from the boardroom. The real changes have to take place in the executive suite itself, which is what happened at Compaq. There a very rare board, containing only one executive (the CEO) fired him as the precondition of a shake-up that produced a turnround of unexampled speed and success. Here the insecurity was injected by a non-executive chairman, Ben Rosen, who had been the company's guru from the very start.

Executives who want to be insecure can easily arrange it themselves, though. No contractual hiring, no compensation for loss of office, no golden parachutes or handshakes, all nominations to the board entrusted to a committee of investors, salaries and other financial benefits submitted for approval to the same committee before ratification by the annual general meeting, executive directors' stockholdings (and those of their families) held in non-voting trust while they remain executives, and no chief executive allowed to double as chairman. Such conditions wouldn't guarantee the break-up of the management Mafia, but they would increase the chances of Our Thing being managed as Their Thing – 'they' being the outside shareholders.

14
The Risk-Taking Delusion

Managers are deeply ambivalent about risk. Top executives who have never taken a risk in all their long careers bemoan the lack of risk-taking initiative among their young. Politicians and shareholders are also advised (by directors) to help make directors rich, so that they can afford to take risks. Theorists teach how to construct decision trees, heraldic devices of scientific management; and how to marry the trees with probability theory, so that the degree of risk along each branch (each branch and twig representing alternative results of alternative courses of action) can be metered. But no manager uses the trees, the branches or the twigs.

They can't be altogether blamed. The measuring is spurious, and, anyway, the best management doesn't take risks. It avoids them. It goes for the sure thing. The greater the risk, very obviously, the smaller the case for embracing the project at all. Risk-taking holds its pride of place among the management virtues only because it's confused with gambling – a sin of which too many managers are guilty. The sinners need no urging to take chances. The most purblind old buffer in the boardroom will cheerfully approve ventures of total insecurity.

The monstrous chances that directors take with other

people's money are often unwitting, but they are still risks. And executives who take great risks, whatever folklore says, are as dangerous to a company as a crooked accountant. The great and fabled business empires, with hardly an exception, were built, not on outlandish bets, but on irresistible ideas of elemental simplicity. This is not just hindsight. From the Model-T and the chainstores to semi-conductors, instant photographs and personal computers, the great entrepreneurs have taken available methods and married them to burning market needs.

A peddler named Michael Marks decided to sell every object on his stall under one slogan – 'Don't ask the price, it's a penny'. From that moment, the main lines of development of the Marks & Spencer chain were fixed: simplicity (the price limited the merchandise), control over supplies (if you wanted to sell everything for a penny, you had to buy everything for under a penny), value for money, and a uniform trading policy. Risk hardly came into the idea.

A marvellous, risk-free whim, such as Henry Ford's mass production to serve a mass market, can survive grotesque mismanagement. Ford lost $8.5 million in the 1930s, as Henry I bungled the challenge of Chevrolet, fell into the toils of the gangsterish Harry Bennett, and tortured his son, Edsel. He still died richer than Croesus – because sales went on proving, in their millions, that it takes a genius even more perverse than Ford's to ruin the commercial career of a great idea.

Terrible disasters (such as the over-sized, over-priced and monstrously designed Edsel car put out by Henry's grandson) likewise result from gross and elementary errors of concept, not from justified risk-taking or marginal mistakes in abstruse calculations like discounted cash flow. Yet corporate executives, all intelligent men, will plump for one project rather than another on the strength of a difference of a few decimal points in the rate of return calculated over the next decade.

All such mind-stretching calculation comes under the lash of the Seventh Truth of Management; if you need sophisticated calculations to justify an action, it is probably wrong (the sophisticated calculations, anyway, are all too often based on simple false assumptions). A rider to this is, 'Shun any project that, if all goes according to plan, will just earn its keep'. In real life, hardly anything follows the script. What sensible executives seek is the project whose margins are so magnificent that, if it actually works out, they can all retire to the Bahamas.

Most businesses meet only three classes of major investment decision – the inevitable, the optional, and the make-or-break. Only the last involves risk in the classic sense. The first category includes embarrassments such as new steel, paper, or cement works. Nobody interested in profits would build such expensive encumbrances today to make commodity products that fetch commodity prices; but failure to expand in step with the competition guarantees slow atrophy in a business to which (because of its deadly concentration of fixed assets) the company is bound in perpetuity.

Factory extensions, modernisation of machinery, even important product changes are usually fixed by market forces, not by managerial choice. The risk here is to do nothing – like Gillette when first confronted with the Wilkinson stainless-steel blade – or to do the inevitable at ruinous cost and delay, at which most Western steelmakers have proved adept. Gillette's forlorn hope that the stainless-steel blade would rust away was matched by the resolute conviction of Detroit car-makers that small-sized imports were a passing fad. The fad passed, all right; it passed into a permanent feature of the market, one that cost Detroit billions in lost sales, and billions more in a belated effort to catch up – not once, but twice.

Part of the effective executive's armoury is a sense of when the rape of his profitability is inevitable. When Rupert Murdoch chose the blunt instrument of a 20p price cut to 30p for *The Times*, his rival Conrad Black at the *Daily Telegraph* didn't respond – at first. Eventually, as his circulation dropped below one million, and Murdoch's rose above 500,000, Black felt forced to follow down to 30p: only to be undercut again. The damage to profits had been compounded by the loss of sales; and the threat had still not been removed. The bungle could hardly have been greater.

The second category is where the company has a choice, and the decision, either way, will leave a viable business. This is where rashes of big mistakes are made – extending a product range into new markets, diversifying into new fields, merging with another company. The basic mistake is often not to recognise that any risk exists – for instance, in mergers, one of the most promising disaster areas. The error is usually compounded by refusal to cut losses. Sir Alexander Maclean, the toothpaste king, knew better. One of his associates recalled, 'Maclean tried all sorts of things, but he exploited those which were successful and cut out those which were not.' It's hardly a difficult technique.

By making really addle-pated decisions in these optional matters, a corporation can even and very quickly disprove the original assumption – that the viability of the company will be unaffected. When Brent Walker bought the William Hill chain of betting shops for £689 million, as *Management Today* later noted, 'analysts were prepared to argue that a chain of betting shops – with their abundant cash flow – represented a brilliant addition'. The deal turned out to mark the turning-point from growth company to bankruptcy.

Many other firms have castrated themselves by purely voluntary purchase of companies they couldn't afford. Financial services have been a major disaster area for big companies seeking to spread their risks. Over at Sears Roebuck, the big push into financial services with Dean Witter turned the latter's investment-banking operation, according to a former executive quoted in *Business Week*, into 'a real mess. You could not have messed things up more definitively if you had tried.'

General Electric must have been feeling the same way when it learnt that its Wall Street bauble, Kidder Peabody, had been gulled into accepting as genuine $350 million of non-existent profits. Even companies much smaller than GE, with its $60.8 billion of 1993 sales and $4.4 billion of profits, can absorb such shocks without losing stride (though not without losing reputation). But in the process of committing their gratuitous follies, the big boys often and sadly destroy or damage the perfectly or potentially good smaller firms which they bought.

More commonly, calamity follows from failures in the third main area of decision-making, the make-or-break variety, where the entire company hangs on success or failure. In most of these cases, compelling truth lies behind management's mental processes. Chrysler had to widen its penetration of the US car market to survive its near-bankruptcy. With defence business in long-term decline, only civil airliners offered Lockheed a growing market for its talents.

To get back into a home-entertainment market swamped by the Japanese, and unable to compete itself in VCRs, RCA had to plunge into its rival disc system, or else get out of its Japanese rivals' way. Rather than do just that – get out – the executive, despite his alleged caution, goes for all or nothing; and nothing is often what he gets. Actually, RCA got far less than nothing – a write-off totalling $580 million when it had to exit, like it or not, with its then chairman, Thornton Bradshaw, making an immortal remark to *Fortune* magazine: 'No one's to blame. This is a risk company, and we're going to take more risks in future.'

It's become increasingly unwise, however, to believe in the economy of scale mentioned above. Size, like RCA's $9 billion of assets, can bury monumental mistakes; make too many, though, and you may end up, like RCA, in the arms of another – in this case, GE. Moreover, the pain must be felt somewhere. Divisions of Ford and General Dynamics both survived the two greatest commercial errors up to then, the Edsel and the Convair jetliner; technically losses of $400 million (especially after tax offsets) can be absorbed within empires whose assets total $9.9 billion or $1 billion. But the shareholder pays the bill; Ford's earnings per share over the Edsel era rose by little more than 2% annually.

Even in big companies, whatever the Bradshaws of this world say, executives don't take brave risks. They make foolish errors, such as his company's foolish belief that it could compete with VCRs. Like politicians, executives have a genius for compounding bad policies with worse execution.

The Eighth Truth of Management is: if you are doing something wrong, you will do it badly. The reverse of this truth is that, if your decision is blindingly right, you will execute it well – or appear to do so, which is much the same thing.

But any executive can massacre his own nonsensical project. The correct decision for RCA was to put its resources behind joining the Japanese in the VCR market, rather than to try beating them – especially with a product that lacked the essential recording facility. In marketing the thing, RCA added mistakes in pricing and estimates of market size to its basic misunderstanding of what the customers wanted. The company never got even remotely near its targets (840,000 had been sold against eight million VCRs when the plug was pulled). Yet its people continued to pursue the impossible like knights after the Holy Grail.

Similarly, nobody in the airline industry believed in the original specifications of one bright new airliner, or in the fabulously low cost of its development, or in massive orders promised by its distributor. This little dreamboat was supposed to carry up to two dozen passengers. 'Sure it can,' grunted one competitor, 'if they're all gnomes.' Ironically, the company had some real-life orders, from the ever-ready Department of Defense, for the greatly changed, far more expensive model with which the British company – Handley-Page – eventually and inevitably crashed.

Make-or-break risks can make it – as Apple had desperate reason to hope when it launched the Macintosh computer in 1983. Rapid acceptance of the new machine, with its far easier-to-use technology, was the only way to ensure the very survival as a company of Silicon Valley's brightest star, the venture capital triumph to beat them all – and which really did beat all predecessors in speed to the billion-dollar turnover mark. In Apple's case, the answers to a host of subsidiary questions turned out to be reasonably encouraging.

Was the Apple name and image still strong enough to sell against the might of IBM? Had it retained enough market share, after being massively clobbered by IBM, to serve as a base for the new range? Could the company finance the project, including an advertising budget immensely beyond its previous outlays? Could Macintosh win enough sales fast enough to promise major profits (which meant, also, could Apple get the new product into production at the right time in the right quantity, with the right quality)? Was the market for personal computers likely to continue growing? Above all, did the Macintosh offer a unique selling proposition?

At Chrysler, Lee Iacocca had to pour everything he could beg or borrow into the K-car. A rise in sales, based on an entirely new automobile family, was the only way to ensure survival as a company; the successful screwing of the banks and the Federal Government was only the *sine qua non* for bringing that family into life. The subsidiary questions were perfectly clear, too. Were the Chrysler name and image still viable? Could the company finance the project? Was the US car market likely to improve in the years of the K-models' life? On reasonable assumptions about demand, could the break-even point be brought low enough to yield a handsome profit?

These were not computer-bending problems. But the greater the primary risk, the safer and more careful your secondary assumptions must be: a project is only as sound as its weakest assumption. Note, however, that companies only reach true make-or-break points because of risky errors. Apple reached crisis point because of failure to anticipate the entry of IBM into PCs, and failure to bring its organisation and marketing up to billion-dollar scratch as its situation demanded.

Lockheed had to go for broke, and in much less favourable circumstances, with the Tristar jetliner because of its flop on the Electra turboprop. It took years of mismanagement and bad autos to reduce Chrysler to the most parlous plight of any major US company. RCA had a history of missed opportunities (failing to seize the dominant position in the colour-TV market it had long pioneered, missing the advent of micro-electronics) and bungled forays into new areas (dropping another half-billion on trying to live with IBM in computers).

RCA was not alone, of course, in thinking that, despite its lack of experience in business machines, it could breach the walls of Fortress IBM. These competitors saddled themselves with projects based on implausible assumptions – for instance, first, that the merits of advanced technology would of themselves sway the market; second, that the machines would get into production on schedule and work when produced; third, that if the first two assumptions were wrong, the company could afford the cash drain. Nobody has calculated how much, if RCA's and General Electric's computer losses are added to those of Honeywell, Bull, Burroughs, etc, such risks cost the IBM rivals; but the number must be well into the billions, and all, remember, for a negative return.

If you seek to eliminate all really adventurous risk, true, you risk something else – eliminating all enterprise and innovation. Nine times out of ten, this may be to the shareholders' benefit. But what about the tenth time? What about those unsung ghosts of American business – the IBM man who turned down the Univac computer, the Du Pont executive who showed the inventor of xerography the door, the Kodak man who turned up his nose at Polaroid? Right back to the men who thought the horseless carriage had no future, business history is haunted by the memories of missed opportunities. But the unsung ghosts weren't frightened away by risk; like bureaucrats everywhere, they couldn't see the opportunity, and they preferred doing nothing to doing something.

General David Sarnoff was their total opposite. He gambled, by the standards of his time, when he pumped $50 million into commercial TV. He took an equal gamble, apparently, in backing colour TV in the 1950s, for $130 million more. But the odds were much shorter than they looked. Sarnoff's RCA was the only set-maker that could take the gamble because its NBC network could transmit (at a loss) the colour programmes without which, clearly, nobody would buy a set. And was colour TV really a gamble? Colour had taken over the cinema screen, and was as certain as anything in life to take over TV.

Sarnoff's only risk was of being too early – as he was, both technically and commercially. RCA still made a mint. Note, however, what happened in a virgin market where Sarnoff was not building on his know-how or his assets – those computers again. Just like GE, RCA had to throw in its hand; all its risk-taking had bought was a $500 million loss, plus huge diversion of corporate time and attention. That lost the company the lead in the very markets in consumer electronics where the General's early, bold pioneering should have given his successors – and not the Japanese – the right rewards for the right decisions.

Faced with a decision, always ask one implacable question: if this project fails, if the worst comes to the worst, what will be the result? If the answer is total corporate disaster, drop the project. If the worst possible outcome is tolerable, say, break-even, the executive has the foundation of all sound decision-making – a fail-safe position. Heads I win, tails I don't lose, may not sound madly adventurous, but that way, the executive never loses. As played in many companies, the game is 'Heads I lose, tails I don't win', and that is a pastime for idiots.

Many a tycoon has fostered his fortune by astute acquisition on the belt-and-braces principle. These canny fellows keep up their trousers by never buying any business unless the realisable assets (cash, the real estate, etc) cover their total cost – so the trading side is in for free. Lord Forte followed just that principle, which is one of the reasons why, in a hotels, property and catering world bestrewn with landmines, the Forte empire still survived prosperously, with a stock-market value of some $2 billion, into the mid-1990s.

Where they make mistakes (and all tycoons do), you usually find it's because they've ceased to obey their own rules – buying earnings instead of assets; Forte's soft mistake was in soft ice-cream. Managers and magnates alike should stick to their maxims. In any business, remember that the object of good management is not just to maximise profits, or growth rates, or market share. It's to maximise those rewarding statistics at minimised risk.

15
Serving the Super-Chief

Call an industrial chieftain incompetent, and he won't love you. Tell him he has laid a Grade-A egg, and he will argue. But call his company a one-man band, and he will be furious – especially if it is. The natural tendency for powerful men is to dominate, and the natural instinct of those who serve them is to be dominated. One-man bands, moreover, are quick to spot each other – what they can't recognise is themselves. They are blinded by the received idea, in a democratic age, that one-man bands are a particularly heinous form of bad management.

When the ideal is some nebulous 'team', nobody likes to admit that they personally make every decision – major, minor, or minimal; that their senior disciples, after years as yes-men, could never rule independently; that they lust for supreme authority and would wither away without it. One such chief executive, whose brilliant dictatorship was as emotional as Wuthering Heights, maintained less a head-quarters staff than a court. The courtiers sat on long into afternoons or evenings listening to monologues that, while fascinating at first hearing, palled by the ninety-first. Yet the tycoon would never admit that his company had little top management, just him.

One day, when the master's behaviour became too erratic to bear, the worms turned. Looking back on the débâcle, the ousted chieftain philosophically admitted the truth. 'The trouble was,' he said, 'that the company was a one-man band.' In any company, and in any area of management, it's better to face the truth at the time when it hurts – and possibly helps.

There happen to be real, though problematical managerial advantages for the one-man band, but self-deception can lose or offset all of them. The advantages are not in any textbook, because the reasons that make them great also make them non-transferable – they harness the working forces of a corporation to one highly personalised and identifiable driving power. The results can be astoundingly good, even though that outcome is strictly illogical.

In logic and in fact, one man can't run a group of 10,000, or 30,000, or 80,000, or 200,000 people – though some do try. There are chief executives who pass on all capital expenditure, right down to typewriters; others who approve all foreign travel; and others who operate a private KGB to discover what's happening before their underling bosses know it themselves. At the up-and-coming Bloomberg Financial Services, the founder, Michael Bloomberg, signs every non-payroll cheque and contract, so that nothing can happen without his knowledge.

All that, too, is totally illogical. But management is not logic. One unusual man can impress his personality on a gigantic organisation not only so that he knows, controls, and influences everything in the present, but so that for years into the future the company will live in his shadow. This needn't be because of transcendent genius. True, the pervasive force of personality will also be generated by the abiding power of a transcendent idea – like Texan Charles W. Tandy's notion of combining a chain of radio and electrical stores, some franchised, with factories making the products they sold. Years after Tandy's early death, that inspiration was still the largest visible and invisible asset of the corporation he built.

Yet when the steam started running out of steam radio,

hi-fi and the like, Tandy was saved by something else – not by another flourish of the Great Man's genius, but by the combination of his personal power with an unplanned product: the home computer. At one point Tandy, through its Radio Shack stores, became the second largest computer company (by units sold) after IBM. It happened only because an engineer hobbyist in Tandy's employ had been playing about with computer kits. The manufacturing people got wind of this and decided to develop the thing into prototype form, just for the heck of it.

The resulting masterpiece was set up in the premises one day when Tandy happened to be passing through. After the computer had been briefly put through its paces, the Great Man said, 'Let's make a thousand. If we can't sell 'em, we can always use 'em in our own stores.' This was taken as the go-ahead. But when the management accountants worked out the costs, a thousand made no sense. So Tandy built 3,000; before very long orders for 10,000 had flooded in for the most expensive product the company had ever sold.

There's a reason why the aura of great men lives on after them, and not just in business – thus the British Broadcasting Corporation, despite the Birtist reforms that have turned it into a quasi-commercial hybrid, is still within the aura of its first boss, Lord Reith; the FBI, likewise, hasn't finally escaped from J. Edgar Hoover years after his final, final curtain. In business, the great founder-entrepreneurs have the same supernatural impact – Henry Ford, or the first Lord Leverhulme, creator of the British half of Unilever, or Thomas Watson Sr., builder of IBM.

The companies were run as their personal property. The continued exercise of their property rights was founded on business genius, personal charisma, and family stockholdings. And if a mighty entrepreneur can raise the earnings and the stock price year after year, it hardly matters to stockholders that he also plays the dictator. It probably doesn't matter to his executives either. Many people love having every decision made for them, and executives are no exception.

At least, the one-man band makes the decisions, and

186

usually at high speed. Delay makes a good decision worse and seldom improves a bad one. If the dictator is a genius, the decisions may even be right. The odds favour him more than the rest of mankind. He, after all, is the company, absolutely identified with its purposes and potential. And he has, by creating the empire, shown the energy that makes a good decision work – and can sometimes save a bad one from its badness. But no man's genius lasts forever, and the longer he reigns, the more seeds of decay get planted.

The travails of Texas Instruments, one of the most talented corporations in the States, are thus widely blamed on the founding management's reluctance to let go; and much the same sad song had to be sung about Ken Olsen's Digital Equipment. At Compaq, a spectacular renaissance hinged on the ouster of the founding boss – just as an earlier recovery at Apple demanded the removal of founder Steven Jobs. While most of the characters concerned were not particularly old, their industries are so new and moving so fast that age has become strictly relative; just as a fifteen-year-old dog is 105 in human equivalent, so a forty-year-old super-manager in electronics may be two decades older in real terms.

Few people now doubt that the supreme businessman/inventor of the early post-war years, Polaroid's Edwin H. Land, hung on too long (into his seventies) for the good of the company. Discontinued disasters like the TI ventures into digital watches and home computers, or long-running failures like Polaroid's declining sales, are monuments to the dead or deathly hand of dominant heroes. Japan provides more constructive lessons – for instance, that of the late Soichiro Honda, who quit at sixty-three (quoting lack of competence in computers and insufficient appetite for sake and sex).

In his valedictory statement, Honda revealed that neither he as chairman nor the president had seen any executive committee papers for ten years. During all that time, though, the two men had guided their successors and the corporate strategy to ensure, as best they could (which was in high degree), that the corporation would outlive them – as Japanese ideology demands. In the West, too, the good that great managers do should be interred in the success of the business they leave behind. That, almost by definition, means that they cannot be total dictators.

Few really able people will work indefinitely under an autocrat. Those who do either lose the habit of making decisions, or never get the experience; either way, there's no adequate succession. Anyway, dictators dislike having strong men behind their backs – though most, for some deep psychological reason, have an *eminence grise*, a long-time, shy associate, whose special expertise, usually technical, keeps him out of power's way. (One tycoon, in a verbal use that would have delighted Freud, called his *eminence* his 'day wife'.)

Management Today, after looking at a series of company disasters (Brent Walker, Ratners, Spring Ram, Tiphook etc) suggested a 'common thread ... one man in charge, usually the founder ... a natural optimist, risk-taker and autocrat'. An extra, and harmful, quirk is that many one-man bands are also bullies – though, again, many executives like to be bullied. But victims won't turn into heroes after the bully quits; they are more likely to be punch-drunk, or to follow willy-nilly too closely in the footsteps of Land or whatever other father-figure used to rule the corporate roost.

A study of successful 'mid-sized' American companies by a couple of McKinsey men, Richard E. Cavanagh and Donald K. Clifford, found that succession was a particularly critical issue: 'The personality and drive of a builder chief executive are so pervasive and important that his loss and replacement can be a severe shock to the organisation. Many of the ones interviewed suggested that no high-growth company has fully proved itself until it has undergone the transition to a new chief executive once or twice.'

It's hard to argue with that thinking. Nor is it easy to contradict the general proposition that an excellent guide to a man's ability is that of his successor. The timing of the succession is decisive, too. The presiding genius may be the last to understand that his best days are over, and terrible erosion can follow while he blindly hangs on. Many companies have known what it felt like in Nero's Rome: the decaying emperor fiddles while the city burns.

In one case, the other directors were just alert enough to take evasive action. They got the founder-chairman to agree that a new executive committee would make all decisions before matters reached the main board. The committee was identical to the board – except that the chairman was left out. But mostly the decision to relax the iron fist has to come from the dictator himself, and this is the one decision he will not make.

It will eventually be made for him, if not by palace revolution, then by illness, fatigue, or death. Then comes the moment of truth. The autocrat has to pass the same test as any director (dead, deposed, or departed); does he leave behind an organisation that (like Marks & Spencer after Lord Marks) shows great continuity, flexible strength, and regenerative powers? Or does he (as in Ford Motor after Henry Ford I) leave behind a shambles, capable of losing $22 million in a single post-war quarter?

The key is that men like Simon Marks, for all their pervasive personalities, are so deeply interested in organisation that their bands are orchestras. They express their egos through the systems they build; they have their eccentricities, but they don't manage through eccentric egos alone. The one-man band, in contrast, rarely has organising ability. He convinces himself that he is an organiser, and easily convinces others – for arguing with success is even harder than admitting to failure.

But what looks like effective organisation is the working through of that tremendous personal urge. Remove the drive, along with the person, or bring the drive up against some unexpected obstacle, and the apparently well-organised company tears apart. Maybe this is legitimate if the company really is the dictator's personal property. What a man creates he is presumably more entitled to destroy. But a great industrialist's empire can rapidly transcend the scale of one ego. Henry Ford I retained the power to destroy Ford Motor; he no longer had the right.

The proprietorial boss may well lack the ability to sense the destructive effect of his own management style on his own organisation. There's a sad little story about Heinz Durr who,

according to *Manager* magazine, 'was a successful Stuttgart
manufacturer of paint shops for the motor industry when he
was brought in by the ailing AEG [a vast and horribly
mismanaged electrical group] to kick it back into shape and
profitability. He seems to have made a success of this
assignment [he actually hadn't], but now has to worry about
his own business, where things have been going wrong and
various plants have to be closed.' The proprietor owes too
much to the colleagues and work-people who helped make
him rich to neglect either the present or the future.

This applies far more to the professional director. The
person who doesn't own the business has a particular
obligation to follow in the footsteps of Alfred P. Sloan, who
created order out of primeval chaos at General Motors, and
to shun the example of Henry Ford. As the paid servant of
the company professionals have no property rights. They
must expect to be judged severely on short-term results
(though they aren't); they must also demonstrate that they
are not indispensable (which they aren't).

Professional executives have no excuse for one-man band-
manship. But powerful forces push them that way; precious
few countervailing forces hold them back; and who can resist
an invitation to play God? That was the internal nickname of
many a chief executive in the bad old days – and is not
unknown in the more liberated 1990s, either.

The difference between proprietors and professionals is
not really understood. The professional is expected to play
the part of the founding genius, without having the latter's
mystery ingredient X, which is that two-way identification, as
owner and creator, with the company. True, the professionals
identify with the upper management and with their own
egos, but that's a different matter entirely.

The public can't tell the difference. It lionises the management hero by instinct; it offers the tempting prospect of a
business magazine's front cover, or a knighthood, or membership of some blue-chip panel of business leaders, or a life
peerage. The public does this because it dearly loves a leader.
This is the one argument in favour of the one-man band that
its critics will accept. Everybody believes that leadership is a

supreme human attribute – it even gets praised in school reports. But in management terms, leadership as understood in the past is a greatly overrated quality.

The British, with their long tradition of war, kings, aristo-crats and empire, have an innate tendency to fall down in worship before chairmen, headmasters, prime ministers, royalty and commanding officers. The Americans are blin-ded by their recurrent desire for 'a man on horseback', their admiration for the 'take-charge guy' and their simple refusal to believe that anybody who has made millions, floated to the top of a large corporation, or both, can be an idiot. But it's essential to be quick on the draw when the leader fails, vital not to stare at the whites of a failed *capo*'s eyes for years – and disastrous never to fire at all.

A sad development for American business in the 1980s was that the bullet-proof executive vest became more common wear. Not only did the authors of unprecedented US aero-space disasters fail to bite the dust in the requisite numbers at the requisite time; but self-evidently failing CEOs at IBM, GM, Kodak and other giants were left *in situ* for years after their failure had become blatant. In such traumas, lack of leadership has seldom been the agent of fate. If anything, the companies have suffered from an excess of being led. Under the one-man command of leaders who could have charged the Light Brigade into suicide, these companies too have headed straight for the enemy's guns.

The story goes that one ennobled, embattled and really leading leader of industry was persuaded to spend three hours with a great and wise guru of real management. The guru emerged, shaking his head, and told the other direc-tors, 'It's up to you boys. I can't do a thing with him.' One of them ventured in and asked the peerless leader how it had gone. 'Very well,' he replied, 'he said the way I manage this company is perfect.'

As the highly led company gets bigger, and the high leader gets more heavily laden with outside activities and honours, he loses contact with reality. (Founder-entrepreneurs are more reluctant to take on outside commitments than professional one-man bands – another vital clue to the difference between them.) Very easily, the dominating concept, the informing element, of all managerial work in the company becomes not what is right, but what will Mr This or Mr That (and very rarely Ms Other) agree to.

This is only acceptable if the boss is consistently correct; but in eight cases out of ten, the boss will at some point become consistently wrong, and the consequences will show in the company's figures – not in calamity usually, but in mediocrity. In the two exceptions, so long as the one-man bands are fit, in form and *in situ*, the company will run surprisingly, even magically, well. But even here their refusal to admit to their solitary power means that no action gets taken to prepare the corporation for their inevitable departure.

This danger can only be countered by a simple rule: compulsory appointment of a new, empowered chief executive when the old one is sixty, compulsory final abdication of the old buzzard at sixty-five, and stick to it. Don't be like J. Lyons, once Britain's greatest eating-chain, where the retiring age of sixty-five was theoretical and 'the older anyone was, the more theoretical it became'. In this sorry instance, the viability of the business became increasingly theoretical, too, and mainly from that cause: ageing, inept management. First dismembered, then disappeared, Lyons merely provided bargains on which other, smarter managers fed.

Never mind that the towering tyrant is still doing ninety press-ups every morning and can outrun, out-talk, and out-deal any man in the room; the earlier he has to go, the more likely he is to think about the succession with an unwarped mind and so create some kind of organisation to go with it. At Beecham, when the founding tyrant died, 'All the performing seals got down from their barrels and began to fight', remarked Leslie Lazell, the exceptional manager who dealt with the seals, turned Beecham into an international force – and then mishandled the succession issue himself.

Lazell's personal choice totally lacked experience of either fast-moving consumer goods or pharmaceuticals, and his reign merely put off the evil day of choosing between the two men who respectively ran the two sides. When the FMCG

leader, Ronald Halstead, finally got the job, it was only to
have it removed from him in a boardroom *putsch*. At AEI,
when the elderly colossus Lord Chandos finally came down
off his plinth, there was no *putsch* – like Lazell, Chandos had
brought in a hand-picked successor from outside. Both cases
broke a simple rule: the more dominant a man is, the less he
should be allowed to name his own successor.

For subconscious reasons, great men select successors who
will not surpass the Great One. Proprietorial one-man bands
usually have this guaranteed for them by nature. Most have
sons, nearly always inadequate copies of the master design,
ready to step into father's oversized shoes. There is an
immortal (and doubtless unfair) remark about Robert Sarnoff, boss of RCA in succession to founder General David
Sarnoff. The son, said some jester, joined the company at the
bottom – but then his father took a fancy to him.

Nemesis followed nepotism. The Sarnoff Mark II regime
was marked, and marred, by the massive losses incurred on
computers before RCA capitulated to IBM; by destructive
office politics, one of whose victims was eventually Bobby
Sarnoff himself; and by the trail of consumer-product errors
which ended in the video-disc humiliation. It says much for
the strength of the General's creative power, if little for his
son's, that RCA survived with $9 billion of sales. But the
negative 1973–83 growth in earnings per share, the fact that
Fortune classed the one-time giant of consumer electronics as
a non-industrial company, the eventual takeover by GE – all
are testimony to the terrible damage that a badly managed
succession can achieve.

Men cannot, though, bear the idea that others will say of
their successor, 'Of course, he's done much better than old
so-and-so'. A Stalin chooses a Malenkov to succeed him, a
Churchill picks an Eden. The one most likely to succeed is
the one least likely to disturb his predecessor's legacy; yet
counter-revolution, no matter how brilliant the past, is
almost certainly a necessity at the moment of inheritance.
This is true even where the ruler genuinely created a superb
organisation.

Counter-revolution was badly needed for years, but not

provided, at Sloan's General Motors, where the corporate constipation of the late 1960s was already causing bad outbreaks of spots in overseas car operations (Britain, the Continent and Australia) and in the small-car market in the US. These spots, clearly visible in those far-off days, developed into a near-deadly, debilitating disease in less than a decade: a disease, what's more, from which the corporation had still not fully recovered in 1994.

The ideally wise one-man band would know these risks. So the third simple rule for producing discord-free corporate music is gradually to disengage – to reach the point of domination from a distance. You don't have to emulate the ghostly manner of Howard Hughes (who, incidentally, was for long a highly effective business leader, even though he never saw, and seldom spoke to, any of his executives). But it is possible to animate a company brilliantly without day-to-day interference.

The most successful mid-century oilman in the US, some believe, was Robert O. Anderson of Atlantic Richfield, who only came near the corporate headquarters twice a month and was sometimes incommunicado for weeks. Unfortunately, self-control is rare in self-centred successes; and absolute power tends, just as Lord Acton said, to corrupt absolutely. The essential weakness of the one-man band is that it establishes a closed circle, in which only the one-man leader can act against his vices. There is no way round this; his ultimate privilege is to be the first Gadarene swine over the edge.

16
The Eighteen-Hour Cynosures

The ethic of Western society dictates that to work hard is good. By extension, to work harder than anybody else is, therefore, to be better than everybody else. Since the only measure of an executive's work is the time spent, the hardest-working executive is clearly the man who puts in the longest hours: the eighteen-hours-a-day paragon. No normal executive would boast that he worked only three hours a day, no matter how superlative his performance. But corporate annals regularly feature the tycoon who (in the words of that great business musical, *The Pyjama Game*) can hardly wait to get to work at eight (or seven, or six...)

Hardly anybody worries about the abnormality (and sheer physical impossibility) of the eighteen-hour business jam session. Once upon a time, it made sense for the boss to get in first and leave last – then he could keep a constant eye on the till. But in the great modern corporation, without a till to its name, the boss keeps shopkeeper's hours for one reason only: to satisfy his ego. In itself, there is nothing wrong with this hobby. A man who has clambered to the top of a business empire deserves some pleasures. But the pastime has unpleasant and sometimes serious consequences for the company and its other executives.

The eighteen-hour chief executive is unlikely to fancy working all alone in an empty office; he wants company. So secretaries and subordinates have to appear at the same unearthly time, but for less good cause. One dynamo, the future Lord Ryder, regularly employed two young management recruits as personal assistants at Reed International. In theory, they were being groomed for future stardom; in practice, they served as early-morning and late-evening acolytes at the great man's altar, and later starring roles were supposed to be rewards for the service. It didn't always work out that way – simply because the brightest and best young men (or women) won't serve as anybody's lackey.

Young people are resilient and probably suffer little ineradicable harm; but their elders, including the dynamo's directors, also get sucked into the same maw. If the chief executive summons a divisional manager to a breakfast conference or a seven a.m. meeting, the subordinate may be brave enough to refuse, but he will quail in his boots. Gradually, the whole working life of the executive suite revolves around the eccentric timetable of the perpetual-motion machine at the top.

One personnel consultant felt obliged to tell a company chairman that the corporate organisation could not survive in the same form after he stepped down. No conceivable successor would work the same punishing routine, starting before dawn had even cracked. Nor, judged by the recent results, would anybody want to. That chief executive was Daniel B. Haughton of Lockheed, which was about to sail into the Galaxy, Cheyenne and Tristar disasters – the greatest triple threat in the troubled history of aerospace.

It doesn't follow that, if Haughton had worked on a saner regime, the company would have got its sums right. But equally, it didn't follow that, because the chief executive was a glutton for hard hours, the company would win success, avoid error and fly into an ever-golden future. In management there is no correlation between effort and effectiveness: a fact so obvious as to be trite. But there may often be a correlation between excessive effort and ineffectiveness – foreign though this is to the puritan ethic.

Yet everybody knows the symptoms of ineffective effort lower down the management slopes: the departmental head whose desk is littered with pieces of paper that he endlessly shuffles as, piece by piece, he mentally sinks beneath them. The eighteen-hour chief executive is the same breed of cat. Only, because of his power and because he has bursts of real effectiveness, the disease is not recognised by its symptoms, by its progress, or by its results. Nobody in any important executive position can find enough work to fill even ten hours a day, day in, day out, unless their operation is badly organised and/or they waste time in what looks like work, but isn't.

Sir John Davis, the prodigious worker who headed the Rank Organisation, garnered most of its growth (and most of its profit) from the operation jointly owned with Xerox. That joint goose in those days laid its golden eggs with no need for much attention, apart from an occasional pat on the head (and the continual insistence of Davis on approving all prices for Rank Xerox products). The rest of the company con-sisted of diversified interests which, like all mixed corporate baskets, included some rotten eggs.

The company created its own problems by buying them; and Davis created his own workload by sending out a stream of memos, manufacturing at one stroke two pieces of paperwork – his own enquiry (which might or might not be relevant), and the reply (which might not be relevant either to the enquiry or to the business of the division). In consequence, his in-basket was always one of the most heavily loaded in world business. His regime, not at all surprisingly, ended in uproar and débâcle.

The eighteen-hour menace hung on long after retiring age, sacked his heir-apparent in circumstances so scandalous that the affronted board secured the menace's departure as well, and left behind the ailing relics of a once-great company. Strenuous repairs by his successors restored the business to more respectable circumstances by the early 1990s: but a firm which in the 1960s had enriched its stockholders by 1,021% in ten years added only 83% to their capital in the entire hyper-inflationary decade to 1983.

197

It figures. The eighteen-hour day is often a symptom of the deep psychic forces that drive their victim, not only to feats of magnificent empire-building, but to destructive and ultimately self-destructive behaviour. In *The Supermanagers* I chronicled the day of one high-technology manager: a mere fourteen-hour run, starting at 7.18 in the morning and ending at home at nine in the evening. This left him with almost no time at all for work with his papers or his colleagues.

The description concluded with this prophetic (as it turned out) question: 'At the time of writing the Super-manager concerned – ICL's Robb Wilmot – is still alive, well, and doing reasonably well. But is his *modus operandi* good for him – or for the company?' The answer to that is presumably written in the fact that the company failed to preserve its independence, despite the fourteen-hour days; while the hero thereof, shortly after the acquisition by Fujitsu, was moved upstairs into a post where seven hours a day were more than adequate to perform his greatly reduced duties.

The truth is that, while superhuman hours will sometimes be needed to accommodate superhuman efforts, the organisation and the human being cannot indefinitely accommodate themselves to the superhuman. More often than not, anyway, the inhuman hours continue long after the necessity for them has passed, with the certain result that inhuman demands are made on others besides the menace himself.

Vicious circles of this kind are hard to break. One merchant bank in the City of London, notorious for long hours, added to the burden on its bankers by the chief executive's memos; one director alone found an escape – he refused to answer the memos on the grounds that he never knew what to say. The longer an executive works, the more time he has to dispatch unnecessary pieces of paper or volleys of electronic impulses, and the more work he makes for the subordinates and superiors who have to deal with them.

Some of the documents may be worth reading, but Parteto's Law undoubtedly applies – 80% of the useful transmissions will arise from 20% of the corporate flow, 80%

of which will contribute virtually nothing. But the communicative proliferation is only a symptom of a disease which has been made worse by the advent of E-mail; now the same message can be instantaneously spewed over the computers in all directions to such an extent that answering it can take a full hour of the managerial day.

Communication overload usually reflects a deadly underlying situation: the executive who gets into too much detail of another executive's job is filling his own hours at the expense of the other man's effectiveness. There are other ways of achieving the same miserable end than flying paper and electronic darts around the corporation. The best-known and most heavily used device is the meeting. Nearly all executives spend a large proportion of their time in meetings (just as their secretaries say).

For example, here is one day's log for a manager in a red-hot, high-technology business:

8.00–8.30: Met with a manager who had submitted his resignation to leave for another company. Took incoming telephone call from a competitor.

8.30–9.00: Read mail from the previous afternoon.

9.00–12.00: Held executive staff meeting (a regular weekly meeting of the company's senior management). Subjects covered at this particular one:

–Review of the previous month's incoming order and shipment rates.

–Discussion to set priorities for the annual planning process (about to start).

–Review of the status of a major marketing programme (scheduled subject).

–Review of a programme to reduce the manufacturing cycle time of a particular product line (scheduled subject).

12.00–1.00: Lunch in the company restaurant.

1.00–2.00: Meeting regarding a specific product-quality problem.

2.00–4.00: Lecture at employee orientation programme.

4.00–4.45: In the office, returning phone calls.
4.45–5.00: Meeting with assistant.
5.00–5.15: Read the day's mail, including progress reports.

The hero of this particular diurnal saga is Andrew S. Grove, the president of the enormously successful microprocessor maker, Intel. In his book, *High Output Management*, the high-output manager explains that 'in a typical day of mine one can count some twenty-five separate activities in which I participated, mostly information-gathering and giving, but also decision-making and nudging. You can also see that some two-thirds of my time was spent in a meeting of one kind or another.

'Before you are horrified by how much time I spend in meetings, answer a question: which of the activities – information-gathering, information-giving, decision-making, nudging and being a role model – could I have performed outside a meeting? The answer is practically none.' Maybe so. But note that Grove seems to equate one-to-one meetings (with disgruntled employees or his assistant) with meetings where more than one participant (numbers unspecified) took part. The two things are not the same.

Simple logic dictates that the more people who attend a meeting, the less effectively the time of its average member is used. If four people meet for one hour and talk for an equal amount of time (an unlikely story), each is active for one-quarter of an hour and passive for three-quarters. If eight people fill the same time-span, the active-passive ratio declines from one to three to only one to seven.

In practice, the time taken expands to accommodate the numbers present, rather than the subject matter. So eight managers take two hours where four take one hour, and so on *ad infinitum*. It hardly matters whether the meeting is formally called a committee, or that the theoretical model is spoilt by all manner of incidentals, such as the proportion of those attending who are asleep (or wish they were). The principle is always the same – the more people present, the more the managerial time consumed and the greater the amount wasted.

The eighteen-hour menace, however, introduces a savage twist as chief executive. His long hours and his detailed interference with subordinate operations imply that he is the dominant personality. The decisions taken at any meeting he attends will, therefore, be the ones he would have taken on his own. The other executives are only present like a claque in a Viennese opera house – paid to applaud the performance.

Actually, meetings can be effective in which one personality does dominate and the others in effect simply endorse what the overlord proposes. Hence the desultory nature of board meetings (a board is nothing but a committee) with non-executive directors present. Etiquette forbids dictation, so the conversation rambles on without direction, and the chairman often has to resort to standard stratagems to get his way (like leaving the only important matter until ten minutes before lunch, or referring contentious issues to a pliant sub-committee).

Probably a company that pretends it is managed by committee, but isn't, is more effective than a company that genuinely is committee-run. Many minds are always better than one, true. But that presupposes a system or framework which directs the individual minds into the highway of collective thinking. The Western style of adversarial debate is not such a system. The Japanese, in more effective contrast, insist on each person present expressing their view without discussion. The leader then pronounces what he sees as the consensus decision.

A very strong chief executive could operate this system as a rubber-stamp; but one who is both very strong and very good will use other minds, not seek to dominate them. If the boss is neither strong nor good, of course, there's no point in continuing his employment. Even the best and strongest executive needs advice and double-checking. But not all the time. Part of a chief executive's essential equipment is to know when to scream for help and when not to; part of his duty is to be as sparing of the time of other executives as of his own, because time is the one irreplaceable corporate asset.

Physical assets can be replaced, financial losses can be recouped, lost production can sometimes be made up, but time passed can never be regained. No company is short of executives. The shortage is of effective executive hours. But what is effective and what isn't? The answers are culturally determined far more than executives realise. Contrast this working routine, for example, with that of Andrew Grove:

- Mr A gets up at about 6.20 a.m. After light exercise and a shower, he breakfasts while reading the paper and watching the TV. His company car is waiting for his 8.00 departure: during the forty-five-minute commute, he continues with the daily news.
- Mr A spends three hours at his desk, checking paper-work, meeting with directors and section chiefs, and finishing the newspapers. During that time, he signs his approval to eighteen papers, representing the final stage in the decision-making process.
- The rest of his day, till 6.00 p.m., is spent in outside meetings with directors of associated businesses or banks, or with economic groups or industrial leaders.
- Three days a week Mr A returns directly home. Other days, he entertains business clients at dinner or for drinks. Reaching home, he bathes, dines and watches TV, then retires early, around 11.00 p.m.

Not counting the entertainment days, Mr A works for a mere $9\frac{1}{4}$ hours, only three of which are in-house. His meetings are not operational in the sense that Grove's clearly are; and his approvals are plainly predetermined. In fact, they are the last stage in the *ringi* process. For this is a Japanese senior executive, who has delegated a wide range of operational duties and powers, and who is occupying a genuinely presidential (or presiding) role.

Where Grove is deeply involved day-to-day in how others do their jobs, Mr A is at a remove. That is the cultural norm in Japanese companies and that alone, not the real executive pressures within the company, explains how he spends his time. All the same, at first, and maybe second, glance, Mr A appears to be disposing of his time more intelligently. Indeed, any Western executive who examines his use of time and delegation dispassionately invariably comes to the conclusion that he is doing much that he ought not to be doing – and *not* doing much that he ought to be doing.

Unfortunately, executives have marked regressive tendencies in the use of time. Several studies have proved that, if the executive day is analysed as above, large fallow periods pop out that, by self-discipline and changed methods, the good manager can promptly fill up with productive labour. Any follow-up, however, would surely show steady back-sliding – probably to the point where as much time as ever slips away like sand through the fingers.

Possibly, in some cases, the eighteen-hour executive, by spending twice as much time as normal in ostensible work, gets twice as much effective time. But this is the wrong answer; the ideal of summit management, and of delegation, is to reduce the job content at the top to the bare minimum. The boss who keeps his desk clear and his calendar empty, for one thing, is certain to be available when somebody really does need him.

Lord Weinstock comes close to this ideal. He turned a near-bankrupt GEC into the only profitable company in the electrical industry's Big Three (and finally turned the Big Three into a Big One) without any outward appearance of undue effort. Mythology had it that between mergers, Weinstock could be found wandering around looking for something to do – and the myth contained some reality.

The blissful state of always having time is easily achieved. First, the executive must avoid outside entanglements like the plague (most big-time executives, not content with squandering time on internal obligations, itch incurably to serve on outside committees). Second, attend internal committees only when strictly necessary, and ensure that board meetings are used effectively and are highly organised. The test of strict necessity for other meetings is whether the chief executive will save more time by being present than he will lose.

The most important step, however, is to delegate – and

mean it. The dogma of delegation is simple – the Sixth Truth of Management again: either delegatees are capable of running the operation successfully by themselves or they aren't. This handy formula relieves the top executive of any responsibility except that of finding, supervising and (at the appropriate time) moving the men and women who are doing all the work. Bosses can then truly manage by exception: involving themselves with judicious rarity in operations that are doing well, but concentrating on the plague spots, where everything, including the management, is going badly.

Human nature is such, however, that the more wondrously smooth and rich a business, the more the head office wants to meddle; and the more dreadful and backbreaking a problem seems to be, the more prepared the head office is to abdicate to any potential saviour – unless, that is, the problem is self-created and trivial. Such were the troubles an American chemical giant's European management made for themselves by buying two tiny and feeble businesses, one in Holland, one in Italy, for the sake of diversification; yet these mere pimples came to absorb most of top management's time, at the expense of far more serious sores.

Many years ago, a company was well along the course of its rake's progress towards a seemingly inevitable takeover by one of its own customers. In this emergency, it turned over its northern interests to a bright young director, who, in his own words, 'rang down an iron curtain' between head office and the factories. Left to itself, without interference from HQ, the business turned round smartly; but as soon as profits again reached respectability, the board started boring holes in the iron curtain.

The director quit, and the company rapidly relapsed into its anti-growth trend. This tale is repeated again and again. The former boss of what was one of the fastest-growing big-company divisions estimated that he spent half his own time insulating his executives from the interference of the multi-hour work glutton who chaired the holding company.

There are plenty of other ways to fill the work-day of a management positively determined to get in eighteen hours

– such as travel. First-class flights across America and around the world rapidly consume time; and the operation of the biological time-clock, which gets thrown out of gear by even the small transatlantic shift, guarantees that few useful results will follow. The electronic revolution has made much of this travel superfluous; but still the travellers throng the air.

Another device that combines maximum consumption of time with personal gratification is the business lunch or dinner. Hours can be eaten away in expensive restaurants or lush corporate lunchrooms on the excuse of conducting business that might take a brisk ten minutes on the telephone. Often there is no specific item of business to discuss, anyway – the engagement is purely social. But it still contributes its stint to the eighteen hours.

Work in these corporate circumstances is more realistically defined as absence from home. If real work is effective application to the purposes of the corporation, nobody has ever worked an eighteen-hour day in normal, non-emergency circumstances. To the extent that they try, they merely create an artificial situation that can't possibly endure, and shouldn't. One American oil company prided itself on the superhuman hours its senior executives worked seven days a week. They argued that as they were no brighter than their rivals in other companies, they would outdistance the competition simply by putting in more mileage.

In fact, the company did grow faster than any other outfit in the industry. But to what end? Any corporation, looked at from one angle, is a club of senior executives who all have lives outside its frontiers. A breed of zombies can always be created; but the corporation is not an end in itself. The sensible company organisation operates successfully within the framework of human (and humane) hours.

In *Up the Organisation*, Robert Townsend tells a revealing tale: 'One of my colleagues once spent a twelve-hour night working on an undated document that turned out not to be the current draft.' Townsend's point was always to date a memo; but the better point is that twelve-hour nights indicate gross organisational failure somewhere along the line. Anybody who has ever launched a venture knows that the early days consume every available hour; later, when the business has prospered and grown greatly, conducting its much expanded affairs is much less demanding – you've simply got much better at its organisation and your own.

If somebody has this strange inner compulsion to spend the maximum time in the ego-boosting security of the office, there is no harm in letting them indulge the urge, provided that, first, they are effective, and, second, that they don't force saner people to adapt to their rhythm. The second trap is hard to avoid, if only because underlings will be tempted to emulate their bosses (and grab their attention) by showing equal enthusiasm for the office.

More often than not, maximum-hour leaders explicitly expect to see effort matching their own. The corporate boss who calls the break-of-day conference, or who rings around on the squawk-box in the evening to tell the executives they can go home, is asking for inferior performance; it takes an inferior executive to submit to what is little more than bullying.

Outside the entrepreneurial foundations (whose founding bosses often have a touch of monomania, or megalomania, in their genius) the eighteen-hour boss is a rarity. The corporation man seldom has this lust for self-flagellation. Yet he tends to work longer and longer hours as he gets older and more senior, as if the corporate executive's ideal was somebody like Harold S. Geneen of ITT or Haughton of Lockheed.

The first-named was once renowned as the most successful of conglomerate-makers. But neither his record, nor Haughton's, says anything for or against masochistic hours; and that was self-evidently true even before Geneen's creation ran into the calamities and errors that reduced its earnings per share growth to a miserable 0.64% in the decade to 1983. Nobody would dream of modelling a corporation after the life-style of a lazy genius, and there is just as little point in building the company in the image of an obsessive worker. But if you have to choose between the ant and the wizard, pick the latter every time.

17
Top Management's Secret Vice

No management school runs courses in mendacity. They aren't needed – executives are to the manner born. Not the deliberate lie: that is reserved for occasional denials of financial deals or other forlorn suppressions of the truth. Not, usually, deception on the criminal scale, like that of convicted thieves, fixers and bribers. No, the kind of untruth that is endemic in management, and potentially fatal, is self-deception. For example, it is well-known that if five firms compete in an industry lacking independent research, and all five are asked to give their market shares, the resulting figures always add up to well over 100%.

The American boss of GM's Vauxhall outfit was once asked about the miserable sales of his new car, a certain loser named (of course) Victor. 'We don't think it's done badly,' he replied. 'It has 70% of its market.' 'Market' had been defined to exclude practically everything else on four wheels, except a few imports. Car-makers are prone to wishful futility; the GM man was eventually moved, or removed, as his charge slid further down the scale of reality.

This habit of gilding the lily, or the weed, is every executive's secret vice, and often his last protection. Executives usually quit after a 'policy disagreement', or 'for personal reasons', or even because of ill-health – seldom for the real reason, such as that they have been sacked for incompetence. One departed chief executive, said to be at death's door by his successor, turned up right as rain in an even tougher chief executive spot the very next week: a cure only less miraculous than that of the Guinness convict, Ernest Saunders, in his progress from incipient senile dementia to apparently perfect mental well-being.

The lies can be personal as well as corporate. *Forbes* magazine discovered one company president who 'listed a BA from the University of New Hampshire, an MBA from Babson College and a master's degree in materials from the Massachusetts Institute of Technology – all of which were bogus'. The culprit kept his job, though: no doubt because he founded the company, and still owned 20%. The managing director of Korn-Ferry International in Chicago was less fortunate when his bogus degree was uncovered – he resigned, not surprisingly given his employer's identity as a large, maybe the largest, consultancy in, of all things, executive recruitment.

Deciding when the secret vice is conscious or unconscious is for psychologists. When a Ford of Britain man said, 'We don't believe they can sell the same car in Germany as we can here,' when the company was about to do precisely that, was the untruth deliberate or instinctive? (Or did the American overlords simply forget to tell him?) Men who apply more or less uniform private standards of morality divide their commercial lives into areas of honesty and other areas (such as future product plans) of total untruth.

Lying in the cause of commercial secrecy does little managerial damage (and little good for that matter, as competitors mostly know what you are trying to hide, even without benefit of industrial espionage). But damage comes when the truth, the whole truth, and nothing but the truth doesn't govern every aspect of the company's internal affairs.

The secret vice can spring from virtue. Enthusiasm is an essential component of the executive's survival kit. Managers have to believe in the product; if they don't, how can anyone else? But enthusiasm shades over easily into obtuseness. A top British shipyard executive once denigrated Japanese competition as that of 'little yellow men with vacant minds', and his company objected violently to being told in public that the little vacant-minded yellow men built ships far faster and much cheaper than the British.

That same shipyard later on boasted that it would sign only profitable contracts, then promptly signed several that made losses in the millions. The excessive patriotism and the gross commercial error are two sides of the same coin. There is no ultimate escape from reality. Executives eventually must come to terms with their real blessings and curses. The longer they delay, and the further fantasies drag them from the truth, the worse their danger.

The fall of Avon Products from a unique and shining commercial beauty to Wall Street dog, with its stock down nearly two-thirds from the peak, is a typical tale of self-deception taken to extremes. Nobody in either cosmetics or door-to-door selling had excelled Avon's achievements in ninety years of non-stop growth. The method hardly ever varied. The door-to-door Avon ladies determined what was stocked; the fortnightly catalogue stimulated the sales; the Avon representative delivered the goods on the next call – and wondrous profits were earned.

So where could weakness and the risk of self-deception possibly lie? The answer lay in the very core of the company – the sales force and the increase in its numbers, which had been the key, the only key, to overall growth. The crunch came when the Avon old-liners predicted that the representative army, having risen to a stupendous 401,000 beings, would advance as always – that year, by at least 5%. A later chairman explained what happened to John Thackray for *Management Today*:

'Here we go again, they said. But they didn't get the 20,000 increase – they got only 7,000. The old system they'd lived by failed. And they didn't know what to do.' The normal, logical reaction, you might suppose, would be to mount a crash course in learning or importing the unfamiliar and now suddenly vital marketing skills which Avon lacked. Not a bit of it.

The management deceived itself with the comforting notion that large increases in the numbers of representatives, despite actual experience, were still available and would still generate all the growth that Avon needed. The forecasts of 10% and 13% in which some executives continued to believe were not only self-deluding, but impossible. They meant that by the early 1990s, every woman over eighteen in the US would have had to be either a current or past Avon representative.

Minor conglomerators have also had to learn the hardness of truth. Mostly, their only talent was to stick together lucrative paper empires and personal fortunes by using fast, fancy, and modish financial glues. They couldn't manage anything or anybody (except Wall Street suckers), but they pretended otherwise. Even some major conglomerators managed to get seduced by their own myths. Litton Industries, basically a successful Pentagon contractor, kidded itself and everybody else that the corporate genius lay in civil high technology.

Just as Goebbels persuaded most of Germany, and the rest of the world, that Hitler's mugs and murderers were statesmen, so corporate publicity men, or external hired hacks, have often convinced the public (and the man himself) that a lucky wheeler-dealer is a super-executive. The misrepresentation needn't be deliberate. Goebbels genuinely believed in Hitler and company, and this real faith made him a fearsome propagandist. There's no evidence that the super-thief Robert Maxwell, even on the point of collapse and exposure, lost one shred of his sincere belief in Robert Maxwell and all his gross ambitions.

Self-deception flourished in more respectable surroundings than Maxwell's Headington Hall hangout. The public relations directed from the Litton office in Beverly Hills (a former movie palazzo, furnished with low-technology antiques) cost plenty, but it worked wonders. Of all post-war companies in the US, Litton was the most flattered and followed. Its emphasis on converting expensive space-age technology into commercial products summed up the ethos of the moon age; and its speciality of 'systems' introduced a new and magical phrase into the salesman's sample bag.

Litton raised the pursuit of higher earnings per share, with the aid of heavy debt gearing, to an art-form. Its stockholders got their dividends, not in cash, but in stock; its executives too got their kicks in stock options; the top two, Tex Thornton and Roy Ash, achieved their higher rewards in the rise of sensational paper fortunes. The whole Litton legend was built around the constant rise of the share price, though Ash said, predictably, in an interview before the inevitable crash, 'It is not an essential or even an important part of our growth for the price of the stock to go on rising.'

Like hell it wasn't. Self-evidently, keeping a high head of steam behind the share price in such situations is the bounden duty of the publicity machine – and everybody else. *Forbes* reporters heard the doomed Charlie Knapp, creator and near-destroyer of Financial Corp. of America, 'screaming into the phone: "You're supposed to be my investment bankers. Why aren't you helping support the stock? You're off the payroll tomorrow."' Institutional investors had dumped Knapp's stock for the good and sufficient reason that they were worried, and with better cause than they actually knew.

As the magazine observed, before Knapp's crash, the 'profit numbers', which showed a fifty-four-fold rise in half a dozen years, 'seem too good to be true. They probably are ...': and so they actually were. At Queens Moat Houses, a hotel group which had the enchanting habit of taking into account profits, as yet unmade, that might result from contracts signed just before the year-end, the true picture was almost too bad to be believable – a record £939 million loss. At another crashed company, Spring Ram, £35 million of previously unrevealed debt was among the skeletons that jumped out of the cupboard.

The desire to match the price of the stock, not to the truth about the business, but to the ambitions of the management, is not confined to operators of the variety involved in the above and like scandals. Even an apparently high-minded company like IBM isn't immune from this mercenary objective. Anybody who thinks that the sudden, simultaneous appearance in major business magazines of stories lauding the new, aggressive IBM in 1984 was a coincidence is underestimating IBM. The stories resulted from a carefully orchestrated public-relations campaign, planned largely to elevate the stock price: as it duly did.

The stories were not so much untruths as exaggerations, which deceived the IBM management as much as anybody else – and with the inevitable long-term results when hubris blinded the leadership to harsh realities. At Litton, though, the truth, as opposed to the untruth, was that Litton as a company was (and is) very like an old-line multi-product corporation such as General Electric. GE, like Litton, pioneered any number of new management concepts; its resources in high technology leave Litton lagging: and it too is heavily decentralised into divisions and business departments, or 'strategic business units'.

Observers once saw this proliferation as a weakness in GE, although it was hailed as a strength in Litton; as the wheel of fashion turned, it came to be regarded as a GE asset, indeed, as an example to others. By then GE had moved from mostly off-colour blue-chip to much-favoured leader among giants, with a CEO, Jack Welch, who got the kind of praise that used to be lavished on Ash and Thornton. In those days, because people believed in Litton's story, they made it believable. After all, isn't any company that increases its shareholders' wealth tenfold or twentyfold in a decade a marvel of management, technology, and diversification?

It's not necessarily so. Litton's sheer growth in sales volume, half at least coming through acquisition, was formidable, but its profitability (the name of the real game) was never up to much. It still wasn't in 1993, when Litton made 1.2% on sales, against 7.1% for GE. By then Litton no longer had a viable myth; no longer could anybody emulate Ash's forlorn response to the first setback in its earnings: 'I regard what happened as a stumbling in the search for growth'. The stumble has lasted so long that it qualifies as a crawl.

Would such managements have operated any more successfully if the myth had not been believed, internally and externally? If, to take Litton again, top managers had not persuaded themselves (presumably) and the public (certainly) that there was some meaningful connection between building ships and making portable electric typewriters? Would IBM have fared better if, instead of promulgating the myth of high innovation, management had faced the crucial problem of slow-development programmes and product lags measured, not in months, but several years?

Since history can't be written backwards, questions like this can never be answered. But when myths swell up in such huge bubbles, their eventual bursting makes a far louder bang. IBM's shareholders saw their investment dive by $70 billion in the decade to 1994. And yet in many respects IBM was truly admirable; so was Litton. The trap lies in pretending to be something you aren't. That's not easy to avoid when outside commentators, even if not encouraged by the company's own publicity efforts, are engaged in lauding its presumed, but non-existent excellence.

In 1990, Spring Ram was hailed by *The Economist* as possibly 'the most successful manufacturer in Britain', and in 1991 by *Management Today* as 'perhaps the best example of both entrepreneurial flair and sheer manufacturing professionalism' produced in the 1980s. The enthusiasm was explained by an eight-year surge in the shares during which shareholders saw their investment return over 2,000%. In 1992 the shares began a decline which eventually wiped three-quarters off their value. Yet brokers were still hymning the company's 'fantastic and probably unique' qualities weeks before revelations that the accounting books had been comprehensively cooked.

Fantastic, indeed. Extravagant praise is almost always the precursor of extreme disappointment. Inside every fat bubble, though, there lurks a truth: maybe a big one. Michael Milken, the disgraced hero of the dismembered Drexel Burnham Lambert, saw that there was a profitable gap between the interest that lesser companies could afford to pay and their ability to borrow by issuing securities. By issuing high-interest junk bonds aggressively, Milken exploited his gap to sensational effect, but at the price of creating a market that could only be sustained by artificial and dubious means.

At the equally ill-fated Investors Overseas Services, Bernie Cornfeld saw unerringly that nobody was using American sales methods to tap the oceans of non-American savings; and his idea of pooling mutual fund investments under the marvellous title 'Fund of Funds' was a stroke of pure marketing genius. All these ideas (like the inertial guidance systems with which Litton first made its way in the world) were strong enough to make fortunes for anybody who exploited them with vigour, whether the men were corruptible or incorruptible, organisers or hucksters, captains of industry or con artists.

Because of the basic myth of management (that success equals skill), the public makes no distinctions. But as the wonder-idea pays off, the wonder-boy's competitors – including the big corporations who missed the beautiful force of his idea – run scared, act jealous and retaliate. Their Cassandra-like carping, however, is always discounted by everybody, including the wonder-boy. This is sheer folly. If competitors say that an Atlantic Computers, leasing out the same machines and paying the same price for its money, can't possibly be earning higher profits than its rivals, it isn't.

Big established financiers, though more than capable of making mammoth boners of their own, really do know the loan and investment markets down to the last decimal of a percentage. And every time an upstart like Drexel Burnham, or Slater Walker, or IOS, appears to be running circles round them, the odds are overwhelming that the new boy is headed for catastrophe, just as the big-company Jeremiahs are liable to say. If an Asil Nadir is reporting stunning levels and rises in profit for Polly Peck from fruit-packing activities which yield little juice for others, the likelihood is not that he has found the alchemist's stone, but that he is bedecking the lily with great globs of fool's gold.

The hero, though, becomes so rich, so successful and surrounded by so many flatterers that he is convinced of his genius at management, as at everything else. He has a lovely growth record, a managerial myth, and money. Money has a magnetic attraction for other money; so the wonder-man, bit firmly between his teeth, typically strays (just like all the conglomerates) into businesses of which he knows nothing, such as oil lands and banking (Cornfeld), or just banking (Slater). The new areas rapidly strip bare the wonder-boy's shortcomings, organisational and personal, in short and horrible order.

Organisation-man types will protest that they aren't a bit like the failed entrepreneurs. Then they shouldn't behave like it. Don't deceive anybody, especially yourself. For a start, listen to what customers, competitors and suppliers say about you, your company, and your products; eight times out of ten it is just as accurate, and, if used properly, just as constructive as the findings of a paid researcher (and much cheaper). What you believe about your own products and performance, eight times out of ten, is untrue.

Second, never trade solely on a personal reputation; observe that entrepreneurial stayers who bequeath enduring empires are usually as close with their mouths as they are mean with their money. And never seek to manufacture a myth. Myth-making can fuel a share boom, making it much easier to raise money and buy up other businesses. But if the record of achievement is genuine, the stock price looks after itself, there are no cash problems, and acquisitions are optional. If the achievement is spurious or inflated, the stock price will collapse one day, the borrowed money will strangle the corporation in its inevitable downturn, and most of the buys, having been forced, will be bad.

Third, never misrepresent the financial facts, internally or externally. If an old, old product is expensive to make, but looks cheap because there is no longer a depreciation charge, the management which keeps churning it out is being misled just as dangerously as the investor who thinks that a change in accounting methods produces a real gain in profits. Don't treat non-recurring profits as operating income, or adopt any of the other methods for dressing up shabby profits in better clothes. Even if you get away with it, the shareholders won't.

Fourth, act on the truth about products, services and the calibre of colleagues. As a rough rule, if nobody ever tries to hire away a company's executives, they are not as good as they or their superiors think. A top executive who starts praising 'the team' is usually concealing the fact that none of the players is of sufficient individual value. As for the product and its production, it is not world-class unless it is demonstrably equalling or excelling the best rivals in the world. Moreover, every product and every service (like every management) could be improved, usually to a marked degree, and should be.

Fifth, never believe your own advertising (after all, nobody else does) or your own public relations (even if everybody else does). The public-relations chief for a Swiss giant once said firmly, 'Our top officers would like to get their names in the paper, but I say no.' He could have been doing them a wonderful service.

Sixth, don't lie gratuitously. When asked, on leaving a secret conference with a company you want to buy, or that wants to buy you, whether a merger is on, don't deny it with your hand on the Bible – as Carnation did twice while happily negotiating its $3 billion deal with Nestlé. That deceit worked to the great joy of the smart money, which knew perfectly well what was going on, and to the deep sorrow of the dumb small investors who were conned by the denials.

When a new product line moves from losing a million to dropping £900,000, don't say it's nearing break-even, either. And when you fire an executive for incompetence, or having his hot little hands in the till, don't say he is resigning for personal reasons or after a policy dispute – just don't say anything. Just make up your mind never to make the same mistake of selection again.

Finally, remember that the ultimate victim of self-deception is the self. Had Avon, for example, seen itself as it really was – no longer a red-hot sales organisation with a magical growth formula but a company pressed hard by heavy competition which it wasn't fitted to tackle – it couldn't have missed the demographic changes in America. That was no mean miss, when everybody in the land knew about the increase in working women, smaller families, and so on.

Rather, discover what the company is really good at, and

remember that there are no such things as technological strength or management depth in themselves. If these claimed assets are not being applied to useful purpose, the company is good at nothing. And if the company really makes its money, not by any real merit, but by fooling the suckers, forget it. You *can* fool all of the people, but you can only do it for some of the time.

BOOK IV:
WAR GAMES

Introduction:
The Global Imperative

Not a day passes without bearing witness to the growing force of global business. The evidence is unmistakeable. The borders between businesses are coming down. What about the borders between people? Global management assumes the existence of global managers, borderless executives whose domicile is as irrelevant to them as to their employers. And they do exist. The most conspicuous example must be Eckhard Pfeiffer, who masterminded the astonishing resurgence and surge of Compaq from its Houston HQ, but goes home to Munich when he can.

His ambitions, too, are pitched in global terms: to overtake IBM in world market share for personal computers in 1996 (a once-tough target now in clear sight). Join a senior group in a Swiss drug company, and you'll find several European nationalities and an American listening to an Israeli pharmacologist. Visit a European car company, and young American managers will be working side-by-side with Britons and Germans. In the new globalism of the car industry, Detroit has surrendered the lead in smaller cars to the Europeans, for the simple reason that they understand the market better.

Several years back, the Taurus cars that dramatically revived Ford's US fortunes were adapted from European

219

mid-range models. From now on, world-wide small-car sales, led from Europe, will fit into Ford's total global organisation of five 'programme centres', each staffed with managers and engineers from around the world. This parallels the evolution of the multi-disciplinary, multi-functional teams which have become mandatory in modern product development. That has worked smoothly, which is no surprise; the old system of hand-overs between functions and departments as projects moved consecutively between stages might have been designed to produce delay and disagreement. Concurrent team-working is plainly superior.

The new cross-border approach is equally superior to the old matrix system – in theory. The matrix subjects managers to triple control. They are responsible to the national bosses in the country where they work; to the supranational heads of their business function; to the leaders, also supranational, of their product group. The progenitors of the matrix were trying to square the circle: to combine independence with dependence without reducing effectiveness. Instead, they produced a recipe for confusion, overlap and turf wars.

At IBM, once the acclaimed maestro of matrix management, the current answer is to create fourteen marketing groups organised by industry customers – banking, retailing and so on – right across the world. According to *Business Week*, this follows a study of ABB, whose boss, Percy Barnevik, is the best-known practising guru of globalism. But the presidents of ABB's 1,300-plus profit centres still have two bosses: the head of the national company which houses them, plus one of fifty heads of business groups, who in turn report to an eight-man executive committee.

That sounds as cumbersome as any matrix, and its validity must remain unproven unless or until ABB starts making more than minuscule profits. But within the system, Barnevik's group heads will 'coordinate globally, overseeing factories in far-flung locations, allocating export markets, realising economies of scale, and ensuring that quality and performance meet global standards'. As these heroes rest on the seventh day (if they can), at least they can reflect on truly global weeks.

Globalism changes the whole management perspective. If there's no home country as such, who's an expatriate, or an underling, and who isn't? The new global managers will follow the task, and that will determine their authority and their location. But what will determine their success? Computer networks are indispensable foundations for firms which want to operate across borders; that currently obstructs Ford's ambitions – its US and European systems are incompatible. But compatibility is also impossible between Detroit managers who believe America knows best and Europeans or Asians who may actually know better.

The odds are, however, that the sheer pressure of competition for global markets will overcome the national, human barriers. The pressure isn't confined to or coming from mighty multinationals alone. Last year *The McKinsey Quarterly* reported on a new breed of smaller Australian company that is 'born global', using the fax rather than the network as founder managements 'cherry-pick the best business and customers' anywhere in the world. In small, medium and large companies alike, that's how markets are evolving, and managers are bound to evolve with them.

The people will be evolving along lines plotted by the late, great W. Edwards Deming. The pre-Deming industrial world now seems as far away as life before the PC. Amazingly, that's only some dozen years back – but it's even fewer years since the factory floor ethos shifted, à la Deming, decisively to training and retraining; constructive leadership instead of order-giving; elimination of fear as a means of industrial control; removal of barriers between functions; and substitution of improved systems for slogans, exhortations, targets and quotas.

With those steps taken, so world-wide experience has shown, pride of workmanship can rise again. The whole process hinges on two further, familiar developments: the extension of education and personal development throughout, including top management, and working in the teams mentioned above. Project-based teamwork is rapidly becoming the dominant organisational mode; the teams, just as Deming insisted, are more likely than not to cross the functional and departmental borders. The spread of his ideas, though, never mollified Deming, who was continually discouraged by the reluctance of Western managers to practise what he preached – and his Japanese disciples gratefully adopted.

Yet in 1994 the Japanese example no longer seems so awesome to Westerners. Under pressure for profits, great global companies like Sony and Matsushita have been reorganising radically to improve the speed and quality of corporate decisions. Management layers are being cut. Whole divisions and departments are disappearing. New internal companies, focused on their markets, are being formed under individual bosses whose enhanced powers will include design, manufacturing and marketing. The standard theme, if you can't beat the Japanese, manage like 'em, doesn't have the same resonance if the Japanese are restructuring in much the same way as constipated Western giants.

But Professor Manfred Perlitz of Mannheim University has been warning Western managers for some time that, by imitating yesterday's Japanese model, they are missing today's challenge: which goes beyond Deming into areas of creativity and innovation. As before, Easterners will probably lead in thought, Japanese in action. Already, maximising mutual benefits by mutual action, globally and nationally, via what's known as 'strategic alliance', is one of the ways forward that doesn't bear an exclusive Japanese trademark as theory; but it does carry a long-standing, powerful and growing Japanese endorsement in practice.

Europe's management contribution hasn't been widely famed in either theory or practice. So it's quite daring of three authors, Helen Bloom, Roland Calori and Philippe de Woot, to produce a book which describes its title subject, Euromanagement, as 'a new style for the global market'. It argues that Europeans have a lead in key areas that include managing international diversity, social responsibility, and orientation towards people. On the debit side, though, product-led management has still not retreated enough before customer orientation, while Europe's management systems are looser than the Japanese would allow.

So why have Sony and Matsushita been pressured into reorganisation? It's the old story. Success locks companies into established ways – and lifetime employment hasn't helped by littering Japanese executive structures with surplus bodies. The West isn't better off, though; merely in the same position. It's true that, in this fix, the European Single Market's own diversity is creating a new style of diverse, truly multi-national management that could well be globally effective. The Japanese aren't mere bystanders in this process, however, but active participants through their European implants.

The necessity for Westerners is to ensure that the established organisations and senior managers simply get out of the way. This means abandoning the matrix and its enshrined centralising forces in order to develop genuine global dynamism. That's a far harder task than developing individual managers who can think and operate across frontiers. Their development is inevitable. Like the new, path-finding businesses described earlier, the new generation of managers has been born global. Their employing organisations have a simple choice: keep in step, or stumble into obscurity.

18
Planet of the Planners

Once upon a time, big business had a new religion: planning. With many sub-cults, it culminated in the long-range corporate variety. This ultimate in techniques had to wait for its moment; earlier managers needed the long view, all right, but they lacked the computers, or the men to feed them. When a new breed of hardware and soft humans was born, corporations could at last cope. Before the computer, the task of gazing into the chasms of the future, and juggling with its endless permutations, would have chained every manager to his slide-rule for eternity. Thanks to the computer, companies could now do their sums – and get them wrong – in comfort.

The chances of number-crunching your way to success remained slim. Thus 'a reassessment of strategies' described in *Business Week* in 1979 and 1980 found that a Naughty Nineteen 'failed, ran into trouble or were abandoned, while only fourteen could be deemed successful'. Among the fourteen 'successes', what's more, history has turned thumbs down on American Motors and its link-up with Renault in yet another of the latter's doomed attempts to find a role (and consistent profits) in the US auto market; while Gould Inc., which shed all its traditional businesses in favour of high-technology operations, succeeded only in being a high-tech flop.

In any event, these failures, along with others like Campbell Soup's attempt to diversify away from food, were based, not on the crunching of numbers by computer, but on human judgment, on broad strategy. Corporations might have headed off in just such directions without benefit of the long-range planners. The latter, though, were following their own strategic plan. They embraced responsibility for strategy after the previous phase of planning's meteoric rise had fizzled out, again in a rash of disappointments. This first phase had gone hand-in-glove with the compulsively reasonable sub-cult of management by objectives.

Of course, directors should know what they are trying to achieve; of course, it's fair to judge them by how far they reach their own objectives. Provided that the aims are realistic, and the genius isn't proposing to outsell BMW with a three-wheel electric mini-car, this wrapped up in one neat parcel the messy problems of appraisal and direction. The trouble started with the misplaced hope that the formality of the dance – in which boss and subordinates go through a fixed waltz of setting mutual objectives, and then assessing performance together – would get rid of the dreaded interpersonal conflict.

You no longer gave your subordinate orders; he gave them to himself. You no longer had the painful task of whipping him for his failures; he flogged himself before you. And if this smacked somewhat of the confessional, so be it. The Catholic Church hasn't found the guilty conscience of the faithful to be a useless management tool. But if a manager hates his boss to distraction, he will hate him no less because they have worked together on his objectives. The second pious error is to hope that all management tasks can be turned into objectives, or that all objectives can be described precisely. The great entrepreneur, for instance, doesn't manage by objectives, but by instinct, and by riding his luck. He doesn't, above all, work on a system.

In the objectives system, the corporation's aims, or plans, were broken down into a hierarchy of lesser aims or plans;

and the grand total of all those objectives added up to those of the corporation. Then all the executives had to do was meet their planned and agreed objectives and – hey presto – the corporation does the same. Perfection in management, at last, had arrived, except that it hadn't and never will. To plan may be divine, but to err is all too human.

The golden years of planning saw errors of strategy and missing of objectives on a macabre scale. Periodically massive over-ordering of airline equipment had jumbo jets crossing the Atlantic more than half-empty; even the despairing support of their bankers hasn't been enough to keep the airlines aloft financially. Steel and chemicals have likewise veered between under-capacity and over-capacity the world over, before settling down into seemingly permanent over-supply. In industry generally, plant after plant, computer after computer, has come in late and at grossly excessive cost; while forecast after forecast has come grievously unstuck.

After oil prices went sky-high in 1973, every planner in the oil industry proceeded on the assumption that scarcity would continue, and prices would go on soaring, forever and a day; Milton Friedman apart, almost nobody, from the CIA downwards (or upwards), foresaw that sharply higher prices would choke off demand – which actually fell, dragging down prices, when all those brilliant planners expected it to rise. In the computer industry, packed with brainpower, both human and electronic, the planners confidently expected the mixture to continue as before; they completely missed the overwhelming swing away from mainframes to distributed information processing, with a terminal on every desk or bench.

Not to be outdone by themselves, the same planners missed the even more significant shift from terminals to PCs built round microprocessors of ever-ascending power and speed. Even the electricity industry, whose only business is to balance supply and demand, has run short of generating capacity or run into gross surplus at critical times. In business at large, annual growth targets have been missed by so many miles that companies have wisely forgotten all about them. One US group, which formed the sensible-seeming, once fashionable objective of 15% annual growth in earnings per share, four years later needed a 170% jump in one year to get back on target. That's some objective.

None of this has done the planning industry any good. The long-range planners had been striving to establish themselves as a separate breed – technicians as essential to the corporate future as a competent accountant is to its present. Some American companies consequently found themselves with brilliant vice-presidents who spent half their year planning and the other half converting the plan into an action programme for the next year. Which conveniently left them no time whatsoever for managing.

Among the top executives who pay the planners' bills, this gap between ideas and action couldn't pass without notice. GE, a pioneering force in the planning endeavour, found that 'the staff-work did not make a good connection between environmental studies and the implications for top management decision or action'. The speaker is the company's own ace planner of the 1970s, Michael G. Allen. The GE staff was cut by around a quarter, leaving a mere 100-odd people to plan the future of this mighty corporation.

That was in 1975. Move on nine years, and *Business Week* reported as follows: 'In a bid to return strategic planning to its original intent – forcing managers to take "a massive, massive look outside ourselves" – GE chairman John F. Welch Jr. has slashed the corporate planning group from fifty-eight to thirty-three, and scores of planners have been purged in GE's operating sectors, groups and divisions. Now the cry is a capitalist version of "all power to the Soviets".'

For Soviets, read the line managers. They saw strategic planners seize authority from the line after the work of consultants like Boston Consulting Group and McKinsey had wondrously sold big US business on a twin concept – that strategy is the key to corporate success, and that strategic planning can be made manifestly effective by the use of relatively simple tools of the consultants' trade. Now a GE man talks of 'gaining ownership of the business', of grabbing hold of it from an 'isolated bureaucracy' of planners; while a GM planning chief, not to be outdone, says bluntly that 'planning is the responsibility of every line manager'.

It may not be a responsibility they covet. *Business Week* also
quotes managers at a Midwest manufacturer who still completed strategic-planning forms that HQ had dispensed with:
'You almost had to rip them out of their hands.' It's easy to
understand why. Taking action is where painful mistakes may
be made and jobs risked; so merely thinking about what to do
may be nicely to an executive's taste. Nobody is to blame for
a plan that is falsified by events – for nobody can foretell the
future, can they? After five or ten years nobody will even
remember who drew up the original document.

Like Lord Keynes and everybody else, the planner and the
executive are both dead in the long run. The long run,
however, is only a series of short runs added together – and
this is vital, as the directors of one big boiler company should
know. Self-described as an unrepentant planner, its boss
(rather, its *former* boss) said, 'The real benefits of reorganisation will be tested in five to ten years' time.' Within just two
years, the company had run into a brick wall and disappeared by merger.

Such relatively primitive failures were supposed to have
been made less likely, if not impossible, by the new sophistication inspired by Boston. Since the consultants had identified
a link between high profitability and high market share, it
followed that corporations should seek to maximise the latter
– but where? The choice of markets was made gloriously
simple by the matrix which, judging businesses by growth
rates and market shares, divided them into stars, question-
marks, cash cows and dogs.

You backed the stars to the hilt, tried to turn the border-
line cases into stars, milked the cash cows and disposed of the
dogs and, hey presto again, you had a corporate strategy, a
planned portfolio of existing businesses. As for new ones
(needed, of course, to replace the old dogs and dry cows),
you found those from a market matrix constructed on the
same principles. Unfortunately, many managements found
that high-share and high-growth businesses could equate
with low profits – and could even bring large losses, if the
competition was too intense, the price of entry too great, or
the corporate experience inadequate.

It often happened that all three adverse factors operated at once – as when Exxon blundered into office automation and electrical manufacture. Look at this and the other nineteen strategic failures mentioned before, and you find the same story over and over again; the strategy failed either because it was based on incorrect assumptions about the environment, or because its implementation was mishandled. In the case of environmental error, corporations can do very little to guard themselves. Error is of the essence, which is why the embattled planners seized on the magic word 'scenario' in a later phase.

Instead of committing themselves to a definite projection on interest rates, winter weather, the supply-and-demand balance for energy or cement or chemicals (to name a few of the factors where gross mistakes made flops of *Business Week*'s Naughty Nineteen), the planners now offer management a choice of alternative scenarios (three, usually). The idea is that the options force managers to think for themselves, to manage, in short; but the scenario approach has the not so incidental virtue of taking the planners off the hook.

They can also hardly be blamed for the operational messups: like the fact that one brewery's great drive for higher market share was vitiated by its lack of needed marketing strength. As in war, strategic success depends on tactical effectiveness, and no degree of planning can lessen management's tactical imperatives. The first responsibility of executives, anyway, is to the here and now. If they make a shambles of the present, there may be no future; and the real purpose of planning – the one whose neglect is common, but poisonous – is to safeguard and sustain the company in subsequent short-run periods.

Every executive should go to bed happy that no omission of his will leave successors without new products in the pipeline, with no cash in the bank, and with an inadequate production plant crippled by crazy labour relations; that's what actually happened in the long deterioration of Britain's top car-makers which ended in the BMW-owned rump, the Rover Group. The basic planning every company needs is intelligent anticipation extrapolating the trends of the business to determine probable needs for capital, cash, new plant, product replacement, and the rest, with a massive allowance for contingencies thrown in.

That foundation isn't enough, of course. The shorter the product life-cycle, the greater the proportion of sales that has to be derived from new products. That demands an utterly different kind of planning, which hinges on creativity and innovation, and which number-crunching can't help. What goes wrong with basic planning, though, is that sensible anticipation gets converted into foolish numbers; and their validity always hinges on large, loose assumptions.

After the first Suez crisis of 1956, the world oil industry, stacked to its eyebrows with planners, concluded that, without a major new pipeline across the Arab world, built at stupendous cost, Western Europe would run dry of oil. For the first and presumably last time in history, every oil company boss who mattered (and many who didn't) met, blessed by the US trust-busters, at a London hotel. As soon as the moguls got back to their desks, they found that, because forecast growth in oil demand hadn't materialised in a single year, Western Europe was oozing with excess oil, a condition in which it remained until the oil producers imposed their cartel in 1973.

As noted above, the cartel merely succeeded in reducing demand to the point where the surplus was larger than ever – so large that the cartel and prices have remained in a state of collapse ever since. The chemical company Monsanto, influenced by the Boston theories, made a large, loose assumption of its own: that, partly because leisure suits would stay in high demand, so would polyester fibre – making the Number Two spot in polyester a great place to be. As the CEO sighed to *Business Week*, 'Our assumption that there was growth enough disappeared in a hurry.'

There's a confusion that easily appears in planning. An exercise that starts in simple prudence – ensuring that you have the resources you need – becomes another gung-ho device for achieving superlatives of growth and profitability. Executives take their eyes off what is going to happen and think about what they are going to make happen. They manage, in other words, by objectives. In the long-range passion, moreover, they even ignore real short-run happenings.

Commonly executives, in the worst examples, have started playing with their 'rolling five-year plans' in the spring of the preceding year. At that point, they can only guess the outcome of the current twelve months. Anything from cocoa blight in the Congo to a strike in Wichita or Upper Tooting might well be about to hit them; yet they plunge into documents of immense volume and tiny detail. The translation-into-numbers defect readily takes over. Once the basic assumptions are made – just as the corporate objectives can be split into atomised individual aims – the entire future of the business can be sliced up, right down to the usage and price of raw rubber in four years' time, or the sales margin on light bulbs in three.

This is tricky enough when executives are simply trying to predict. Better to heed the experience of the Beecham drugs-to-foods group. 'We found a five-year forecast was pie-in-the-sky and it tended to encourage excessive expenditure. The forecasts were nearly always way out because one cannot legislate for failure.' When executives are attempting to achieve, as well as forecast, the corporation has a potential tiger by the tail. Since the mercy of God is infinite, however, there is a self-correcting device. Executives soon catch on to the notion that, if they are being held to a plan or objective, the plan had better be one they can meet.

The Russians, though they lagged behind Western management technology in every other respect, pioneered this subtle art in the Soviet days. The only yardstick of a Soviet executive's performance was whether or not he made his plan. So, not being a complete idiot, he spent most of his ingenuity on getting an easy plan. One Communist executive whose screw factory's output plan was set by weight, switched, clever lad, to making heavier screws. When the boss of a plan-happy American corporation says, 'The [planning] numbers are getting better all the time', he cannot know whether the executives are improving as planners or as time-servers, Soviet-style.

That quote came from Honeywell, whose own plans, anyway, can't have envisaged the jettisoning of its hard-won computer business. The plan to become a mini-IBM with IBM-style growth rates misfired to such an extent that management in Minneapolis decided to rebuild its strategy round the non-computer interests, instead of the other way round. A decade's growth in earnings per share to 1983 left Honeywell strictly in the middle of the road, with a 6.3% figure: almost exactly half that of IBM. Restored to sanity, Honeywell in the following decade returned to effectiveness; earnings grew by 14.3% annually, the sixtieth best figure of the *Fortune* 500.

Locking executives into detailed plans and objectives, self-fulfilling or not, has a saving grace. At least, managers are made to think about what they suppose themselves to be doing and what the consequences will be. Companies part at the seams, not because executives don't plan, but because they don't think. Planning and forcing managers to set objectives have much point as devices for compelling thought, so long as executives don't forget that any plan worth making is inaccurate; the longer a plan takes to write, the worse it is – just because of its consumption of time; and the more they change plans to suit events, the better they will manage – if you've made a mistake, you had better admit it.

Even businesses into which the long-range planners have never burrowed need these three lessons; even in such firms, unless they are stuck fast in pre-history, annual budgeting (really a one-year corporate plan) and capital-spending approval (the crunch part of any planning activity) are bound to crop up. Even annual budgets are a post-war fashion, in many companies. Plenty still have inadequate controls, barely worth the name, even on costs; and some only have a tenuous handle on profitability. The surprises are only occasionally pleasant, just as capital-spending plans do sometimes pay off according to schedule.

This isn't for lack of sophistication. Investment appraisal was one of the first fields to receive the full force of would-be scientific managers. Worthy tomes soon abounded on discounted cash flow, net present value, and internal rates of return. All of these sets of numbers, however, rest on anticipations of the future so dubious that the use of the technique, according to some statisticians, is little more effective than picking projects with a pin. This won't worry most executives – for expansion projects are all but unstoppable.

Boards of directors are always claiming that performance will be 'greatly' (or 'significantly' or 'substantially') improved when the new wonder-factory starts producing, in March, or August, or whenever. In case after case, it doesn't produce then. When it does, for month after month all that pours out is trouble and loss. The only thing that doesn't emerge is the promised rate of return. If the board sets 20% or 25% as the minimum return on investment, the managers cook the futuristic figures to fit the target and get the project approval they crave.

Every company has beloved projects on which, if prices had held up, if the contractors had finished on time (or finished at all), if the plans hadn't been altered, if the thing had actually worked, the planned return would have been earned. But since some or all of these calamities usually happen, any manager who neglects to allow for them is not planning – merely thinking wishfully. Desire for the project has, as usual, overtaken desire for profit. Letting the wish be father to the accomplishment is only one route to a false objective. Another is to start from a false premise – say, that the company really can achieve some dazzling growth rate or return on capital. Like setting subordinates a 'stretching' objective (i.e. one they can't reach), this guarantees failure.

Managements regularly survive many years of missing announced targets without much damage, even to their self-esteem. That's hardly surprising, if John Thackray is right in saying that 'Planning is, of course, first and foremost a security blanket of both practical and symbolic value. A great deal of planning is an occult and highly plastic activity . . .' As always, though, executives who don't require artificial security, or occult aids, can make the most out of what weaker men misuse. These days, the best corporations, in Japan or the West, plan no further ahead than they have to.

In the majority of businesses, that's no more than three

years. Only the first of those years is hard and packed with
figures – as it must be, since that's the annual budget. The
whole three-year view, though, starts with objectives
expressed in words, not numbers: indeed, a Japanese president wouldn't feel happy without an initial statement of the
corporate philosophy – and never mind about cash cows and
stars. This idea of the sovereign importance of 'vision' has
now been widely, sometimes slavishly, adopted in the West.
You couldn't have a sharper contrast to the once all but
universal, inherently defective American game of picking on
arbitrary figures and then working back.

Take 15% annual compound growth in earnings per
share; and forget, for the moment, that since earnings per
share is a very funny number, it can be manipulated to
produce 'growth' from the wild blue yonder. Even if the 15%
is translated into real, honest growth, what grounds are there
for expecting this jacket to fit the corporation? And if it
doesn't, what then? The saner executive would surely plan
and develop each component business according to its
potential and settle for whatever group growth turns up.
Then, so long as the business can coin the requisite money,
growth will look after itself.

If only it were so easy. That's the Du Pont way. The net
result for the heavyweight leader in the world chemical stakes
was twenty years of dismal performance. Net earnings in
1961–70 rose by only 20.5%, which compared (almost
unbelievably) with 176% for Britain's supposedly sleepy old
ICI. Thereafter, Du Pont transformed itself only by the
megamerger with Continental Oil – a gigantic strategic move
which looked less and less wonderful with every downward
lurch in the petroleum market. In consequence, Du Pont
stockholders didn't even double their money in the 1973–83
period which saw ICI's investors get a near fivefold total
return on their money.

Even that Du Pont decade looks good beside the ten years
to 1993. As noted in an earlier chapter, earnings per share
dropped by 6.4% annually as the once-brilliant business
ended the period with piffling returns of 1.7% on sales, 1.5%
on assets and 4.9% on stockholders' equity. As for ICI, while

its billion-dollar losses of 1992 were only a quarter of Du Pont's, they were the precursor to the protective bifurcation of the group: the abrupt end to a corporate strategy that any Japanese, or any schoolboy, could well understand – to be, according to former chairman Sir John Harvey-Jones, 'the best bloody chemical company in the world'.

How executives plan or what numbers they choose doesn't count; what does is the standard of performance they are ready to exact. The essence of any objective is that reaching it should be reasonably difficult. The precondition is that you expect it to be met. But corporations settle on plans and targets with little idea of how to react if the objectives are missed. If the whole company undershoots its targets by the width of the Atlantic Ocean, the directors are unlikely to take the extreme step of firing each other. This weakens their position when it comes to firing others for the same offence – which consequently rarely happens, except in time of earthquake, when the system has already (and long since) broken down.

Every executive has one dual objective, to do the most possible with the least possible. Don't concentrate on the end – the earnings – to the exclusion of the means – the capital. An executive who is being tyrannised by his boss into raising return on capital from 10% to 15% grows ulcers trying to lift profits by half. You can get the same effect by reducing capital employed by one third. Don't start from statistical objectives and work backwards, either. Begin from the premise that whatever the company is doing could be done better, and start moving forward by making the improvements that are always waiting to be grabbed.

Under the threat of recession and the Japanese example in the 1980s, many firms discovered, as if for the first time, age-old truths about capital. Left to themselves, companies use far more of it than they need. They hoard inventory that is too hefty and slackly controlled; they let unnecessary fixed assets pile up; forgetfulness about cash flow leads to regular and excessive borrowing; they tie still more money up in businesses that never have produced a worthwhile return, never could, and never will. Anyway, all capital generates costs, so cutting out capital must eventually cut expenses. Other things being equal, the capital cutter will improve profitability simultaneously on both sides of the hallowed ratio of Return on Capital Employed.

The process is as near as anything in business management to ranking as a golden rule. While managing capital has helped to produce spectacular results for companies like Coca-Cola (18.1% on assets in 1993, with an astronomical 47.5% on equity), it is less thrilling than planning a five-year future. The future, however, is pure uncertainty, limited only by the constraints of possibility. The manager must understand those constraints, and can limit that uncertainty by thoughtful anticipation. But if you want to master the future, you have to find out first what is really and truly happening right now; to make sure that it is happening right; and then use the inevitable right outcomes to make the future happen in the same right way.

19
The Motivational Misfits

For many years, the most emotive word in management's vocabulary was motivation. Those four syllables motivated companies so powerfully that they shelled out huge daily fees to have some high priest elucidate the mysteries of motives. These hot-gospellers all trod in the footsteps of Frederick Herzberg, an academic consultant, who (as a founding thinker) was reputed to pull in $6,000 a day from some corporate admirers at a time when, to most gurus, such fees were pure dreamland.

The high noon of these hero-thinkers has passed, but not before their ideas have become a pervasive, inescapable influence on management life; that's hardly surprising, given the sheer height of that noon. To quote John Thackray, writing in *Management Today*: 'The allegedly humanistic psychologies of Douglas McGregor, Abraham Maslow, Frederick Herzberg, Chris Argyris and others' made them 'the chief spokesmen for a liberal attack on traditional corporate authoritarianism and hierarchies'.

In their 'promised land of greater voice and personal fulfilment for the individual', wonders would flow. 'Participative management and "enriched" jobs, they claimed, would foster worker happiness, and also boost productivity and profits.' The paradox is that, at the time when these comforting theories were being promulgated, in the 1960s, productivity and profits were not the besetting concern of US management. They should have been; but when the crucial nature of the American productivity crisis was realised, under the extreme dual pressure of recession and Japanese competition, the ideas of the motivational sages mostly went out of the window.

The next most conspicuous school of thought (if that's the right word) sought to embrace the principles of JABMAS – the Japanese business and management system which had done so much of the damage to American pride and profits. Through this gate passed quality circles, and Total Quality Management, and the doctrine of *kaizen* (or continuous improvement), and *hoshin kanri* (Policy Deployment), and much else. But as these influences coalesced into a general rethinking of management, so did the principles of motivation; it no longer hinged on intervention, but its opposite. Now the key was to allow the forces of self-motivation to come roaring through.

Is the difference real? Motivation – like all psychological insights – contains its fair share of truths, or rather truisms. Its blue-chip purchasers basically got an insight that they could have obtained as easily (and much more cheaply) from peering into their own interiors: that money is only one of the forces that motivates people to work effectively. This truism burst upon companies like a blinding light because of their deep yearning for a universal key to unlock their everlasting problems.

The 'behavioural scientist' offered a kind of philosopher's stone, an explanation and solution rolled into one, with which to attack the irritating refusal of men to act in the best interests of the corporation. The late-twentieth-century executive feels his pains more than any predecessor. He is also more convinced, after being inundated by a Niagara of business theory, that cures exist for any corporate condition. Man, he believes, is a perfectible animal. So, if the management is not developing marvels of entrepreneurial initiative, drive, and speed, or if the workers, instead of churning out untold productivity, are militant, grudging, and alienated, the solution is plain.

They all want (because all normal people do) to achieve; they are just not properly motivated, or so the gurus explained. Press the right motivating buttons, and the machine – at last – will whir off into beautiful action. Even the language of business began to change. Companies didn't 'employ' executives any more. The standard phrase was to 'attract, retain, and motivate' them. In this Holy Trinity, motivation must loom largest; it's no use having a splendidly attracted and retained executive who won't work. The behaviourists were able to show, which wasn't hard, that management's approach to employees had been misguided and muddle-headed for decades.

Better still, they could apparently show – 'scientifically' too – how to get elevated results by amending the approach. But the question 'What are your motives?' isn't objective. The answer varies wildly from person to person and day to day, and people lie about their motives, even to themselves. In the days when British scientific brains were draining across the Atlantic in flood proportions (just in time for the first great aerospace and computer recessions), the deserters never admitted that doubling or trebling or even quadrupling their living standards was a prime reason for going West. No, the confessed lure was always the wider scope, the richer research and development budgets, the more lavish scientific equipment.

Those disinterested scientists who would have emigrated to the US for unchanged standards of living could have been comfortably hijacked in one small executive jet. But in Western society some shame still attaches (even after the Great Greed of the 1980s) to doing anything (even something perfectly respectable) just for the loot. How often does a multi-millionaire allow that making still more millions is his dearest hobby and most pressing motive? That he simply loves to roll around in the green stuff? On the contrary, the money, he will say, is just 'figures on a piece of paper'. The man clings to those pieces of paper like a starving octopus.

Self-made tycoons are highly acquisitive and retentive: the

proprietor with millions in the bank gets wild over wasted paperclips or secretaries paying for cabs with his cash; the professional executive, with little more to his name than a big mortgage, never minds at all. Greed is a great motivator, in all its forms, and you can't disentangle greed, for money or anything else, from non-financial motives of equal force, such as ambition.

America is well-stocked with rough and tough entrepreneurs whose ideas on motivation are closer to those of Attila than of Argyris. Indeed, roughness and toughness are much admired; *Fortune* annually runs a feature on 'America's toughest bosses', which isn't meant to be pejorative. Their 'toughness' might be construed by others, less as virtuous managerial drive, more as the manifestation of an unpleasant ego. Most of the tough guys have also minted money in equally ego-satisfying quantities – and which comes first, the money motive or the management drive, is exactly the same question as the old conundrum about the chicken and the egg.

The boy who sets out to be president of the United States is motivated by personal ambition, desire to better mankind, lust for power, and other drives. He also ends up rich, with a fine white pad on Pennsylvania Avenue, an army of servants (and a real army too), a fleet of cars, a high salary, and after these delicacies are removed (by the voters or the end of his second term or even, as with Richard Nixon, by disgrace), a huge pension and rich sales of his ghosted memoirs.

The corporate man who wants to achieve is likewise a bundle of powerful motives, which include desire for the personal benefits, in wealth, prestige, and their companions, that await those who reach the top. But that man's motives are of little interest or relevance. Motivating an ambitious, able executive isn't the problem; the difficulty is often to retain him. The real problem of the corporation is the motivation of the vast majority – people who don't have any particular wish to achieve.

The large corporation is traditionally structured more for time-servers than as a springboard for the ambitious. Big companies long adored to offer a lifetime career to those they hired, still moist behind the ears, straight from the universities. Lifetime hiring meant a steady progression on grounds of years alone from one rung on the ladder to another. The ladders would all come tumbling down if the corporation became a gymnasium for the ambitious, all vaulting over their seniors in a mad dash for the top.

But come down the ladders must. The gee-whizz companies of America's electronic belts have led the way in flattening hierarchies and replacing command-and-control systems with self-managed teamwork – impelled not only by the necessities of their high-tech trades, but by the eagerness with which employees have motivated themselves right out of the company. From one aspect the spin-offs have acted as a spur to create cultures that can retain free spirits; from another angle, they provide a necessary safety-valve.

Average ages in these companies may well not climb out of the twenties. When the Apple founder, Steve Jobs, was in harness with his president from Pepsi, John Sculley, the latter was a veritable ancient by these standards – and by those of the twenty-nine-year-old Jobs. In 1993, when Sculley, having ousted Jobs, was ousted in turn, both men were still at an age when big company bosses are still only on the threshold of CEO status. Sculley, as the Old Man of Apple, was no doubt right in claiming that 'There's incredible interest by young people in Apple ... What we're finding is that we can take young people out of university, train them and put them in positions of great responsibility much earlier than was ever thought possible.'

That's hardly the most novel insight to come out of Silicon Valley. But what happens to the college kids when they grow up to Sculley's age? If a company opts for a board of go-getting high-fliers under forty, what age will the next tier of management be? If that is thirty-five (allowing five years before they high-fly on to the board), the next rung down will be thirty. What does the great and good company do with everybody over forty? Shoot them? And what about the forty-year-old whizzkid directors when they in turn reach the rotten old age of forty-five?

The emerging answer is to substitute horizontal careers for

the vertical – for managers to move from project to project rather than rung to rung. But the big organisations have not yet adjusted to this change in career patterns, even inside high-tech industries. Even after its multi-billion losses, collapses of market share, and handover to top managers recruited from outside, IBM still maintained a massive global hierarchy. The hierarchy needs its medium-fliers and even its earthworms; it needs them so that the relatively few high-fliers can have somebody else to manage.

But there's bound to be a leakage; some of these low-voltage managers will seep through into the highest levels of the company. Arrived at the top, panting and unprepared, they seek more motivation for the company, when they really need it for themselves – and the managers who have to ask for motivation are not the most suitable cases for treatment. Every force in the organisation presses them into the conservative mould that their own temperament prefers. This long-service, low-volatility element dominates most large corporations, and rarely with wonderful results.

At General Motors, the chairman and president of 1983, Roger Smith and James McDonald, had soldiered on for nearly eight decades of service between them. Their Praetorian guard of vice-presidents were similarly distinguished by their long years of loyal service: to be precise, 32.6 average years per Praetorian. Not surprisingly, Smith presided over a deterioration in corporate effectiveness only exceeded by IBM. When he retired, the board turned to an equally long-in-the-tooth veteran, Robert C. Stempel. The only unpredictable outcome was the poor man's ouster as the crisis manufactured by Smith utterly defeated his successor.

In this pattern of organisation, mere survival and the submerging of personal ambition into the corporate ethos set up the motivational norms. Managers such as GM's at least have their public exposure and awesome responsibilities to stimulate them. But how does anybody motivate the equally long-toothed managers who lie secure lower down in the corporate bosom? As the behavioural scientists have said, money alone won't do it, partly because these people earn too much, too easily, anyway. But nothing else will ever change them into human dynamos; dynamism isn't in their character, or in the corporation's prescription for their behaviour.

If someone is uninterested in money, he can't be made to be interested. If he is unambitious, he can't have ambition thrust upon him. The unsurprising corollary is that, the more highly motivated managers are, the easier they are to motivate. If they love money, they will try twice as hard to get twice as much. One danger of the motivational movement, however, is that the cardinal motivating importance of loot can get mislaid. James Thurber tells how Harold Ross, his great editor at the *New Yorker*, tried in vain to hire the old *Herald Tribune*'s star writer. Finally a new managing editor snagged the prize by offering the man three times his *Tribune* salary. 'You're a genius,' said Ross, 'I never thought of offering him money.'

Every man may not have his price. But corporations customarily pay the price irrespective of what, in performance terms, they are buying. If an executive is paid adequately for being adequate and loses nothing by being inadequate, money has very little chance to show its power. Don't think that material bribery will get you nowhere. Rather, unless the bribery is skilfully calculated, or the bribee (like some computer salesmen) is highly bribable, it won't get you far enough.

Herzberg ('I am an achievement bug. I think the most rewarding thing is achievement') distinguishes between the environmental 'hygiene factors' – a curious phrase, which suggests brushing the managerial teeth – such as pay, and other factors to do with the content of the job itself. The latter, according to Herzberg, are the motivators: achievement, responsibility, recognition, advancement, the nature of the work. But what if the manager's idea of achievement is to earn $200,000 a year by the age of forty? What if the recognition sought is a fat pay increase, a lavish stock option, or a more profoundly carpeted office? One manager's hygiene is another manager's motivation.

The motivation prophets also preach, 'You don't hire a thumb, you hire the whole man.' But you can't activate one motivating factor, you hire the whole lot. You can only motivate the entire man, which means the whole complex of his personal drives. Equally, you cannot motivate a manager beyond the potential of the organisation. Put rapacious, ruthless egotists into the typical large company – the kind of people who become millionaires by thirty – and the organisation will squeeze them out before they are twenty-eight.

The key to motivation is not only the manager, but the company. Place executives in a well-found company with whose objectives and style they can identify, and whose growth and drive create personal opportunities and challenge, and where the executive feels secure, appreciated, properly rewarded, and constantly under fair test: there you have the conditions for marvellous motivation.

That description was once thought to fit a company which also used to be a byword for conformity: IBM. In the early 1980s it briefly and partially showed that neither size, nor market dominance, nor strong cultural norms, needed to be an obstacle to creative management. In other words, the characteristics which give a corporation the stability which the organisation man craves can also give it the foundations for discontinuous initiatives. The saga of how IBM stormed Apple's personal computer market, starting from scratch, by setting up an organisationally independent group with authority to override all the preconceptions of the tight IBM world, is still a chapter in the history of great business achievement.

Tragically, IBM never absorbed the lessons of its own creation. Instead, it absorbed the PC business into the system and stamped out much of its vitality. The tale of the electronic typewriter is equally enlightening. Missing the early years of personal computers was wrong, but understandable. Making a mess of electronic typewriters was bad and inexcusable; that's exactly what IBM did in 1978, losing the electric customers on whom it had a stranglehold to electronics, primarily from the Japanese.

Responding with its typical time-lag, six years later, IBM started churning out competitive machines from a $350 million automated plant capable of 4,000 units a day. It was hailed as certain to crack what had become a key market. It was just an expensive finger stuck into the dyke. Eventually the typewriter business, once the leading force in the industry, became the first IBM business to be sold off, the first overt admission of failure. The lifetime employment policy which was thought to underlie a wonderful degree of motivation proved to contribute to stagnation and complacency across the board, and in their wake the lifetime promise and IBM's famous high morale died too.

It wasn't the lifetime employment of an IBM manager which motivated him at the corporate zenith. The security, the corporate ethos and the excellent conditions of employment were combined with rotation around demanding jobs under an all-embracing corporate strategy. That produced an outfit in which the individuals either assimilated their own ambitions with those of the organisation, or left. So long as IBM's financial results were excellent, this system seemed equally good. But in the 1990s the organisation man has lost his foothold; the structure must be one that gives individual men and women their freedom, not their orders.

The number of corporations fitting this description is small, partly because the organisation needs two pairs of elements that are in continuous conflict: security and appreciation in one corner, contradicted by challenge and testing in the other. Top managements incline to concentrate on providing the first couplet rather than the second; they have their own security and comfort at heart, and they hate the psychological traumas of demanding good performance.

The typical executive, myths to the contrary, hates firing, doing it rarely, and usually after long and pointless delay. Few can face the terminal interview, even though most candidates for firing know they deserve it, feel guilty in consequence, and can only have their guilt expiated (to their enormous relief) by being fired. If companies don't fire when firing is essential, they do injustice to their other employees. They also lose a motivator which traditionally has been almost as powerful as money: the stick, as opposed to the carrot.

The stick has fallen behind the carrot for both practical

and theoretical reasons. Caning sits uneasily with the ideas about humane and collaborative treatment most popularly expressed by Douglas McGregor's Theory Y, which holds that work is as natural as play. Theory X fans, who reckon that man only works when forced, face certain difficulties. Apart from firing, a company has very few canes in the cupboard. Cutting a man's pay or demoting him is tantamount to firing; he may quit, and he is unlikely to be an effective servant of the great company after the act. The corporation is like a dictator who has only one legal penalty to control the rabble – sudden death; the difference being that most dictators are less namby-pamby than directors when it comes to capital punishment.

Hire-and-fire companies, in contrast, are run by neo-Nazis, not by namby-pambies; and their malevolent dictatorship usually has to be balanced by high pay. Too much benevolence and too little money are the worst motivational combination; but malevolence and too much money can work wonders. One company boss thus surrounded himself with well-paid weaklings who periodically had to be fired for their weakness. Over a long-drawn-out dismissal, the boss would sadistically strip the victim of his last vestiges of self-respect. Rebuking a man violently and cruelly in front of others never fails to demolish the current target and soften up later candidates.

Finally, the victim would yearn for dismissal as a condemned man longs for the scaffold. The irony for humanitarians is that investors in this company multiplied their fortunes tenfold over a single decade. As a rule, and for a time, hire-and-fire companies have disagreeably good growth and profit records. At first sight, this seems to prove that the stick can motivate more magically than the carrot; and it is true that, used alternately, the two produce a positively Pavlovian response to stimulus. The chief demon of one growth company, for instance, found one technique highly effective. He would wait at some highly paid subordinate's desk and go through the latter's papers; the sight of the dreaded boss metaphorically laying bare the executive's soul was correctly calculated to produce a quivering, malleable subordinate.

Motivational expert Saul Gellerman once called the carrot and the stick 'the oldest management theory in existence', adding ruefully that 'the rationale of the carrot and the stick is not altogether unrealistic ... some people are motivated by the lure of wealth or the fear of being fired all of the time and all people probably are so motivated at least some of the time'. But don't conclude from this that the neo-Nazi corporation truly has an advantage. That's the same mistake made by pre-war commentators who ludicrously thought dictatorships were more efficient than democracies, because Mussolini made the trains run on time. (He didn't even do that.)

Hire-and-fire companies grow, not because of their addiction to carrot-and-stick management, but in spite of it. The carrot guarantees that they attract mobile, hungry managers; the stick, however, also produces a large quota of murderees, born victims who lust to be whipped by those to whom they act as yes-men. The sadism of the corporate Führer eventually motivates the better managers to leave, as soon as they can match the pay in some more benevolent climate. And the sadism doesn't generate the growth; that's done by the sheer personal drive. Part of the drive is expressed in the autocrat's despicable personal behaviour, but the two are not inseparable. Both the leader and the company would be better off, if possible, to keep the drive and lose the whip.

The most you can say for carrot and stick is that a good executive heading into this variety of company has the self-confidence to accept risk, welcome insecurity, and be judged on results. The standard corporation operates on a different philosophy: carrot and comfort. The executive who makes it to the top makes it financially and in every other way; executives who miss still have few material complaints – except that, if their last two working decades coincide with a recession or with the now all-too-familiar 'downsizing', he or she could be (maybe gently, but still shatteringly) put out to grass.

Far better, for all concerned, is the carrot-and-carrot company – if you can make it work. The first ardent advocate of the greenfield company, which starts off with no organisational ideas, save belief in having as little organisation as possible, was Robert Townsend. His *Further Up the Organisation* thesis was explicitly 'down with the organisation', utilising the motive power of challenge, managerial independence, profit-sharing financial rewards and plain fun. With those, you could obtain the kind of growth that Wilbert Gore won with Gore-Tex, the rainproof material that breathes (and which, typically, was turned down by Gore's employer, Du Pont).

According to Townsend, Gore's objective was to make his company as little like Du Pont as possible. Without question, this rejection of big-company norms, this turning to what Apple's John Sculley calls 'no-manager management', is of itself a powerful motivational force. Having something to kick against always is, especially if the object deserves kicking: and managers in the mighty corporations have been through a mighty bad time. The wholesale firing of those whose services are no longer required is one harsh example of the disrespect in which middle managers are held.

As Boston management consultant Emmanuel Kay has observed, 'To them this is grim evidence that they are not in a uniquely favoured and protected position just because they are the echelon immediately below the top executives.' Managers who survived with ease the threat of the computer are now anxious that the electronic office will undermine their positions. Some hope that the networking of personal computers and the attendant 'groupware' will enhance managers' individual freedom of action and decision as they operate more and more in self-managed teams; but in most organisations that is hope, not reality.

Back in 1981, that acute observer John Thackray noted that, rather than improving the human interfaces, 'most large corporations today are bent on increasing their organisational scope and anonymity through further mergers, acquisitions and consolidations'. Thirteen years later, the observation is still valid and is strengthened by every passing mega-merger. The high-tech mavericks and their imitators are growing in number, and are bound to seem increasingly attractive. But it isn't their free-and-easy ways which will ultimately call the tune.

The proof of these motivational puddings isn't how well they're cooked, but what they taste like – to the market-place, not the managerial palate. The issue always comes back to the motivation of the firm. How individuals respond to treatment depends above all on the behaviour that is the organisational norm. Where the bland are leading the bland, all the behavioural scientists in the American universities will not improve performance. However, it's important to note that their ideas have obtained impressive results below the managerial line, by allowing workers to plan their own operating schedules or salesmen to organise their own selling.

Under the stimulus of Japanese competition, and in the sporadic lust to imitate elements of Eastern competitors' methods, ideas like Total Quality Management and 'quality of working life' programmes have paraded the surely obvious truth that the more you involve men and women in their work, the better the results of that labour will probably be. The behavioural scientists and the Japanese management experts should try persuading a few more corporations to allow their executives actually to execute. Then the behavioural geniuses will really come into their own – though it shouldn't require a posse of expensive professors to teach chief executives how to suck that particular egg.

20
Centres of No Profit

The idea of the profit centre, of slicing a business into the optimum number of accountable components, took its time to work through the capitalist system. It didn't start to penetrate the nether regions of Du Pont, the first bastion of American capitalism and of decentralisation, until the start of the 1970s. Few large companies have since missed the trend; but many missed the message entirely. In the most benighted cases, the profit centres didn't make any profits, and they weren't centres. The device satisfied a great managerial yearning to imagine that every cell of the corporate body is a business like one's own. It often accomplished little else.

The basic idea behind the profit centre and its development, 'the strategic business unit', was to provide a cure for corporate flatulence, a medicine to revive the flow of entrepreneurial blood in stiffening arteries, a means of ideal progression for executives – earning their spurs in their very first little unit, moving on from lesser to greater until they arrive at that big profit centre in the sky, the chief executive's suite. This ideal hankers back to the golden past when the business was small enough for one man to run, and the founder in his buggy could supervise his first clutch of salesmen from the end of road. The business unit, with its one man and his show, is a spiritual snub to corporate bureaucracy.

But the unit is no more a manager's own business than a self-drive car belongs to the customer. Like Hertz or Avis, the company leases out a piece of its property; but it retains full possession, and it exacts a heavy toll. The centre can't be run like one's own business because the real owners (not the *de jure* ones, the shareholders, but the *de facto* ones, the managerial Mafia) don't want it run that way, whatever their brags.

The small businessman must answer only to himself, his family, his conscience, his professional advisers, and his tax collector. Nobody makes him submit an annual budget, plus his plans for the next several years, for scrutiny and approval. Nobody tells him how much he can take out of the business or put in. Nobody vetoes his bright new ideas or his choice of staff or his business proposals. But the powers kept by top management include all this – and more.

In any event, the profit centre can be so arbitrary a creation that it isn't a business at all. In chemical companies this little fact is at its nastiest. Much of the work in these groups is for a sole customer – the company itself. Profit Centre A sells all its output to Profit Centre B, which sells all its output to Profit Centre C, which finally offloads the stuff on the public. At this stage, the company at last makes a profit.

The game is played to well-known rules such as, 'Never make anything inside that you can buy cheaper outside.' Philips Lamp of Eindhoven was famous for playing the game more than most, since it had diversified into almost every component under its sun. But what happened if Philips satellite A, buying component X from satellite B, found that Xs are a drug on the outside market and selling for peanuts? Would B give up its Philips business? Not on your life; it cut its internal 'transfer' price down to the outside level, and the shareholder was left with yet another unprofitable chunk of turnover.

Earnings per share at Philips fell by 22% over the 1960s.

Much the same dismal tale of sales growth failing to generate tolerable profit expansion was retold over the 1970s. The next decade, after a promising start, saw the group stumble towards heavy losses – $511.6 million in 1992. Simple arithmetic shows that adding profit margins along a supply chain with twelve profit centres will result in a far higher and less competitive price than simply transferring at cost. It reverses the arithmetic which explains why, if all dozen units make 95% of their deliveries on time, 45% of final deliveries to the customer will be late; multiply 95% by 95% eleven times, and 55% performance is what you get.

The business system must be viewed and treated as a whole, not as separate pieces. Any striking of profits down the line is merely an imaginative hobby, at which corporation executives pass many an idle hour, day and week. What's more, profit centres are normally lumbered with charges for central overheads – basically the costs of the head office – over which they have not an atom of control. So even their accounts bear very little relation to those of an independent company, especially since units A and B may largely depend for their sales growth and investment projects on how those bastards in C make out in the market-place.

The consumer markets witnessed the most contorted attempt to slice up the corporate cornucopia – the concept of the brand executive. The 'business like your own' was a brand, and the lucky manager (normally young) was responsible, in theory, for everything from its packaging and pricing to its advertising and distribution. If the brand was a proud and treasured heirloom, however, the company tied the brand executives to its apron-strings so tightly that they could hardly breathe.

The only brand executives who were allowed real freedom were those with products on which the corporation had given up; and then, if the bright young manager put real management muscle behind the baby, the profit centre came up against the sound barrier – the corporation wouldn't provide any more spending money. It was all earmarked for Daz, or Nescafé, or some other boring product without which the whole corporation would cease to be a centre of profit.

The total profit centre (the corporation) won't genuinely atomise itself, for mechanical and emotional reasons. This hard fact matters most to those who share the ideal of the small business. The theory is that the large business breeds inefficiencies out of its size (true), and that small businesses are therefore more efficient (false). Most small businesses are just as incompetent – that's why they stay small, and why so many go bankrupt, passing over unnoticed and unwept to the other side. Every now and again the true course of events in a small business gets known outside, and the picture can be quite fantastic.

There was one modest-sized, fast-growing company whose boss demanded only one management accounting statistic – weekly turnover. So long as turnover was rising, this happy entrepreneur was tickled pink. After all, he knew his percentage profit, didn't he? He didn't; in any case, the turnover figure was inflated by double-counting whenever (as it largely did) the sales division sold to the hire side. The company duly descended into bankruptcy, turnover figures still bounding upwards, as the result of infantile errors that any competent accountant, if allowed, could have eliminated in an afternoon.

Small firms are always publicised as the backbone of the economy; in Thatcherite Britain the idea of the little entrepreneur became as emotive as that of John Bull himself. But small firms only sway the economy to the extent that they become middle-sized or greater still. They dominate numerically, but in qualitative and quantitative terms the clumsy mammoths are in an invincible lead. Without the giants, the G7 economies would still be stuck at the Greek level of economic progress.

This runs counter to much modern economic philosophy, fervently espoused by the Reaganites in America as well as the Thatcherites. This school of thought was greatly heartened by David Birch of MIT at the start of the 1980s. He opined that most of America's jobs were not created by the giant corporations, but the modest employers: to wit, firms with under 100 employees had generated 82% of the entire mass of new jobs over a seven-year period. This was most remarkable, not to say odd, at a time when total employment in small business seemed unable to budge from 40% of the jobs total.

In fact, the true figure for small-business creation of jobs appears to be around half: a creditable performance, to be sure, but one for which, according to a White House report, 'a fraction of small firms' is responsible. The most conspicuous contribution comes from small firms sponsored by the venture capitalists, who in a good year backed 1,500 different US businesses. But that was a drop in the numerical ocean of all new business formations (10,000 a week). True, the impact of that venture dribble gigantically exceeded its initial scale. Venture capitalist Ben Rosen has calculated that a mere $50 million launched Intel, Apple, Microsoft, Rolm, Genentech and Tandem.

For that sum, among other goodies, the US economy gained the microprocessor, the personal computer, and memory chips (all developed, significantly, in under two years, against the thirty-year gestation period for radar). But those half-dozen companies are highly atypical. Only one of them failed – Rolm, and that might not have happened but for its hamfisted takeover by IBM. Far more typical are the 85% or 90% of small firms which, as John Thackray writes, 'go through long fallow periods when they don't create a single job'.

The record of one small British textile company is representative of the way that little firms merely cling to life like limpets on a rock. After fifty years it was earning less profit and making fewer sales, in real terms; its investment in new plant had ben negligible; what there was had been wasted; and much of the energy of its management had evaporated in internecine disputes that made boardroom politics seem like cosy parlour games.

No big corporation would want any segment of the business managed as a small company really runs; and it is stupid to moon over a non-existent ideal. The profit centre cannot work as a way to make managers think like individual businessmen. It is only another good, vain try at resolving the conflict between the corporation as a decision-making entity (i.e. head office) and the corporation as a business (i.e. the sharp end, the places where the money is made).

As H.G. Lazell, the great marketing man who brought Beecham to the States, once said, 'That's the struggle all the time, the battle between head office and division, the battle for power.' The profit centre is a fiction to give the divisions the idea that they are winning the struggle. But the divisions know the real score; and they resent the millions that (as they think) they shell out for central expertise, control, and direction, which in divisional eyes seem more like expense and interference.

The question about whether head office adds any value, of course, is only answered by its heads, and their answer is a foregone conclusion. The truth, though, emerges with total clarity from a simple question. In 1994, thanks to a stunning three-year surge, Compaq's sales were roughly equal to those of IBM's PC business, though its profits were very much higher. Can you think of any value that IBM's central establishment could conceivably add to Compaq's business if the IBM services, from chief executive Lou Gerstner downwards, were made available for free? Plainly, Compaq wouldn't gain a thing. Nor does the IBM PC company.

The only difference is that IBM's central apparatus, with all its potential for interference and delay, doesn't come free. ICI executives used to jest about the Millbank headquarters in London as 'Millstone House'. The weight around the divisional necks (now removed by the splitting of ICI in twain and departure from Millbank) helps explain why that bifurcation became necessary. An aggressive divisional boss in Unilever says about central charges, 'You have to pay your club subscription . . . but there are few operating skills of our sort sitting in the middle.'

There does, in fact, seem to be an uncanny correlation between the size of the head office and the effectiveness or ineffectiveness of the company. It was a richly symbolic gesture when ICI, under the new chairmanship of the iconoclastic Sir John Harvey-Jones, announced (very prematurely, as it turned out) that it would sell the Millbank building. The message was unmistakable. As Harvey-Jones told *Newsweek*, 'The thing I'm really interested in is how you make large organisations work.' That meant, in practice, not only cutting out still more superfluous employees and unwanted products, but also reducing the board by a third and decentralising the authority to make decisions. Killing the centralisation of Millstone House was essential if ICI itself was to live – and even then the new-found vigour didn't last far beyond the brief reign of Harvey-Jones.

By the same token, Helmut Maucher of Nestlé, another new boss, knew exactly what he was doing, and what it symbolised, when he sold off a pristine building, designed by I.M. Pei, in Purchase, NY. As Maucher, another keen decentraliser of decisions, explained, the old building was 'good for a long time yet'. Maybe somebody had told him that a large company's shares often nosedive when it moves to spanking new offices. The Vickers engineering group, which put up what was then London's most ambitious skyscraper, and saw its shares promptly halve in half a dozen years, is one awful example.

Union Carbide, tragically accident-prone, is another – one year its Park Avenue skyscraper had to stand in suspended animation until earnings picked up again. Both Shell and BP, too, ran into profit constipation and organisational purges after they moved houses; and there is clear managerial logic involved. Overheads always shoot up, because the new building invariably costs much more, and it's temptingly easier to add more central staff, more central departments, and hence still more central costs. So it was a good omen for the Vickers shareholders (and divisional managers) as occupancy of the tower shrank from the original thirteen floors to a mere half-dozen.

Conversely, it was a bad sign for the owners of the British steel industry (the Labour government) when their newly nationalised British Steel Corporation moved next door to Buckingham Palace. The same offices had housed one of the most notorious cost centres in Britain, headquarters of the defunct AEI (its 800 central employees compared with 160 in its purchaser, the three times larger GEC). The UK steel industry promptly lost some £140 million in four and a half years.

257

Even that was a bagatelle compared to the £1 million a day the Corporation was losing later on, at the height (or depth) of its powers. The losses were only stemmed by staging a command performance of the Incredible Shrinking Steel Industry – to which the grandiose headquarters seemed increasingly inappropriate. None of these moves and expenses are undertaken at the request of the profit centres, note. The head office, the cost centre par excellence, imposes its levies whether the divisions like it or not. And the levy is never light.

In modern times only a brilliant giant has pre-tax profit margins of 10%; so incurring £10 million of extra central costs, in effect, cancels out at least £100 million, very possibly £200 million of profitable turnover. It's more than symbolic that BP, having moved from Finsbury Circus to a shiny new skyscraper nearby, moved back to the circus as the pressure on its costs and efficiency mounted. Yet in normal times the onus is never on the head office to prove itself; the onus is always on the divisions, and that onus is to pay on demand.

Executives shouldn't be held to account for expenditure that they can't control. They can never run their bit as if the business were their own, because it isn't. The recipe, however, is to let them run it as if the money were their own. The money isn't theirs either, and don't let them forget it, but it can be made to look that way. Start off by imposing no central charges except for specific services which can be charged for specifically – and which the unit can always challenge. After all, the head office ultimately collects all the loot, anyway, and it can afford to pay its own expenses.

The counter-argument is that excluding the central overheads gives a false view of divisional profitability; but so may the arbitrary allocation of that load around the joint. The most remarkable operation of this kind was at Du Pont in Wilmington. There the theoretically decentralised divisions shared the same monumental offices as the headquarters. Elaborate apportionments of the central costs had to be made continuously, as if the divisions were headquartered in distant places like Nome, Alaska.

The typical big-company principle is that of Robin Hood,

stealing from the rich to give to the poor. Because a division is making a bundle of money, it doesn't mean that it can spend a lot. It follows, of course, that even though a division is making no money at all, it may be authorised to invest like wildfire. In logic, a high earner should cash in on its luck; an unprofitable unit should suffer the pressures of its own misfortunes. The notion of running a business as if the money were your own demands no less.

Running it when it truly is your own brings powerful lessons in reality. Today Saatchi & Saatchi is held up as an example of pride running before a fall, a proof on the grand scale that advertising agencies didn't lose their notorious talent for managerial incompetence during the growth splurge of the 1980s. It's almost forgotten that the two brothers, Charles and Maurice Saatchi, in fourteen years magically multiplied under a million of billings into £2 billion. During their reign as the world's largest agency, they showed what prizes could be won by keeping separate agencies just that way: separate. And for all its turmoil, the Saatchi & Saatchi of 1994 was still a very large and effective advertising business.

In service industries like advertising, the business is typically of recent foundation and founded with the entrepreneur's own limited resources. The own-money philosophy tends to come on hot and strong. What hurts with your own money is not the earning of it but the spending. Profit centres are strictly speaking cost centres, and it's costs that executives should agonise over. But in real life the detailed head-office control is over one kind of spending only – investment. A divisional director must line up, cap in hand, to get permission for a £500,000 extension while, out in the sticks, a factory supervisor is incurring extra current costs of exactly the same amount, without the head office (and maybe the supervisor) even knowing.

That problem is supposed to be dealt with by the budget. But nobody can accurately predict all costs for a year ahead. Targets too are seldom set in cost terms. Managers were rarely assessed on their cost-cutting ability until the advent of Total Quality Management, business process re-engineering and other new names for what is often old wine. Competition, led by the Japanese, has gingered up the sluggishness which for decades retarded value engineering; this expressed exactly the same devastatingly true idea – that no product is ever designed for manufacture in the most economic way possible – which is now common currency under different labels.

Executives are natural spendthrifts with other people's money. One great company chairman excused his company's total lack of control over a trade investment – this 'profit centre' had to be saved from dire losses and bankruptcy – because the pounds involved were only a few million, compared with, say, £450 million for sales of a major division. This was a man who would have been hurt by a personal expenditure of a few hundred. If he had been taught to think of the company's money in the same way as his own, that few million might never have been lost. The relative amounts are irrelevant – it is all money, and other people's too.

When the big corporation director starts to think of millions only as numbers, the termites are in. The head office's prime duty is to remind executives that money is real, which naturally means that the head office must take the same unpalatable view. In fact, directors do customarily treat the corporation's money as if it were their own – but not in the proper sense. They spend as if in recent receipt of a rich uncle's legacy.

Few firms reach the opulence of one British company that kept three kitchens for the directors, each offering a different national cuisine; owned a grouse moor; provided two houses for the chairman; and hired private trains for the board's annual pilgrimage to its Midlands factories. But few companies follow the austere standards of one chief executive who bars all fringe benefits and all padding of expense accounts, even with tiny sums. (He somewhat spoils the picture by refusing to work for a company that won't provide a decent car – meaning Rolls-Royces all round.)

How the director in the profit, cost, or loss centre down the line behaves is a function of how the executives at the top behave and of what they expect from others. They should start from a known truth: that head office is an unnecessary evil unless proved otherwise. They should confine headquarters functions to those central areas that are central by definition (patents, law, finance, and the like). The executive directors, kept as small a band as possible, shouldn't attempt to duplicate in any way the operating functions in the divisions. They shouldn't spend their time second- or third-guessing the operating directors to no good effect, or waste money providing services that the divisions either don't need or can perfectly well, and much more cheaply, supply or buy for themselves.

And the head office shouldn't become a luxurious, no-subscription club for the chosen few; nor should expense accounts be high-class pocket-money. Nor should the inhabitants pretend that central expenses are low because only a few people work in the West End pad or Manhattan glass mansion. Many a company has a tight headquarters only because all the central staff are stacked up around the main factory site. But that is where staff should be wherever possible – not in the company's Taj Mahal, but close to where it's all happening, close to the factory, or to the market, or to both.

A head office can be every bit as bureaucratic at the plant, of course, as in White Plains, Westminster, or New York City; and the bigger the plant, the better (or worse) the chances of bureaucracy building up. Wilbert Gore, the Gore-Tex inventor, is only one of many people who hold strongly, convinced in part by experience, that when it comes to plant size, small is very, very beautiful. As soon as Gore found he had 180 persons working at his first plant, he started another factory, and another, and another – and none of today's Gore plants has more than a couple of hundred people, all highly motivated and allegedly all having fun, just as Robert Townsend, the prophet of small virtues, would hope.

But it's not only smallness that helps give a real sense of ownership: it's ownership. Townsend argues that any executive worth his salt should march into the owners of the business (pretty difficult if it's ICI or BP, but never mind) and demand that 15% of the profit be set aside forever, for distribution to the employees. What if the owners say 'No'? You politely shake hands, say goodbye – and move to some other company which has the sense to realise that 85% of a fortune is worth vastly more than 100% of nothing very much.

Indeed, companies with a brilliant record of motivational management do tend to share the spoils – or to insist that they are shared. At one literally high-flying company, each employee had to buy company stock as a condition of employment. This insistence went with an organisation to match. 'Everybody has manager status in a flat structure,' according to *Management Today*: 'Employees work in small teams which set their own goals and are self-managing within the company's objectives.' That's the new management at its best. There's only one problem – the company concerned was People Express, the cut-price airline which cut its own throat.

There are multitudinous cases of failure despite employee shareholding, and there will be plenty more of new-fangled management ending in old-fashioned disaster. Share ownership isn't the only form of possession that counts – not by a long chalk. Owning the job is at least as important. The sense of job ownership is concrete and a real force for managerial good. It's facilitated, too, by going beyond the profit centre, breaking down corporations into small, discrete units, capable of making both managerial and economic sense. That's the prevailing mode among managements which think about their managing – but there are essential consequences for head office.

In this recipe, head office functions as banker (you can't leave cash lying around all over the corporation) and almost as an independent investment trust, whose business is owning operations, taking in dividends, and reinvesting the money. But this banker has the unique advantage of being able to demand performance from the executives running its investment. If the profit-centre concept is to mean anything, this is the only role reserved to the head office.

By minding their own business, the management Mafia would in truth be able to run the company as if it were their own. But they want passionately and insistently to manage, and to manage the wrong things. Consequently, the executives under their authority feel that nothing is their own – and they manage just as you would expect.

21
Merchandising the Future

One electronics tycoon, famed as an emperor of automation, hated to be told that he made and marketed hardware. He would retort with heat, 'I'm selling the future.' His firm later became more and more unprofitable until it was sold (at too high a price) to an even larger and equally troubled seller of futures, which duly disappeared in exactly the same way. Those who sell the future, like those who buy it, face a heavy risk of being sold a pup. No law, economic or moral, holds that all technological advance must provide rewards.

The larger the leap, the greater the chance that the company will end in the most uncomfortable, exposed, and expensive posture of all: sitting well ahead of the market. The post-war history of the aircraft industry should disabuse executives who believe that if you look after the future, the future will look after you. The jet engine saw action in the last war. Large pure-jet bombers were flying in the late 1940s, but Boeing's 707, itself a development of a military tanker, made its first flight in 1954. To win orders, Boeing felt it had to price the plane to the bone.

When the wide-fuselage jumbo (embodying even fewer path-finding technological advances) flew along, this difficulty was repeated with much the same financial results. You could argue that Boeing's biggest stroke of luck came when Washington denied funds for the next great leap forward in technology – the Supersonic Transport. That left the world market wide open for Britain and France, who proceeded to scoop the pool: all of sixteen aircraft, built and subsequently flown at losses horrendous even by aerospace standards.

The industry's troubles stem partly from the conviction of its managements that, like Everest, the next technical peak must be scaled, because it is there. Aerospace managers love their technology even more than their money. That being so, nobody (including their financial backers) should be surprised when technological effort ends in financial failure. What's more, disaster strikes even though the companies are largely spared the bugbear expense of research and development. Fantastic largesse has been invested in this group of businesses by governments, especially in the US, all because of their importance to national defence and technical prestige.

Europeans commonly cite the American figures as the most unfair disadvantage under which European competitors labour; their complaints have, however, carried considerably less force since their own governments poured billions into the Airbus project to provide a fully competitive, but heavily subsidised rival to Boeing. In fact, the so-called spin-off from military work is small both in absolute terms and in relation to the total US federal spending on research. The military is a highly specialised customer; and, in any case, executives rarely prove competent at transferring technology from one market to another, even within the same company.

The men making missiles and space shuttles are not interested in machine tools or refrigerators, even if the advanced technology is cheap enough to be of any use (which it isn't). Rockwell, big maker of automotive components, had the hilarious notion when it bought North American that the latter's aerospace know-how would help Rockwell itself. Al Rockwell later sadly admitted, 'We did over-anticipate that there were some products at North American that we could tool up and take off the shelf and manufacture.' British Aerospace offered (and may even have believed) the same delusion when it purchased the Rover Group car business.

The most advanced technology is often worse than expensive – it may not even work. Take the record of electronics in weapons systems supplied to the Pentagon; six out of eleven major systems begun during one ten-year spell achieved 25% or less than specification and only two came up to snuff, which does not inspire faith in applying defence goodies to mass-produced goods. The spin-off from civilian industry into military technology is probably much greater than the reverse spin; for instance, all the Du Pont products in the Apollo programme had originally been developed for down-to-earth sale. The Japanese, moreover, have swept to the front in industry after industry without benefit of defence bonanzas.

True, a few industries (data processing and electronic components, for main examples) have been utterly transformed by advanced technological developments which found their first applications in military uses. But none of the crucial breakthroughs that have changed the world – the personal computer and networking, just for a start – offer any evidence, so far, that the rich economic prizes go hand-in-hand with technological pre-eminence alone. On the contrary (but perfectly logically), the greater the leap forward, technologically speaking, the greater the risk.

This isn't only a fact of microelectronics. Look at any industry, and you will find at least one example of ambition overreaching itself. Thus Dow Chemical constructed an ethylene plant in the Gulf of Mexico, based on the brilliant idea of using crude oil direct, without the intervention and cost of an oil refinery. For all anybody knows, the process was a brilliant success; but the plant never operated (resulting in a loss to the company of half a billion dollars), not because of technological defect, but because Dow couldn't get a big enough supply of the requisite crude at the requisite price. Aim for the moon, in other words, and you may hit the ground.

West Germany's record in high technology is about as

inspiring as its low performance in management education. Yet until the oil-price shocks it had the world's second most successful economy, the most brilliant being a Japanese economy led originally, not by space-age whizz-products, but by super-tankers (which are nothing but floating boxes), motorbikes, cameras, portable radios, hi-fis and cars. And how about hovercraft, carbon fibres, metal oxide semi-conductors, fluidics, and glass transistors? All of these are technological marvels of the 1960s on which, well into the 1970s, any investor would have lost most of his shirt. Only in the 1990s are one or two of these technologies coming into their expected glory.

None of this will stop a director from bragging about his R & D spending, as if the money itself promoted something beyond the continued employment and well-being of scientists. The latter's controllers are sure that R & D is intrinsically good and absolutely essential; yet its results in big companies are generally disappointing. Rather than conclude that there is something wrong with the management of the whole company, directors decide that the fault lies with the specific management of R & D. Consequently, quantities of intellect and trouble have gone into attempts to make this activity live up to its billing as a fountain of profit.

The least productive of these pastimes is 'brainstorming', in which the participants are encouraged to throw in every idea in their heads, however irrelevant; and that's what you get – irrelevant ideas. The most intellectual game is known as technological forecasting. The object is to show companies where, given the likely developments, they should concentrate their own efforts. The names of the technological forecasting techniques (Delphi, morphological research, relevance trees, and the like) are a poem in themselves; their weakness is that, by the time the forecasts are proved right or wrong, it's too late. If you back a wrong horse (for instance, if you happened, like the manufacturer of the Stanley automobile, to choose the steam-engine in preference to internal combustion), excellent R & D will inevitably go to waste.

Technological forecasting won't solve the problem that

makes R & D genuinely baffling to the directors: that its results are so hard to predict and to measure that its paymasters cannot quantify what they want. This vagueness has its charms – the executive can (and usually does) merely avoid making any sensible calculations at all. Investors have the same entranced rapture in face of the future. The case of Viatron can stand as their monument. The hot-technology idea was to apply MOS (metal oxide semi-conductors) to LSIC (large-scale integrated circuits).

Investors who couldn't tell an MOS from an MTB, or an LSIC from LSD, rushed to buy the stock on issue – even though the prospectus said candidly (as US law insists) that the management had no reason whatsoever to suppose that it could make anything but a shambles of the business, which it duly did. Under the banner, 'Never before have mass production methods been applied to the computer industry', Viatron offered to lease its System 21 wonder-terminals for $39 a month. This low, low price, in a typical hot-technology gambit, was not justified by economics, but by the necessity to get high orders, without which the price of the MOS magic could not be lowered from sky-high levels.

The inevitable end was a collapse all along the management line, a switch to selling the terminals at much higher prices and a bankruptcy that stranded all the stockholders high and dry – and nobody could say they didn't deserve it. The moral of such cases (so numerous that by the early 1990s venture capitalists had virtually bowed out of high-tech investments) is that greed is no substitute for intelligence. The company's own statements made it clear that Viatron was a monstrous gamble, which in any context save that of high technology and buying the future would have been shunned like Central Park by night.

The Viatron backers, like countless others since, got mugged. Any attempt at purchasing the future can be reduced to figures, and all that most high-tech start-ups offer is a prospect of sustained losses well into that future. Against this known chasm, their managements and supporters (above all the stock-market claque which profits from the share sales) set the prospect of entirely unquantified Microsoft or Intel-style gains – if, that is, the technology, marketing, general management, and following wind are all set fair. That's like jumping out of an aircraft without a parachute.

But sums fly out of the window when the future comes in the door. At a more prosaic level of technology, and of market appeal, the Nimslo camera succeeded in uncovering a whole lake of naive eagerness. What the *Financial Times* labelled as among the ten greatest technological flops of all time ran through enormous sums of money: $43 million of losses in just two years, on top of $38 million of capital supplied by investors. They might have been able to read balance sheets, but couldn't apparently understand simple facts: like Nimslo's need to capture a market share, ridiculously high by Polaroid standards, with a 3-D product that plainly had less appeal.

The market sums just didn't add up. But to those intent on the hope of emulating Polaroid without a Polaroid, sums are unimportant. Even in the death-throes of the Nimslo apparatus as a consumer product, the latest management was cutting the price while lowering production to fit a financially crippling shortfall in demand. To innocents in these matters, the more reasonable course of action might have seemed to be (a) a price-cut accompanied by higher or unchanged output, or (b) a price increase linked with lower production. But when you look at life through three-dimensional spectacles, the results are different. The logical alternatives didn't apply, because the product itself was illogical: i.e. there was no advantage in 3-D photography that would attract more than an insufficient minority of the public. The backers made the fatal mistake of being seduced, not by the market potential, but by the technological promise.

A few lessons should be engraved on the hearts of all futurologists, high and low. In estimating costs, work out an honest number and then double it. Nor is the future priceless; there is always a point where the price becomes too high. Whether the cost lies in R & D or in operating losses in a new business, the question is always the same. How much can current earnings be sacrificed for future benefit? In this context the only sensible (and often only too accurate) way is to treat R & D as pure loss. The minute a company starts to kid itself that scientists' wages are an asset, it is writing its doom on the wall.

How much a company shells out depends on the dynamics of the industry and the quality of its R & D staff (a quality that non-technical managers, being ill-equipped to judge, are prone to exaggerate). Given that R & D is always to some extent a game of chance, it is dangerous to spend less than the other players; you may as well have the same number of throws. The R & D write-off can also be regarded simply as a firm's subscription to the industry club, as the licence fee that entitles it to stay in business – provided, that is, that the same logic and intensity are applied to its management as should run throughout the whole company.

Whatever the firm spends, executives must do the kind of back-of-an-envelope sums that far too many managements either fail to scribble down or else ignore. It's no use putting big money into a transistorised combination electric toaster, tea-maker, and radio clock; the likely demand for such a toy will never generate the needed earnings. (Britain's General Electric Company, no mean technological cornucopia in most of its activities, actually did once produce a combination portable radio and camera, which is just as weird.)

If a company is going to lose £10 million this year – or spend it on R & D – the financial pain is only worth incurring for a sure extra £2.5 million profit after a five-year wait. 'Anyone who enters the Continental computer market must be prepared to stand a loss operation for five years,' said a Honeywell man sagely. He didn't add (because he didn't know) that the five lean years would not be followed by the five fat ones that would have made the losses worthwhile. Obviously the longer the wait, the larger the return has to be. Any executive who lets money drain away today without knowing which tomorrow will bring the pay-off, or even what size that bonanza will be, is leaping into the dark with somebody else's cash.

Expensive research work can be sorted out by a simple question: 'If it succeeds, what is the maximum potential financial benefit?' Once the spending has passed the point at which the return is worth having, the answer is equally simple – halt. A new and potent danger sign pops up at this point: the just-around-the-corner complex. Just as prosperity was always around that next bend during the Great Depression, managers persist in believing that the loss-making business, the failed new venture, the great R & D programme, is going to pay off – any moment now.

The complex has a sub-syndrome: 'We've spent so much already that it would be silly not to go on.' If £100 million has vanished without trace into a project, and 'only' £10 million more will bring the breakthrough to a £5 million return, the investment seems marvellous: only £10 million for a £5 million annual pay-off! Gosh! But the return on the total outlay is still hopelessly inadequate. Even supposing that the latest forecast turns out to be right (and it won't), simple payback will take twenty-two years. The result is a permanent drag on the business; or, when the same argument gets applied to some prestige aerospace venture such as Concorde, a heavy permanent tax on the national economy.

The Beecham group learned how not to research, and how to, in the most telling way, which is the hard one. Its former chairman, H.G. Lazell, believed in the goodness of research. For years he defended and sustained Beecham's research effort single-handedly, with no valuable results at all. Then Lazell saw his error. Nobody had decided what Beecham wanted from research; therefore, the company could neither concentrate its efforts nor define them. A chastened Lazell chose to concentrate on one of the lush pharmaceutical markets; taking expert adviser Ernst Chain's expert advice (another rare virtue), he put all Beecham's research money on fermentation chemistry, and came up with a well-bred, wealthy family of synthetic penicillins.

Beecham could still have failed. Its research was still undiluted risk; rumour says that a rival penicillin fan was only narrowly beaten to the tape. But Beecham knew that it could easily survive the loss if the project failed. Just as important the reward, if success came, was certain to return the R & D investment many times over. That is much more intelligent than spending money you haven't got to achieve an objective that is either not worth reaching or impossible to attain.

The Ninth Truth of Management is: if you are attempting the really impossible, you are bound to fail. Worse than that, you will fail abjectly, because the Eighth Truth – as shown in the deeply sorrowful saga of Digital Equipment and the personal computer – also operates its malevolent magic. Because what you are doing is wrong, it will be done badly. DEC brilliantly attacked the scientific and engineering markets with its mini-computers; with its VAX line, one of the largest risk investments in the history of R & D, it had stolen a huge march on IBM in business computing with machines that could work together across any distance. Yet its attempted strategy in the new PC market failed abysmally.

The market consisted of new customers who could only be reached by massive advertising – and could only be convinced by technological novelty and prowess. Setting off in the wrong direction, DEC was too late, too lumbering, too constipated. In consequence, it won no significant position in personal computers or work-stations. It thus had little protection when the market for minis began to weaken under the pressure of much cheaper and increasingly powerful PCs. By the 1990s the company was in an even weaker position than the gravely beset company, IBM, which DEC romantics once hoped to excel.

The implausible, if not the impossible, can be achieved. Sometimes the process is romantic, random, unplanned. No big corporation, being prosaic, routinised and formal, could have contrived, say, the extraordinary encounter of two Hungarians and a German. They created Syntex and the whole birth-control pill business by processing progesterone from the barbasco root, a yam grown wild in the Mexican jungle (into which the shy German later retreated as a recluse). The Japanese, however, have proved, in cases ranging from copiers to memory chips, that implausible breakthroughs can be achieved – if, that is, the competition is fast asleep.

The pursuit of the impossible explains the long, lugubrious record of airline manufacturers outside the US. The back of an envelope used to say that projects could only coin money at a production rate of eight a month, with the break-even somewhere around 300 copies. (This was the calculation which proved to the satisfaction of everybody, except Lockheed's executives, that their beloved Tristar was a financial flying bomb.) Because no outside manufacturer, given the predilection of US airlines for buying American, had any hope in this world of that kind of order, all their projects were doomed to economic failure, either relative or (mostly) absolute.

The equation held good right up to the end of the 1970s. Even then, the US sales of the European Airbus didn't disprove the point. The mould-cracking Pan Am order came about, in part, only because so many 'white-tails' had been built with the citizens' tax money: planes for which there were no visible customers. That situation only arose, not because anybody seriously believed the Airbus consortium would make serious money, but because the governments involved couldn't bear to stay out of airline technology.

Whether this was justified by national economic needs is very doubtful. But in several industries in the 1990s the need to stay in the most advanced, sophisticated, versatile, and technically interesting product areas has become unavoidable. Even an electronics giant like Matsushita, which for decades followed the technique of letting its rivals make the costly breakthroughs, and then surpassing them with its lower cost production, has been forced into the vanguard. Lag for six months, and you may be behind forever. Once, foolproof, rugged, purpose-built and technically boring products would sell in huge volume on those humdrum qualities alone: no longer.

The electronics industry above all has shattered the mould of both producer and customer expectations. When IBM, Apple and Motorola pooled their resources to create a new technology rival to Intel's dominant microprocessor family, nobody doubted that the new chip would work. The question-mark hung only over its market-place potential. Not a day passes without American hardware and software manufacturers spawning new products which all work perfectly well, and which in some respect or other advance the state of the art.

This particular industry wonderfully suits the real strength in US technology, which always lay more in improving established commercial products, processes and production techniques than in genius in the labs. Post-war Europeans were always wise to whip across the Atlantic to see what new productive wizardry the Americans had wrought. Great fortunes were built in this elementary way in the days when the US ruled the production roost. Now it's often the Americans who travel hopefully abroad in search of the technological advances made by others – for instance, almost every post-war innovation in steel production.

The ultimate blessing of technology, though, is that you can buy what you cannot invent. So do it. The Japanese have developed this to so fine an art that they have long been licensing back to America products and processes originally bought from the United States. One of the little ways in which Western competitors love to deceive themselves, however, lies in arguing that the Japanese are not creative technologically. Any camera enthusiast knows that this is nonsense; so does anybody who has operated a personal copier, or donned the earphones of a Walkman, or switched on a video recorder.

Japanese manufacturers have an incurable itch for invention – they often insist on building their own production machinery; and it's their makers of robots and other advanced automation equipment, not the Americans or the West Germans, who have the numerical lead in world markets. The prime characteristic of Japanese innovation, though, is that it is genuinely market-led. The Japanese are less interested in the technology than in whether they can sell it.

Steel's basic oxygen furnace is a wondrous illustration of today's real technology race – invented in Austria, applied widely in Germany, taken up late by the Americans, perfected by the Japanese, and adopted last by the British. Today the virtue in coming first – like Intel with the microprocessor – is pre-eminent. Like everything in management, of course,

273

the virtue depends on the price; but coming even a very good second will seldom now be better, richer and safer. True, Glaxo was later into the anti-ulcer field with the only marginally superior Zantac; but it outmarketed Tagamet so effectively that it was the latter which had to accept second place.

The technologists will love having to try for firsts. But they will also oppose any new idea that didn't spring from their own brains. Don't let them get away with that idiocy. Technical experts are always wrong until they prove themselves to be right; and it's the layman, not the scientist, who is most likely to spot a market opportunity or sweep aside some technological road-block put up by well-educated blockheads – like one executive who made his name by rightly refusing to believe that drop-forging couldn't be made continuous.

You're not after a Nobel Prize, but an innovation that is useful and thus commercial. The zip-fastener has made far more money than the vast majority of high-flying products of high-spending labs all over the world. Bear in mind that, leaving out oil, inheritance, real estate, and other accidents of nature, the greatest fortunes in America have lately been made in investment (Warren Buffett), discount stores (Sam Walton and WalMart), computer facilities (Ross Perot and EDS) and PC operating systems (Bill Gates and Microsoft). Even the two that are technology-based are far removed from the higher technological risks. Which, of course, is why the fortunes were made.

22
The Conglomerate Capers

The shocks and shake-ups of the last two decades have had
several salutary effects on management – not least the death
or diminution of the myth that managers could be experts in
nothing but management itself. Today wise executives go no
further than calling themselves 'professional'; meaning that
they are paid to apply professional aptitudes and attitudes to
performing a management task. Their professional background may encourage transfer from cola to computers –
and John Sculley's move in leaving Pepsi for Apple proved
that success can follow.

But there's a world of difference between such transfers,
the bread-and-butter of the executive headhunters, and the
old conglomerate claim that it doesn't matter at all whether
the product is pop or personal computers. Part of your true
professional's equipment is the knowledge that different
businesses require different types, styles and techniques of
management, that only the rare (and maybe unborn) genius
can manage whatever is demanded with equal success by
applying expertise in the wizard's real business, which is
management *per se*.

That gave an irresistible selling pitch to the conglomerates. Since management does not exist, however, neither did

the conglomerates, not in the sense in which they sold themselves to a fond public. Even the conglomerate-makers seem to have suspected their image; at least, some affronted aces in this hole did their best to escape the name. They coined futile phrases such as 'multi-market company', though conglomeration described their activities rather well. All conglomerates, the respectable and disreputable alike, use financial techniques to pile together unconnected businesses. They manage the results in the way of all holding companies since their time began (which was long ago).

The purchases are shoved into common accounting and reporting systems and generally left to paddle their own canoes, leaky or buoyant, subject to varying degrees and forms of helpful and unhelpful head-office intervention. The basic financial techniques of conglomerate accounting are no more a business innovation than the management method. Financiers have been able to work out simple sums for a long time, and few sums are simpler than the one by which $10 million Company A, earning $10 million a year and valued in the market at $200 million, buys $10 million Company B, earning $10 million, but valued only at $100 million, and so neatly boosts its own earnings per share from $1 to $1.33.

This performance should not have fooled the management professors. But very few foresaw, as Peter Drucker did, that the red-hot conglomerates would in time become corporate hulks. By 1994, ITT, the biggest of them all, had lost most of its industrial interests, and had presented its shareholders with a miserable 5% annual increase in earnings per share over the previous decade. At least that was better than Litton, which also recorded 5% – but that was a *negative* figure. Others, like SCM and Teledyne, have fallen prey to predators themselves.

There are transferable management skills, and there are transferable executives. But it doesn't follow that all management skills transfer, or that one central team can possess all necessary skills, or even that all conglomerates had management skills of any kind, or that all executives can shift easily between all businesses. This fallacy has been cruelly exposed, again and again, in the lust for financial services. It's understandable – almost inevitable – that industrial companies like Xerox and Control Data should burn fingers, even whole arms, by meandering into investment banking, business centres, reinsurance and so forth: about which they knew nothing and for which they paid plenty.

But what about those already in financial services and the like? How could clearing banks blunder hideously by buying investment banks? Or building societies and insurance companies shoot themselves in both feet by purchasing estate agencies? A life-insurance company surely isn't too far removed from property insurance, either; at least, that was the thesis behind the Connecticut Life merger that formed CIGNA, topped up by the investment banking buy of Blyth Eastman Dillon. That deal didn't work out, because (as CIGNA's chairman confessed) 'We had a difficult time integrating Blyth ... there may be some companies that will be successful, though we certainly weren't.'

Undeterred by that experience, or by CIGNA's miserable performance (a 7.4% compound annual loss over the decade to 1994), others have tried and tried to prove the CIGNA man right. American Express doubled its bet with no less than two investment banks, mutual funds and international banking; the cost of this prize package was $3 billion and a great deal of pain. That resulted partly from having no less than eight outfits jostling each other for the money-management business of the institutions. As an Amex man said, mildly enough in the circumstances, 'The risks are that we don't pull it together. The risks are that somewhere the process breaks down, and that we don't benefit from having all these parts.'

That's the same cry that marked the death-throes of the old conglomerates that were in unrelated businesses. 'Two-and-two makes five' synergy and transferable management have proved just as hard to obtain when executives are dealing in the ostensibly homogenous commodity known as money. Not only did Amex lose the wizard who built its recently purchased Geneva bank, it lost so much money on casualty insurance that, for the first time in thirty-five golden years, the Amex parent suffered a decline in earnings (which presaged the eventual fall of its CEO, James Robinson). In Britain, the afflicted buyers ranged from National Westminster Bank and the Prudential to US investment houses. All should have known better than to buy stockbrokers. Similar woes have been won instead of glittering prizes; and yet all the managements concerned were deeply experienced in what is loosely (too loosely, as it turned out) known as 'financial services'.

Given the billions lavished on these buys, this episode of conglomeration has been a hideously expensive proof that companies are only effective at managing in a certain line of business, and that some of their skills are non-transferable, intrinsic and essential to that racket. Because this is so, large corporations are bound to find diversifying less diverting than it seems. But at least diversifying is extraneous to their main activity. For the conglomerates, diversifying was their only business, and in the long run, that's generally a bad business to be in – or so the majority of US experience would suggest.

A couple of *Harvard Business Review* writers, Salter and Weinbold, took a look at the capital productivity of thirty-six widely diversified companies – like Norton Simon, ITT, FMC and Bendix. The diversification strategies that were supposed to raise performance actually brought down their average return on equity between 1967 and 1977. Compared to the *Fortune* 500, the demon diversifiers had made 20% more on equity at the start of the decade (thus obtaining the wherewithal for their diversifying). At the finish, though, their return was 18% less than the 500 average. Over the whole ten years, the dirty three dozen produced returns a fifth or more below those of the 500.

To descend from the general to the particular, diversification proved to be so bad a business for ITT that one year, according to an analyst, nearly all the profits reported by the giant existed only on paper; its assets, estimated *Business Week*, were selling at maybe half their break-up value; the dividend had been cut; and in the wake of that last trauma, a financier was preparing a raid on the wreck. ITT's CEO,

Rand V. Araskog, had cut the dividend to finance the investment badly needed, and shamefully overdue, to restore ITT's strength in its base market, telecommunications. It was too late; ITT had to sell out of telecommunications altogether.

But the entire rationale of conglomeration was to enhance the financial strength of the whole by combining its parts. In ITT's case, the strategy plainly had the reverse effect. Yet ITT is a senior conglomerate citizen, which, like its fellows Litton and Textron, hated being tarred with the same brush as the sharper conglomerate-makers. So did the industrial establishment, which was offended by the sharp practices of the latter, and said so. But just as conglomerate-makers lied in claiming to be a new form of business, so did the established companies who swore they were anything but conglomerates.

All but nineteen of the 200 largest US companies were in at least ten different manufacturing categories as long ago as 1968. At the height of the conglomerate passion, no avowedly multi-market company had such multiple markets as General Electric. And even staid old citizens such as Du Pont saw no reason why they should stick to chemicals; like the conglomerates, and with no more reason, Du Pont thought its skills and resources to be universal. After all, didn't it build the atomic bomb?

Large companies mostly decide to diversify at the moment when their profits from the businesses they really do understand are wilting. New sources of profit are the standard prescription at this juncture. But relative failure in fields you know is no great qualification for success in strange pastures. General Mills was the world's largest flour-miller when it decided, under the stirring leadership of an Air Force general, that milling was a no-good, low-margin business, and that it would shift to emphasis on growth in earnings per share by risk-taking diversification.

After costly purchases of food companies and European businesses as far afield as fashion and toys, General Mills ceased to be the mightiest miller. Its earnings per share in the 1960s rose by precisely 69%. A later generation of management got religion. Instead of whoring after strange flesh, or even after new products, they would concentrate on developing their established brands (age-old items like Jell-O jelly) with all the enthusiasm and money that are generally devoted to the new. The result, in the latest decade, was a 21.8% annual return to investors and, in 1993, a smashing 41.5% return on their equity.

The many failures of diversifiers suggest that the best business is surely the simplest: a firm that markets one product in one market in one way and lives happily ever after. That phrase comes from fairy stories. Real life is different. True, at the start of the 1970s any executive in full possession of his senses would have traded an Avon for a GE any day. Avon's elementally simple idea of door-to-door selling by agents yielded almost one third of GE's profits on one eleventh of GE's sales, with a tiny proportion of GE's anxieties.

Yet, as reported in an earlier chapter, Avon's day was about to be done. As its market worsened and its method became obsolescent, Avon slipped – until on a ninth of GE's sales it was earning only a twelfth of the giant's net. Likewise, Dr An Wang's single-minded concentration on processing words by computer once produced for the Wang company a quarter of ITT's net on a ninth of the sales. But Wang was one of nineteen companies singled out by *Business Week* for strategic failure, and rightly so; the idea ('become the leader in the office-of-the-future market by introducing new products to combine data and word-processing') had misread the rise in personal computers. The results were eventually fatal.

Even a champion one-marketer is bound to get nervous eventually about the golden eggs sitting in that one beautiful basket. It begins to diversify, to stretch its market span, to spread (i.e. to increase) its risks. The more bets you have on a race, the more bets you are likely to lose. True, because the industries are widely spread, if some components are down, others will be up. But executives seldom spot the opposite truth – if some parts of the company are up, it follows inexorably that others will be down. The company is condemning itself to mediocrity, and to more conglomeration; for one diversification (like the first step on the primrose path of sin) leads to another.

Before top management knows where it is, its preoccupation has ceased to be thermostats, or tyres, or computers, but has become the management of diversity. A brilliant Harvard Business School team, primed to the ears with accurate information about UK companies, came to the conclusion that British management's prime failure lay in mismanaging diversity – as if the Americans have proved any better. The confessed conglomerates and the diversified non-conglomerates have discovered alike that management doesn't work in the abstract.

In practice, the many-eggs-in-many-baskets corporation either has to fall back into today's typical rut of unhappy compromises, or to abdicate a management role on classic lines and settle for a banker-investigator-stimulator function. In the 1990s, rather than abdicate, managements have settled for strategies built around their 'core' businesses or, in the most sophisticated cases, 'core competencies'. The echoes of Ted Levitt's famous question of long ago ('What business are we in?') are unmistakable. The core concepts all have the effect of making managements concentrate, selling off some assets, but only to buy others to strengthen their 'critical mass'.

After all this moiling and toiling, they may still be highly diversified businesses. Some effective examples of the genre do exist. Even though most businesses make odd bedfellows, strangeness doesn't rule out a happy sex life. Clothing companies shouldn't even dream of going into food. But after the war, Marks & Spencer, second only to Sears Roebuck as a textile retailer, did so, and with more success than in its basic business. The company had abilities, premises, and policies that fitted both lines, and over time it steadily capitalised on those genuine strengths, not on its mythical talents. Its all-food High Street stores are genuine and wildly successful innovations.

Tobacco companies, in Britain and in America, had reason (à la Levitt) to think that their core competency lay in marketing packaged and branded consumer goods. Rather, they were truly adept at selling cigarettes, a very different commodity from food, being neither necessary nor always competitively priced. At R.J. Reynolds Industries, the transformation from tobacco, and to the new name of RJR Nabisco, could ultimately be achieved only by the wholesale import of executives from the consumer businesses which had tickled the tobacco men's tastebuds; the latter's marketing abilities, it appeared from some damning with faint praise by the imported chieftain, lay mostly in market segmentation.

You can crash in from scratch, as IBM did with electric typewriters and personal computers, and get away with it, but that depends on having a decisively better product and a transferable asset such as IBM's indoctrination of office bosses (and secretaries) with its name. The further out a new line is (Rolls-Royce once even tried making saucepans), the less chance there is of making it succeed (Rolls couldn't even get the thing to stand up). Another giant military contractor started unpromisingly on its dismal peacetime trail in 1919 by investigating the market potential of 'boy rabbits (squeaking)' and 'girl rabbits (non-squeaking)'.

As at the tobacco giants, food has attracted more diversifiers than any other dreamland, on the unsubtle argument that people will always eat. But even in inexhaustible markets a rule of thumb usually applies to all companies in all fields: only the two largest competitors and one specialist make big money. The price of becoming Number Two from scratch, let alone Number One, is so ruinous that often executives run their legs off to budge not one financial inch. If it's a virgin or *demi-vierge* market for the diversifier, he must buy his management experience. The lack of this asset, which can only be acquired over time, ensures a costly initiation.

This might seem to endorse that famous work by the Boston Consulting Group which suggests that the greater the market share, the richer the accumulated experience, and the more profound the ability to extract the highest profitability from a market. So buying a small unit to get your feet wet – or developing one – may not be such a masterstroke after all. Don't rely on something your company doesn't have, transferable management skills, to develop something else it lacks, a worthwhile share of the market. But the purchase of companies with a lovely plump market share comes no cheaper.

One American diversifier has kept its nose reasonably clean by refusing to pay more than fifteen times earnings for any purchase. On that none too demanding criterion (it means a pay-back over seven years, assuming, as you must, no increase in profits because of your own brilliant management), many diversifications by acquisition would never have been made, to the eternal benefit of the shareholders – and even of the executives.

Company executives seldom reflect that nobody forces them to diversify. They can afford to be greedy, to wait for opportunities where the criteria are all satisfied – rate of return, degree of risk, use of real existing strengths. That last criterion almost certainly restricts you to vertical acquisition – buying firms that fit on to existing interests. In a study of mergers by John Kitching, no vertical amalgamation failed, but 42% of the conglomerate mergers went phut. And while executives wait for the right buy, they can concentrate on their central assignment – making the most (just like the General Millers) of existing major markets.

These foundation businesses can be so mismanaged (witness the hash IBM made of data processing) as to undermine the entire corporation. But given reasonable management, such huge core activities make the accidental conglomerate a better bet than the deliberate multi-market, whizzkid creations. The basic, solid sectors, however, bore executives. They want to pioneer new commercial frontiers. They love to quote the progress of new businesses, to boast how acquisitions have blossomed under their gardening – though a one-point drop in margins on the bread-and-butter business would wipe out the profits of every new jam-tart in the group.

This gross disproportion encourages executives to hang on to their errors, in the forlorn hope that some miracle will avert the admission that they have boobed with stockholders' funds. Something about losing money warms an executive's entrails. It proves that he is doing what executives are supposed to do – building for the future. Capitalist mythology holds that all great businesses start by losing money, until the tide turns, the risks pay off, and the risk-taking company or entrepreneur finally get their just glory.

Since most great businesses started small, this must be untrue. Small businesses can't survive years of loss – or couldn't until the mid-twentieth century. The bull market of the 1960s saw the American invention of the perpetually loss-making potential growth star; one hot Wall Street tip was an electronic tape firm that had lost money for fourteen successive years. That's not how the truly great and good product performs. It pays off early and piles up wealth incessantly. Where the pay-off takes years, only a handful, like RCA's colour TV, are genuine gambles against time.

Mostly simple management mistakes spoil a perfect set-up. Just as Boeing underpriced the 707, so did Du Pont originally sell and manufacture Orlon acrylic for the wrong uses. Neat little financial tricks are used to ease the pain of diversification losses. If managers buy companies, they don't calculate the return on the actual capital expended. Standard British bookkeeping practice used helpfully to allow writing off the 'excess over book value' of assets purchased (the difference being laughingly known as goodwill).

If managers start new ventures, they work out returns only on the capital spent – the current losses made before that elusive corner is turned are forgotten as if they had never been. The exception comes when the firm's current profits aren't big enough to bear the strain; then the losses are 'capitalised' as development spending. But these pigeons always come home to roost when the management is finally forced up against the reality that its precious venture is *kaput* – stone-cold dead in the market. Then the only financial recourse available is the write-off or write-down: slicing a chunk off the corporation's assets and throwing in the accumulated operating losses.

If you're really unlucky, that may mean a sum like Texas Instruments' $660 million. It was lost in a home-computer business founded, not on an accurate perception of a market gap which TI could exploit, but on a desire – irrelevant, in market terms – to offload some more of the company's own gigantic output of microcircuits. The company may bravely take the 'hit' in one year, and carry on as if nothing had happened. But the damage will still be there, buried in the balance sheet – and the corpse has a disconcerting habit of rising from the grave when the next calamity comes along.

The secret of conglomerate success (after first confessing that you are conglomerated) is to be far more exacting and sharp financially than that – and to insist that money is paramount. If an operation justifies itself in money terms, you have executives there who clearly know their business. Don't bother them too much so long as they go on proving it. Save top management time for operations on which the group prosperity really swings, and for those that are going wrong. The easiest way of dealing with diversity is to take this easy route, though executives much prefer to have dramas and excitement instead.

The above principles aren't theoretical, but proven in practice. Two British groups have come from out on the touchline to achieve very substantial scale, not least in the US market. Hanson, which has tucked US conglomerates under its belt with great relish, has used exactly this approach to grow the sixty-fifth largest business in the US, with excellent 9.4% sales margins and a respectable 12.1% return on stockholders' equity. Hanson's world-wide performance over the 1980s was outdone by BTR: 29.6% annual growth in earnings per share, inflation-corrected, against 23%. But both figures speak for the same theory.

These groups are diversified with no logic at all, but organised on strictly logical lines to extract the most from the acquisitions that have been the key to their super-growth; their business is buying and managing diversity – and their looming problem is how to sustain the growth when the buying has to stop. By 1994 finding suitable targets had become more difficult for both companies; at £12 billion of market capitalisation, only gigantic purchases could make a sufficiently large impact to equal that of much lesser buys in the past.

The same point must be made of successful diversifiers who don't rely on acquisition skills. Procter & Gamble was widely applauded as an ace organic diversifier, building up its paper products business with rare success on the base of a relatively tiny acquisition. But these examples are good only as long as they last – General Mills was also praised for its rapid development of the Red Lobster food chain; it became one of the corporate drags. Philip Morris was hailed for years as the most successful of the tobacco diversifiers because of its work on Miller beer; by the time this had gone flat, the Seven-Up purchase in soft drinks had proved a humbling failure.

The fatal error is to diversify merely because deep strategic thinking, or deep strategic thinkers, convince the board that diversification is essential. That approach converted a respectable and respected engineering contractor like Fluor Corporation into a conglomerate with a sky-high stake in metals (it paid $2.3 billion for St Joe Minerals in handy time for a major slump in metal prices). Fluor had enormous difficulty in showing a decent profit: all because the management wanted a cushion against the ups and downs of the capital-investment cycle.

Ten of the nineteen failed strategies reported on by *Business Week* involved major diversification. In contrast, of the fourteen plans classed as successes, nine involved increases in concentration, often with disposals of past diversifications thrown in (or out). Like the chief executives of the nineteen flops, any fool can end up with a corporation that has nothing for anybody – its backers, its shareholders, or its employees – except the ability to grow bigger and broader like a fat lady in the circus.

Wide industrial spread is generally a misfortune that piles burdens on managers as they struggle to achieve genuine expansion in earnings. The irony is that, for a spell, some conglomerates set about the management of agglomerated multi-market companies in a realistic, demanding, and financially alert style. Their tragedy was that they came to share all the follies of the established and conglomerated non-conglomerates, including that of believing their own myths.

23
The Computer Comes Clean

One change above all has dramatically refashioned the world of management in the last decade; the unpredicted, all-pervasive and omnipotent revolution in computery. From a point where even the pocket calculator didn't exist, management has moved in a couple of bounds into the age of the user-friendly, ultra-versatile, enormously powerful personal computer: sitting on his desk, even lying in his briefcase, responsive to an unlimited number of demands. The powers of these devices, their ability to communicate, compute, inform and remind, have changed (and will change far more) the lives of managers and the nature of management.

This time there's no 'maybe' about the computer revolution. In the past, qualification was necessary in the light of previous failures and disappointments. The computer used to scare managers stiffer than any other invention – even the allied myth of automation, which is now taken-for-granted reality. The early prophets of what wasn't even called information technology were well ahead of their time: thus business throughout the West ran into its worst post-war troubles with human labour at the end of the 1960s, which was about the time when, according to the more eager soothsayers, advanced mechanisation would be making the two-legged factory staff redundant or servile, or both.

The computer industry likewise ran into its first recession around the same date, when managements, according to the less realistic pundits, were already supposed to be recasting their entire corporations around the machine. That machine, though, was the huge, number-crunching mainframe. With its satellite robot terminals, the mainframe was supposed to allow chief executives to recentralise their corporations – to reduce middle executives to mindless functional roles; to concentrate the information flows of the company into one glorious 'on-line, real-time' system, in which to know was to obey – with the computer issuing the orders.

The threat, though, never materialised. IBM and its competitors (called the Seven Dwarfs before they shrank to five) did try to sell customers on so-called management information systems – huge, ambitious complexes designed to take the guesswork out of management and, incidentally, to sell rich quantities of computer hardware. Never mind that the few commercial examples of these wonder-complexes were unconvincing. There were famous horror stories like the automated MIS at the California Department of Motor Vehicles, a masterpiece that in 1969 was not expected to break even until 1978, and which provided absolutely no information for management.

Never mind that the experts themselves, secluded in their 'software houses', dreamed up monster projects such as Speedata (for automating grocery movements), which proceeded to collapse – in this case for $20 million – because time and cost were underestimated. Never mind the aftermath when Univac sent some hardy pioneers to Europe to publicise its achievement at a plant in Marietta, Georgia. The Georgia customer, too, added some of its men for the ride, so proud were both sets of managers over this ultimate in centralised management control systems.

The wonder was designed to reap extra profit from tight control by, among other things, giving a running account of actual expenses and updated estimates of production costs, keeping the programme on schedule and even building in

automatically the financial results of any change in specification (the plant's major product was a gigantic, complex job
whose cost history was critical). That Georgia company was
Lockheed Aircraft, and the project, the C5A Galaxy monster
transport, overran its budget by $2 billion, worked none too
well at the end of the process, and would have sunk the
company without trace in 1970 but for a Washington rescue
act.

It was a spectacular demonstration of the truism that any
computer is only as good as the assumptions and information
fed into it. Human beings determine what results their
marvellous machine can produce; more than that, they
determine what use to make of the results. The common old
complaint of executives that they were 'disillusioned' with
computers was pathetic – these people were really disillusioned with themselves. Appropriately, what gave executives back their self-confidence wasn't just technology: their
own independent high spirits greatly helped.

When the Apple II computer was born, its creators had no
notion of cracking the business market where IBM and its
mainframes reigned supreme. The personal business computer was invented by its users: executives who dodged the
computer overlords by buying Apples and other micro-
computers for their very own use. Not only did IBM miss the
beginning and significance of this revolution; it was still grossly
underestimating the scale and importance of the PC when its
own model, after a remarkable crash programme, hit the
market. Notoriously, IBM's first-year sales vastly exceeded its
projections for the entire US market.

Since then, the revolution has been spreading, like a series
of forest fires, all over the world. According to International
Data Corporation, there were only 11,800 personal computers being used for business and professional purposes in
Europe in 1978. Five years later, the numbers had swollen to
nearly three-quarters of a million – a sixtyfold surge. By the
end of the 1980s, some 100 million IBM-compatible PCs were
in existence. By 1994, the pundits were seriously predicting
that before long microprocessor-based devices would out-
number human beings in the developed countries.

As PC sales in their billions of dollars rolled in, IBM was forced into sweeping change – not just in its marketing organisation (for the small devices had to be sold through the retailers IBM had almost never used before); not just in its manufacturing (for all the components, even whole assemblies, had to be purchased from outside); the corporation's entire strategy cried out to be reconstructed round the micro. That strategy's failure to win the battle for the intelligent terminal market condemned the whole mighty company to loss of its pre-eminence. Its brand, for years one of the world's most valuable, sank to bottom marker out of 100 in one consultancy's 1994 rankings.

Victory over the mainframe has gone unequivocally to the intelligent terminal: the desk-top unit (and its portable sibling), that doubles as personal computer and entry-point to formidable powers and data resources. In the triumph of the micros, the mainframe market first stagnated, then started to decline. For years makers clung to the fact that, to quote *Management Today*, 'developments in the area of mainframe general-purpose computing have been at least as great as those in other areas ... over 70% of expenditure on data processing is represented by large general purpose computer systems'. By 1993, however, IBM's sales of PCs were virtually equal in value to those of mainframes – and IBM had little more than an eighth of the world PC market.

The only consolation of the mainframe's decline (for the customer, rather than the supplier) is that purchasing powerful and even super-powerful computers, still necessary for some important purposes, is relatively much less expensive and should no longer be traumatic. More managers know better how computers work (thanks to their own experience with personal computers). The technology and the technologists have advanced to the point where performance as planned ought to be routine; it takes major mismanagement (at which British public authorities have been quite adept) to repeat the wondrous fiascos of the past.

The builders of the liner *Queen Elizabeth II*, for instance, blamed their IT installation for an almost overnight collapse into illiquidity, with $37 million of liabilities against only $4.3

million of assets. The accounts, said the boss, had all been put on the computer, and it took six weeks to get them out. At Lockheed the delay was measured in months, not weeks; it took from December to September for the cost projections to catch up with unexpectedly rapid wage-price inflation on the Galaxy: 'fully integrated management by real-time computer' thus proved unable to signal a crisis of $2 billion dimensions for nine months.

Managers very often took it for granted, without even doing their sums, that investment in computers would save money in the present while storing up even greater benefits for the future; no wonder that something between 40% and 70% of computer users – depending whose figures you fancied – were disappointed; or that, according to other calculations, 80% of installations didn't show an economic return on investment. In 40% of cases the experience was far worse; these users reported a significant degree of deterioration of performance in computerised areas.

Computers were bought that didn't match each other, or match the purpose for which the management wanted them, and stood around for ever more, idle, costly, unloved, and unmated. One British group had four main subsidiaries that opted for four separate, incompatible sets of hardware. As a result, one executive found his overheads up by the equivalent of three research chemists or four salesmen because his payroll had been computerised – to fill up computer time. Companies that badly needed the improved systems which a computer could provide poured huge sums into computer set-ups, but not into the systems.

Rolls-Royce, Lockheed's partner in crime with the Electra airliner flop, invested millions in IBM computers (with its usual eccentricity, it had forty-six of the things, all bought instead of leased) and spent $2 million a year on running them; yet its cost control was painfully weak. Any management which, in this age, is not in control of its computers, as well as its costs, is not only naked, but should be deeply ashamed. Yet the new dawn has brought new problems – some of them looming as large as the old. One is the sheer pace of technological advance.

There are plenty of monuments to past errors in this unavoidable form of technological forecasting, like the airline which built a whole new multi-storey building to accommodate its future computer needs, and in the mid-1970s found itself with a wholly adequate installation (obsolescent at that) occupying just part of one floor. What phenomenal computing power, in what size and convenience of packages, will be available at the end of the 1990s? As one expert wrote, 'Data processing has always had a strong body of futurologists, keen to explain what will eventually happen in a computerised world, but their predictions have a way of remaining predictions.' In other words, nobody knows.

Fortunately, it no longer matters in most circumstances. It's a long time since managements agonised over typewriters and telephones; and computers have passed into that same realm of purchases cheap enough to be expendable – indeed, the functions of typewriters and phones are already merging into the computer, and managers ain't seen nothing yet. The argument over the office of the future concerns how fast and how far to move; but no corporation will be risking its own future, nor any manager laying his on the line, in deciding which supplier to use or what systems to computerise. Electronic data processing is now part of the furniture: literally so.

Similar developments are racing ahead in the plants, where actuality is surpassing Lockheed's failed Galaxy dreams. The control of inventory and production is already routine: robots are on the march; and computer-aided design, tied in with manufacturing, is a fundamental of modern output – even of corporate economics. The Iacocca renaissance at Chrysler, for instance, was powerfully aided by the CAD system; without it the crucial line of K-cars couldn't have been produced at the same vitally low costs.

For the next line, Chrysler used CAD for two-thirds of all components; twenty-eight mainframes, eighty mini-computers and 1,000 terminals comprised the hardware for a gigantic system which, according to a consultant quoted by *Business Week*, gave Chrysler 'a ten-year jump on the rest of the industry'. Even with manufacturing systems, though, companies can still very easily make the same brilliant boobs that office users perpetrated in the past; the Raleigh bike company pole-axed itself, in the midst of a desperate drive to emerge from years of losses of markets and money, by installing a system which, by delivering the wrong parts to the wrong places, brought the entire plant to a grinding halt, at ruinous cost.

Ironically, but predictably, some of the major snafus have occurred at the very microelectronics plants which are at the heart of the factory and office revolution. Over at Apple, there was a nasty moment when failures seemed briefly to threaten the totally automated output of Macintosh computers on which the company depended for its very survival. Yet Apple won through. Despite extreme volatility in the technology and the market, the great majority of hardware and software firms that hitched their wagon to the microprocessor saw the 1990s in – which is more than could be said for the Seven Dwarfs.

One after the other, IBM's seven mainframe competitors threw in the towel; and all of them were too spent to see the glorious opportunities seized by little firms like Apple and Compaq. Control Data once seemed to have the business of fighting IBM taped. 'We had and have the best strategy in the industry,' it boasted. 'We didn't hit IBM in the hardest part of their big belly.' After a series of massive mishaps over many years, this highly rated, high-performance player in high technology turned itself from manufacturer to service company. At least computers were Control Data's business; that couldn't be said of the other dwarfs – yet their fatal presumption was echoed in the microprocessor era.

When *Newsweek* produced a supplement on office automation in the early 1980s, it was sponsored by companies whose core products were, respectively, copiers, cameras, computers, telephone exchanges, radios, typewriters, electrical goods and printers. That list only scratches the surface of a competitive line-up which had never before been seen in business history. How could all these would-be office automators make a living, let alone wax rich? The answer, as in mainframes, was that they couldn't.

The first batch of the inevitable drop-outs included the biggest entrant of them all: Exxon. After a total investment of $600 million or so in office systems, the company may have lost as much as it sold one year – $70 million. Not surprisingly, at the end of the year, the oil company bowed out of a market in which it literally never had any business. Yet still they come. Eastman Kodak astounded one and all by announcing at almost the same time as Exxon quit that it was to compete in the business telecommunications market. Kodak is to telecommunications what Ronald Reagan is to flower power; and what went for Kodak applied to most other diversifying runners in the new computer race started off by the microchip.

The inside track had to be held by those with the strongest positions in personal computers and their software. Even strengths in products that seemed to be close allies, like private-branch telephone exchanges, or facsimile, or copiers, or word-processors, proved insufficient. Only the insiders could keep up with the pace of developments that by 1994 were bedazzling the average senior manager with concepts like virtuality, groupware, the electronic boardroom, and CSCW ('computer supported cooperative working').

Tomorrow's manager in tomorrow's company will be less dazzled, for this is the new wave in the IT revolution – a new wave which, for IT revolutionaries, of course, is already old hat. The pattern of development in this on-rushing field is that the nerds and the cybermen use routinely what the routine manager regards as state-of-the-art. When management starts to catch up, the leaders are already moving far ahead. But that's becoming less true, on one researched view: 'the gap between IT and business', it avers, 'is shrinking rapidly'.

The gap was a great divide. In 1988, according to the *Times*/Arthur Andersen survey, only 10% of all directors thought it worth their while to know anything whatsoever about IT. Today's picture, as uncovered by Sema Consulting Group, is radically different; 83% of the directors and managers surveyed 'felt that they understood the potential role of IT in their business', and '92% agreed that such an understanding was necessary'. The old moans (which reinforced the desire for unblissful ignorance) have dwindled; instead of long litanies of complaints about overtime, overcost, prematurely obsolescent and underperforming systems, two-thirds of the survey 'had confidence in IT in their organisation based on a history of successful projects'.

What's more, IT was ranked second only to finance (85% v 95%) in making management contributions that are 'significant' or 'very significant'. The picture glows less brightly, though, when IT uses are examined. Two-fifths of the Sema respondents 'agreed strongly that IT was adding value' in automating procedures. But only a quarter felt the same way about the provision of new information. And 'sustaining change' attracted a lower score still: a fifth. That's the area where the newer and most sophisticated hardware and software makes its contribution: in enabling business transformation through cultural change.

The most extreme transformation creates the 'virtual organisation', in which products are made to order with near-instantaneous delivery, and with the most effective use of resources right through the business system – meaning not only the ultimate seller, but everybody along the entire supply chain. Neither that ideal nor the increasingly necessary approaches to the ideal can be achieved without simultaneous group access to information and decisions. The business logic is compelling; but managers also have the best of personal reasons for moving off the IT sidelines.

According to research by Alan B. Krueger, who teaches economics at Princeton, computer-users, including executives, outearned their computerless counterparts over the 1980s by a minimum of 10%. There's an obvious chicken-and-egg question: did the brighter, higher-potential managers take to the computer more readily, rather than the computer creating the potential? But the answer hardly matters. If the brightest and best are wised up to the computer's management powers, less starry managers dare not compete with less electronic back-up.

Second, two ineluctable trends are forcing managers into the IT age. To quote *Fortune*, 'The core of the new economy consists of converging telecommunications and computer technologies, and to succeed you will need to use them'. Moreover, 'more and more work will be done by teams addressing projects that have a beginning and an end'. Vauxhall's new Omega executive car actually used, not one team, but thirteen teams within the team, each one composed of representatives from the same ten corporate functions – with finance and marketing alongside the technicians and stylists.

Cooperative teamwork can be conducted without groupware, just as airlines used to operate without computer terminals, or store chains without electronic point of sale. But only a managerial masochist sticks to outdated ways – and these days, that won't be for long in management itself, any more than it was at the check-outs. That's simply because the business will be run out of town by its far more competitive rivals. Resistance to the electronic tide would only make some kind of sense if its acceptance involved great understanding of tricky technology. But the technological wonders can now be taken for granted; the non-technical manager can happily ignore the acronyms and neologisms.

The essence of advances like groupware is simplicity itself. In the words of Microsoft's Bill Gates: 'It's simply allowing everyone in your company to collaborate, allowing you to track everything you've done on a new product design, everything you've done with customers.' Put like that, with any major function in the business system inserted for 'new product design', the concept is both simple and irresistible. After all, what are progressive organisational leaders trying to achieve as they advance towards the new century? They seek greater speed of execution and response: to mobilise all the talents in the organisation and assemble them selectively to tackle its challenges; and to collect and analyse all the facts relating to those problems and opportunities.

The new IT powers can't and won't of themselves prevent managers from making as massive a mess of their corporate affairs as ever. The computer will never eliminate the executive's need to think for his or her living. But managements can get usable information about what is happening as and when it happens – as a matter of course, and wherever they themselves happen to be. The information capability that any big company already has is multiplying enormously; but the critical success factors, even when (or if) the 'expert systems' start taking more far-reaching decisions out of managers' hands altogether, will remain in the hands of the all-too-human executive.

The sheer expansion of information is already causing human difficulties. It isn't just a question of deciding what in a huge database is actually useful, or even wanted, but of marrying different sets of data which today may reside uncomfortably in incompatible systems. Tomorrow will be a different story as the on-rushing changes confront managers on both sides of the revolution, the customers and the suppliers with both huge promise and high challenge. They have a tiger by the tail. The saving grace is that it is now, by and large, a friendly tiger.

Those who get bitten, or eaten alive, will have asked for it – not so much by mistakes in the technology itself, more by straightforward management boobs. Monumental mistakes in computerisation were made, not because computers were unmanageable, but because they were badly managed. In a way, managers could be excused; the computer had added considerably to the complexity and perplexity of management at a time when it was becoming more complex and perplexing for other reasons – as it still is. There's now plenty of evidence, though, that the friendly computer is actually reducing complexity and perplexity by making them much easier to handle.

Having built the right handling platform for decisions, the vital next stage is to share those decisions and (partly by that means) to mobilise the support which turns decisions into actions – fast. The Sema prescription fits these conditions: 'flexible client/server architectures, networked PCs supporting groupware applications: wide-area networks for sharing information: advanced telecommunications to support constantly changing needs'. If top managers aren't investing in these blessings, they're heading for trouble. If they don't know what the words mean, they're in trouble already.

BOOK V:
SHELL GAMES

Introduction:
The Age of Panaceas

Pity the poor manager. As if companies don't face enough difficult choices in their businesses, they confront an unprecedented embarrassment of promised riches in management itself. Do you place your trust (and money) in Business Process Re-engineering (BPR)? Or Total Quality Management (TQM)? Alternatively, how about becoming a virtual corporation? If that doesn't appeal, you could try the learning organisation, if you're not too busy with time-based competition, continuous improvement (*kaizen*), core competencies or organisational architecture (OA).

Each of these approaches, moreover, comes complete with its own guru or gurus. In TQM alone, those not content with the doughty old names of Deming and Juran can try Crosby, Taguchi, Ishikawa or Imai. Managers who can reel off the concepts listed above probably also know the attendant gurus: Michael Hammer for BPR, William Davidow for virtuality, Peter Senge for learning, George Stalk for time, David Nadler for OA and C.K. Prahalad for core competencies. 'Reel off' is the right phrase; the assembled ideas look so many and so many-sided as to make the mind reel.

The reeling isn't just in the mind. As top managements latch on to these concepts, so they seek to install them in their organisations. That can all too easily lead to a condition that Mike Freedman of consultants Kepner-Tregoe has named 'initiative fatigue'. Those inside companies know the phenomenon as the 'flavour-of-the-month': the latest 'programme', wished on them by top management, that will be given some fancy name, involve them in fancy training, and then, after contributing negligible benefits to the business, fade gently away into memory, to be succeeded by the next whim.

The pursuit of panaceas has long been a favourite management hobby. The classic case is Management by Objectives. MBO built on a powerful insight of Peter Drucker's (that managers perform better if they know what's expected of them and have agreed to do it). It promulgated a cascade of aims, all with numbers attached, which in theory guaranteed perfect performance and corporate success. In practice, MBO generally produced neither, and its day passed – though more than the memory lingers on.

In very advanced TQM something called 'policy deployment' is at first sight very similar. PD is defined by PA Consulting Group as 'a fully integrated top-down, bottom-up management system through which the two or three critical breakthrough targets and means are identified and implemented with the full participation and alignment of all managers' – or (as at Rank Xerox) all staff. Like MBO, it cascades down the organisation so that every larger objective is fed by the achievement of lesser objectives.

There is a difference, and it's crucial in making sense out of what looks like a managerial Tower of Babel (or Babble). The title *Liberation Management*, coined by Tom Peters, another highly popular guru, strikes the relevant note. Wherever they start from, whatever brand they place on their product, all the gurus end up at the same destination. They all subscribe to the idea that corporate achievement rests on maximising the contribution of individuals, not by imposing controls, but by removing restraints.

The philosophy was beautifully encapsulated by a speaker at the CBI's launch of its competitiveness initiative in the spring of 1994. Asked how other managements could emulate his people's productivity and quality achievements, the speaker replied simply: 'By getting out of the way'. What managers need continuously is faster performance of stream-lined operations to higher quality standards, leading to greater customer satisfaction, achieved by people who use their own initiatives to realise those shared aspirations.

Policy deployment therefore allows people to share in determining objectives and, at least equally important, to set out what improvements they plan. MBO set targets, but wasn't overly concerned with how the numbers were met. PD is deeply concerned with process, with the how of perform-ance as much as the what. Also, its theorists don't make the MBO mistake of believing that a perfect system will produce perfect results. They know that there are no panaceas – that things will go wrong and require correction.

'Flavour-of-the-month', though, leads off with the gung-ho certainty that this 'programme', unlike its predecessors, will achieve the wonders required by the board. Even the word 'programme' is suspect, because it suggests a one-off initia-tive that will one day be complete. Any management approach worth its keep will require many years of sustained effort. If 'programme' is one bad sign, though, another is a cast-iron guarantee of failure – top management refusal to join the party.

The issue here isn't just the hardy perennial of 'commit-ment': every peddlar of panaceas, along with every seller of genuine corporate essentials, has always insisted on top-level commitment as a *sine qua non*. The trouble is that, with a finite number of senior managers, and only one chief executive, a finite level of commitment is confronted by an infinite variety of choice. The choice must be made – but the chosen approach must be one which embraces the choosers.

The reaction of employees whose leaders won't apply TQM training and methods to their own work, for example, won't differ from that of a sports team whose captain won't join the training sessions. Refusers may believe that they're so superbly equipped and performing so well that efforts to improve their activity and skills are superfluous, if not downright demeaning. The argument misses the point (a)

301

because it's invariably untrue and (b) because it harms the collective performance of the team and the system.

'System' is another key word. Any of the approaches mentioned here, and others besides, are capable of producing sharp, even lasting improvements in aspects of performance – in the processes with which policy deployment is concerned. But those improvements need to be integrated with all the other processes that constitute the business system. That isn't the same as the company or the unit. It goes outside their boundaries to take in the customers at one end and the suppliers at the other.

Inside the boundaries, systems thinking takes in all departments and functions that relate to whatever's in hand. Most of the new approaches depend in common on multi-disciplinary, cross-functional team-working. And here the optional element disappears. This isn't another flavour-of-the-month programme adding to initiative fatigue. Such self-managed teams are accounting for more and more activity within organisations, whether top management likes it or not – or even knows that it's happening.

By the same token, as I stressed in Book III, information technology is driving companies in the directions favoured by the gurus. The IT revolution and team-working are connected – literally connected, because the networked PC is linking managers and others in ways that rule out the old ways of working. As *Fortune* writer Thomas A. Stewart puts it, 'Networks irrevocably alter the nature of managerial authority and work' as their use encourages working together across the old boundaries.

Stewart notes that 'A person might spend most of his day with an interdepartmental team led by someone from another part of the company in another part of the world, doing a project his nominal boss knows little about. Then what, pray, is a chain of command?' One 1993 study of seventy-five networks found exactly what you'd expect. Once the networks are used, a company's structure starts to change – even if an 'organisational architecture' guru has never come near the place.

You can see how that results from a *Business Week* definition of OA: 'a metaphor that forces managers to think about organisation in terms of how work, people and formal and informal structures fit together. Leads to autonomous work teams and strategic alliances.' And autonomous work teams and strategic alliances lead to, and are fed by, the IT network. To exploit that to the full, managements really do need all-inclusive, system-wide concepts that deliver quickening speed, rising efficiency, increasing effectiveness and happier people – customers, employees and suppliers.

Which concept is adopted is less important than obeying the rules. First, aim high and system-wide, providing a strategic vision which will give process changes the required direction and leverage. Second, insist that all senior managers believe and participate in the chosen approach. Third, seek and win large, revolutionary outcomes fast; but within, fourth, the context of a long-term commitment to evolutionary change. Some companies have been deeply involved in TQM for a decade or more; you need time to consolidate your advances.

Michael Hammer's firm, CSC Index, did a survey of re-engineering which showed many companies breaking all four rules – and thus wasting the time, trouble and cost of their reforms. Reporting on the survey in the *Financial Times*, Christopher Lorenz wrote that 're-engineering works best in organisations where employees really trust their managers, make many of their own decisions, believe they are paid for performance, operate well in teams, share information freely, and take risks'.

The cynical response is easy: if you've got all that, who needs gurus or their preachings? To that there's only one answer. To obtain and retain these invaluable assets, which will be more and more decisive in the competitive wars, organisations are going to need all the help they can get.

24
B-Grades for B-Schools

Executives, the most extensively educated group of adults in society, are very possibly educated to the least effect. Any executive could spend 300 working days a year – and several thousands pounds of company money – at individual seminars, without coming near to exhausting the rich table that consultants, academics, training firms, associations, publishers, and other do-gooders spread before the business world. Their altruism is spiced with lucre. The teaching of executives has been the best-paying branch of education, and by a very long way.

The figures are awe-inspiring. In a decade, the number of new business titles published in America (each presumably promoting at least one idea) has increased by nearly two-fifths to 1,831: that's five a day. They're being bought, too; sales have more than doubled since 1982. Whether they're being read by managers, of course, is another matter – though you can be sure that some are being studied by the 80,000 MBA graduates (up 33%) at the 670 management schools (up 23%), and by some of the millions of employees trained at an annual cost of $45 billion.

That sum represents a 350% rise over 1982. The stupendous sums raise a pair of questions fit to test any business school academic or graduate. Can you name an expensive, over-supplied product whose suppliers and customers alike are deeply unsure about its value and specification? Would this product be on the crest of a continuing wave, or the slippery slope of decline? The answer to the first half should be easy. It's the business-school degree, the MBA, itself. The second is trickier. But demand for MBAs has softened somewhat, and their worth and training is being questioned – by employers and academics – more deeply than ever before.

Questioning itself is nothing new, though only a few heretical voices have ever questioned the general principle – that you can teach executives, that is, make them better at their jobs by a general course of instruction, short or long. Top managers have been uneasy about the specifics; that's why they've gone on biting the hands they feed. Yet they have gone on feeding, hiring MBAs in great numbers and at great salaries. What's new in the early 1990s is the fundamental nature of the argument: that management has changed, but B-schools haven't; that the age of the 'quants', highly numerate analysts, is over; that the era has arrived of the visionary, multi-faceted, team-working leader who makes things happen.

In fact, this conflict between the academic and the pragmatic has been rumbling away for a long time. The Harvard Business School is the ark of the tabernacle in management education. Many schools more or less ape it, especially its 'case study' method of instruction – though mulling over out-of-date business anecdotes is even less helpful in actual management than waging war by tramping over old battlefields. When Harvard's Dean publicly queried the relevance of the method early in the 1980s, the effect was roughly similar to the Pope casting doubts on the validity of his Church's attitude on birth-control.

Any particular discomfiture suffered by Harvard can't be confined. Even those business schools that self-consciously follow a different route do so by reference to the Harvard standard. These others have also mostly concentrated on 'quantitative' studies; in other words, as a maverick educator,

Reg Revans, pointed out, they teach much the same subjects that students of economics or statistics have always read. The specific management element in these mind-bending studies is hard to isolate. Although executives should be numerate (and many are not), they don't require skills in higher algebra, and many great businesses have been created by men who all but count on their fingers.

The business world is full of successful entrepreneurs who live, not by their calculators, still less their personal computers, but by knowing the difference between a buying price and a selling price. It is also full of clever fools who work out elaborate discounted cash-flow sums to justify projects and products that a real businessman would laugh out of sight. The clever-fool syndrome would explain why one controversial study of Harvard students found that, after a flying start, the alumni (presumably among the ablest young people of their day) gradually slipped back to the general level inside their chosen management hierarchies. Harvard graduates have no reason at all to suppose that they will manage more effectively than less instructed contemporaries.

The Harvards can only claim that they are more highly educated; and high education and high achievement in practical affairs don't necessarily go together. John F. Kennedy found that assembling America's brightest brains in Washington neither got bills through Congress nor avoided the Bay of Pigs; and many companies have discovered that business-school diplomas are a thin defence against incompetence. True, an overwhelmingly large proportion of the highest and best American executives did study business. All this proves is that an overwhelmingly large proportion of business-minded undergraduates got the real message, which is that a diploma will be good for their careers, starting with starting salaries.

It does not follow that the education was of any other direct benefit either to the executive or the firm. Nor does it follow, of course, that the schooling was wasted. As a general rule, wise recruiters pick the finest intelligences they can find; and good minds are far better for good training. The question is only whether academic training in subjects that seem to have some connection with management is the best education for managing, and that is something that nobody can prove either way.

The business school is really great at teaching future business-school teachers. But teaching the raw young is only the start of the money in management education. You can detach experienced managers for hours or years, and you can attempt any form of education, from familiarising them with computers to changing their entire personalities. Attempt is the critical word; for some of the objectives are very curious. They start from an odd proposition: that management is a body of abstract skills, like those of mechanical engineering, which can be applied equally successfully to any number of practical situations.

Once you've built one suspension bridge, very possibly you've built the lot – although the modern history of bridge accidents questions even that. But the abstract principles of launching a new toothpaste are too loose and vague for analogies to apply. And once you've launched one new toothpaste, it doesn't mean that you can launch the next in the same way, much less that you can use the same methods for a cake-mix. The absurdity of the educational proposition is stunning when applied to personal relationships. Prepackaged courses for managers designed (like Midwest evangelism) to change the behaviour patterns of the human beings involved still flourish despite lack of evidence that any beneficial results have flowed for anybody other than the packagers.

In the supreme (so far) development of this art form, the evangelists seek to change the behaviour pattern of the entire company. This was known as organisation development, or OD. In its purest form, this religion had a creed so extreme that, as with the harder-nosed heresies of the Middle Ages, true believers were few, far between and fervent. The OD consultant might never actually talk about people, preferring 'human factor management' or 'human resource development', as he practised 'a process for implementing the improvement of the organisation, particularly the effectiveness of relations among its members'.

Writing in *Management Today*, Paul Rowlandson listed some of the ways in which OD human factors set about this daunting task. There's the 'Intimacy Programme Questionnaire', whose fifty-five questions included 'Have you ever been tempted to kill yourself?' and 'What do you think about nudity?' These very naked managers were submitted to exercises like 'kneeballing' (you sit directly opposite somebody with knees touching and stare into his or her eyes); 'yelling' (you yelled); or 'elimination' (you nominated another group member to be eliminated from the group, and so did everybody else).

Psychologist Carl Rogers defended such processes as a necessary way of 'stripping the self', so that 'in time, the group finds it unbearable that any member should live behind a mask or a front'. The umbrella name of 'sensitivity training' was inapt for a process that was often insensitive to the point of butchery. By confessing to shortcomings in front of others in 'grid sessions', 'T-Groups' or similar gatherings, the executive became psychologically purified. The North Korean brainwashers and the hippies at the Esalen Institute shared this same belief in inducing spiritual change by humiliation. Even if some came away feeling better and wiser and more effective, all uplift wears off, and it wears off long before the uplifted one has any real chance to transform his performance through his transmogrified personality.

The same, or very similar methods are still earning rich revenues for practitioners who appeal to the more gullible purchasers of management training. But the times have turned decisively against indoctrination. OD has been superseded by 'culture change', in which companies embark on long-range programmes intended (just like OD) to produce a brave new corporate world, with brave new men and women acting in brave, new ways. The emphasis, though, now rests on encouraging (rather than challenging) the manager's self-esteem and persuading psychologically secure leaders to share power with others who are similarly motivated to seek cooperation and achievement.

The cynics would argue that the programmes involved

merely substitute one set of conformist pressures for another – and that this is the main, if undeclared, purpose of much so-called in-house training – when groups of executives from the same company are herded together at some away-from-it-all location. The pressure at such occasions can be quite intense. There's an American venue at Starved Rock, Illinois, of which a man once remarked: 'Executives don't leave Starved Rock and become better executives without working at it. How do you get to it? Feedback, results, tests, self-appraisal, counselling – you're the salami in the sandwich.'

Today, high-level in-house courses seek to avoid the smell of the sausage factory and the smack of indoctrination. They aim, rather, to be carefully monitored sessions designed to improve management performance in measurable, practicable ways. Not only do such sessions give middle executives a close-up of their bosses, but the best courses will give them the opportunity to influence the latter's decisions, by working on real-life strategic concerns. In-house education has greater, mostly under-exploited potential. Outside courses can only get at an executive by taking him away from his job; inside courses can teach men and women in the best place of all – which is on and for that job.

Long ago, the aforementioned Reg Revans argued for 'action learning', in which students study real-life problems in other organisations and, most important, produce real-life solutions. That was seen as a threat by the academics – and rightly, because it challenges the need for a school. Some companies, all no doubt also customers for the B-schools, have followed this lead: thus twenty-one powerful organisations, ranging from British Telecom and Marks & Spencer to the Civil Service and the Metropolitan Police, now belong to the non-scholastic International Management Development Consortium. Two of its annual seminars are built round live consultancy work. The younger potential high-fliers – managers, specialists and administrators – imbibe the pure milk of action learning, with assignments occupying all but three days of a two-week 'business management seminar'.

An MBA, of course, takes far longer: in some opinions, too

long. The great Peter Drucker, hearing that a friend's daughter was going on the MBA course at Insead, the highly international school near Fontainebleau, grimaced and said 'that won't do her any harm'. The friend protested that it was only for a year: 'that's why it won't do her any harm', said the sage. You can, of course, learn far more in two years than two weeks – but that isn't the point.

Action learning teaches above all the application of management knowledge in practical situations (without which, obviously, the lore is useless). IMD's business-management seminar does have a faculty; teachers work alongside the teams for one or two days apiece, assisting in the initial definition of the project and the subsequent analysis, and challenging the findings. The whole idea is to equip team members with practical skills and attitudes that they can apply in their own companies.

That is echoed by new developments at the Wharton school in Philadelphia, where, according to *Fortune*, 'professors from previously unrelated disciplines are coordinating lectures so that students learn to grapple with business problems in new, multi-disciplinary ways'. The academics, though, admit to deep uncertainty over whether coordination is being achieved. In contrast, the forty-five-plus firms, ranging from publishing to air-conditioning, who have received IMD project teams are thoroughly convinced, to quote one sponsor, of 'the value of action-learning live consultancy work'.

The most radical of the threatened B-schools, the University of Michigan, is imitating this approach with a 'medical school' model that sends students out to get practical experience inside businesses. These B-school heretics are plainly right. In developing better managers, action is where the action has to be. That lesson was learnt the hard way at British Petroleum, which launched a massive culture change programme: profits fell, the chief executive was fired, and it became clear to his successors that a fundamental error had been made. The culture-vultures hadn't decided what business results they wanted the oil giant to achieve.

But note that, once this grievous fault had been corrected,

BP could use the acquired strengths to build an impressive recovery. There's no question but that managers, just like workers on the line, learn best in real-life, properly directed work. That simple principle has been translated into a significant new emphasis on 'coaching', the manager's responsibility for developing his subordinates by using their work as an educational tool. While the idea is extremely sound, and while some form of coaching is inseparable from any relationship between the boss and the bossed, neither the pressures of the former's own job, nor the predilections of most managers, are truly conducive to enough or good enough coaching to develop a manager's ability and equipment fully.

What is certain is that the company, like it or not, is an educational establishment, good or bad. The phrase used by Apple's John Sculley – 'We're trying to create a unique learning institution' – has become another piece of B-school jargon. But the principle of the 'learning organisation' is inescapable in times which demand continuous adaptation. Organisations, of course, can't learn; only people can. But the organisation provides the boundaries within which managers can develop and apply their skills and talents – and they in turn are the real people who can develop the organisation.

Any training which is directly related to work is more effective than education outside. At one-day external seminars nobody notices if the executive dozes off into languorous half-sleep, opening glazed eyes just in time to sprint for the early train. Even if the seminar's subject is relevant to the participant's job, even if the listener has absorbed a significant part of the information (both unlikely conditions), even if (instead of an indigestible battery of speakers) one or two days' enlightenment have been provided by a brilliant teacher, the audience still faces what is known as the re-entry problem. The students may have found a better way up there on the managerial moon, but will unenlightened colleagues back on earth let them disturb the even, set tenor of the company's ways?

Will they, hell. The more executives are exposed to

312

external ideas of how a modern business should be managed, the longer they spend away from the shop at this university or that seminar, the more alien and obtuse the actual real-life conditions in the company can seem. The company, unlike the business schools, is enmeshed in real life. The academic inevitably teaches of an ideal world in which the personalities of all chief executives (to take one illusion) are equable, open to persuasion, and eager for change, and in which (to take another dream) markets respond logically to logical plans logically arrived at.

There is no other basis on which the academy can operate; but it is not the basis on which a company works. The main criticism of business schools and their graduates is precisely that, and has been for years: that their education and their attitudes are not fitted to real-life business. Many of the graduates, anyway, don't head in that direction. In 1983, nearly a quarter of the Harvard graduating class went into consulting. As John Thackray reported in *Management Today*, one MBA, back for his fifth reunion, was 'shocked that very few of my classmates were making a product, running a plant or drilling a hole in the ground. Almost everyone was on the financial side.'

By 1994, consultancy was booming as never before. The big action had moved to huge projects, attracting $30 to $50 million apiece, in which large teams of MBAs spent up to three years inside companies. The result of this 'consulting gold rush', reported *Business Week*, was that 'MBAs are being lured into the profession at record rates'. Nothing much has changed since Thackray reported that 'One of the more frequent carpings of business today is that MBAs show an over-reliance on mathematical techniques and quantitative methods (usually computer-based) which business doesn't want (or doesn't know how) to utilise effectively'. But who else are the consultants (and the great corporations) going to employ?

Following much the same logic, Exxon, in 1983, once informed the University of Chicago that it wanted the entire graduating class. Very simply, the best brains in America, and increasingly in Europe, if they have an active interest in business enter the B-schools. As with students in Japanese universities, it isn't what they're taught that counts so much as gaining entry in the first place. The more highly educated they are, true, the harder it will be to assimilate them into a manufacturing or marketing business as opposed to a consultancy or financial institution. But this is a very unconvincing argument for putting up with second or third best.

But what happens after entry or re-entry into business life is the real issue. External training must be treated like good in-house education; that is, it should equip men and women to do their jobs better, and as they move to another mystery, equip them for that in turn. That's why the best companies do make an intensive educational effort, using internal and external courses, as well as changing and challenging job progression, to inculcate what professional management means and to provide the professional equipment. Few companies in the West, though, take the process as far as Japanese groups like Hitachi or NEC. In fact, an NEC executive unconsciously echoed Apple's boss when he told Gene Gregory, a Tokyo professor, that 'work in the age of information technology is permanent life-long education. The enterprise has become essentially as much an educational institution [that phrase again] as it is a place of work.'

The education provided at the Hitachi Institute of Technology or NEC's Institute for Technology Education is exactly what the titles of these top-ranked institutions suggest: to a Japanese, education for managers is highly specific, highly technical. A company president won't just know about statistical quality control in general: even a man with a finance background will know the technicalities in depth, and will be expected to. In many Western corporations which spend heavily on management education, neither the expectation of knowledge nor the knowledge are present.

That expectation presupposes that the executive has been taught how to learn and think, possibly the most valuable gift that education has to offer. Those who lack this general lesson are prone to take experience as a substitute for thought. All knowledge is the result of inquisitiveness – of asking why. Experience is another name for ceasing to ask because the answer has been prejudged. 'We've always done it this way' is the worst reason of all, unless, that is, there genuinely is no better way; and that can only be established by enquiry.

Helping executives to think, by giving them the necessary tools and training, isn't the need that most business courses publicly try to fill. But it is the central issue, more so than the defects the schools themselves now confess – for instance, that they can't teach executives how to make decisions under stress. Nor can they. But before making a decision, under stress or at ease, it's essential to have been guilty of constructive, creative thought – which requires processes that are eminently teachable.

Apart from any other factors, thought helps the decision to make itself – which is always the most desirable way. Saying that executives can't be taught the power of decision at business school, in any case, is tantamount to saying that you can't teach managers to manage; for initiating action under uncertainty and pressure is one of the activities for which executives are paid. Individuals can always be taught to manage more effectively; the issue is whether they will be allowed to do so – whether the uncertainty and pressure come only from the market-place and the competition, or stem from a counter-productive internal culture.

In the too-typical situation, where the manager is under-employed, over-managed, and constantly let off the hook, a half-failed manager in a half-failed organisation, education of any variety won't help. And total failure must follow from the unpleasant delusion that classes can transform the adult mind and personality like some fairy wand. The less companies and educators expect to turn an incompetent into a polymath, or a bully into a Boy Scout, the more they are likely to achieve. As it is, too much of what now passes as management education isn't education; it is indoctrination, entertainment, or occupation of vacant hours. And it has very little to do with the management of business, which is the real business of management.

25
Conundrums of Consultancy

There was once a snappy catch answer to consultants, management professors and other tradesmen who tell others how to mind their own businesses. 'Ah yes,' executives could say, 'if you know so much, how come you're not rich?' There are variations to this arresting theme: 'Those who can, do; those who can't, consult', or 'He's never met a payroll in his life'. The last gibe skirts round the fact that most executives have never met a payroll either, not in the sense of having until Friday to find the cash.

The gibes also look beside the point at a time when consultancy itself is big and booming business. True, even $17 billion a year (the sum which the 80,000-odd American-led management consultancies carve up between them) is small potatoes by the standards of big business as a whole. But within that sum groups of clever men and women have been able to accomplish little masterpieces of niche-building, market segmentation and repositioning: the very arts and crafts they enjoin on their clients.

Examples like Boston Consulting Group's invention of portfolio planning built round market share, or Bain's branding of corporate strategy, or Harvard professor Michael Porter's leverage of 'competitive advantage' into the $90 million Monitor consultancy, are a joy to behold – and have proved financially joyful to the partners involved. But the most conspicuous joy must be that of the $1.3 billion McKinsey & Co and that of the two consultants, Thomas J. Peters and Robert H. Waterman, who created a mountain of money with a single book, *In Search of Excellence.*

Its seven million-plus sales make it the greatest non-fiction publishing phenomenon of modern times – no management book has remotely approached such numbers. Not only did Peters (now ex-McKinsey, with personally owned companies grossing many millions a year) and Waterman (also ex-McKinsey and much in demand as a lecturer) become personal successes; McKinsey also cashed in. Having funded the research into corporate excellence, it reaped enormous and continuing benefit from the publicity, while raking in half of Peters' royalties – and all of Waterman's.

Even the most grasping of client businessmen must envy so shrewd a bunch. Plainly, the entrepreneurial juices run high in the bosoms of many consultants – more maybe than in those of the men who pay the bills. Executives rest in the safe arms of the corporation, which always (or nearly always) makes sure that the payroll gets met and the creditors paid. These days, true, many executives are more like consultants – shifting from assignment to assignment, spending their time largely on reports, meetings, and investigations. But like those mentioned above, many consultants are more like businessmen than many executives in the great corpocracies.

The lucrative boom in 'management', as opposed to 'managing', has made large numbers of consultants and professors richer than any divisional general manager. Very few are festooned with Rolls-Royces, Cadillacs, or Lamborghinis. But consulting is paid well enough, and distributes enough of the swag in partnership devices, to retain men who could amble into richly paid jobs managing some client company. Consultants like to say that it's not the money that retains them, but the intellectual challenge. They seldom mention another significant factor – consulting is much less risky than management, which for an ex-consultant can be very dangerous indeed.

The risk may only be that of losing a posthumous reputation, if, like a former boss of Westinghouse, you die in office before the mess you made of the company lands at your door. Profits halved in half a dozen years, partly because of exactly the kind of snafu that consultants are supposed to clean up in their sleep. 'The major problem of the company,' said the successor CEO, 'in its management structure, was the fact that they had too many people reporting to the top operating man ... A bottleneck at the top is the worst place to have one.'

Westinghouse, however, is not the only company (RCA was another) to discover that, while good consultants are good at business, they are especially good at their own, which is a very specialised and lucrative form of service industry. In that industry, the marvels of marketing performed since the Second World War have elevated their status and profitability by strategic strokes that any entrepreneur would envy. The market has advanced to meet them, a usual phenomenon with hit products. Executives perplexed by the problems of operating their own clumsy corporate creations have cried for help, and they have really needed it in areas such as computers where technical advances left companies floundering in strange waters.

That's why Andersen Consulting is by far the largest consulting business in the world. Information systems are the backbone of its $2.9 billion revenues, more than double those of runner-up Coopers & Lybrand. The consultants have been around in these quasi-technical jobs for decades; but the rewards of such humdrummery are limited by an obvious ceiling – the amount for which a company can acquire its very own full-time specialist. Even so, it may be unwise to maintain in-house strengths when outside expertise is available off-the-shelf. Consultancy rewards in general, however, stayed unexciting until the sharper minds in the game raised their sights to a more sublime level, the holy of holies, the boardroom itself.

Advising on marketing strategy or corporate organisation has one shining economic virtue. The consultant breaks away from the constraint of fees related to the time of his own employees and climbs towards more gratifying levels of remuneration based on the expected future worth of his services. Consultants General Systems, for example, charged Tenneco $15–20 million during a 'cost of quality' programme that's thought to have added $461 million to operating income. Nice work; but why not a $10 million bill? Or $30 million? There may be some difference between this approach and charging what the traffic will bear, but not much.

The results can be most gratifying. To quote one US expert, 'there's been a tremendous escalation in the fees for quality consulting by the big firms'. Where once a few hundred thousand dollars was a good fee, GTE, America's largest utility, paid Boston Consulting Group $2.4 million for re-engineering work in 1991 – just for starters. The next year, which saw the start of implementing the recommendations, BCG charged $10.9 million. 'Implementation' is crucial these days. Consultants used to be severely criticised for completing their fat reports, charging their even fatter fees – and walking away from the client to the bank. Now the good ones stay with their recommendations, theoretically to make them work.

In the process some consultants get so close to the management that, for a time, they become indistinguishable. That's how the mighty eight-figure fees are achieved. To quote *Business Week*, consultants are 'forming teams with executives at client companies and working together to analyse problems and develop solutions. Assignments that were once narrowly focused have evolved into nineteen–twenty-four month efforts that encompass strategy, operations, organisation and technology.' Which doesn't leave much else for the actual management to tackle by itself.

The broader the assignment, of course, the harder to prove its success. That's always been the case. After McKinsey consultants visited Shell in the early 1960s, the latter's profits swelled gigantically – but how can you prove that a chain of cause and effect links the consultants with the profits? The story of Shell and McKinsey started in Venezuela, where two brilliant young consultants, Hugh Parker and Lee Walton, worked so impressively for a subsidiary that they were invited to look at Shell's head-office problems in London and The Hague.

McKinsey at this time was still US-centred. But its adoption by Shell, widely supposed (and with some good reason) to lead Europe's management élite, was a gilt-edged visiting card into Europe. If Shell, bristling with internal consultants, needed that extra something from McKinsey, then McKinsey obviously had something extra to give. Old-line British boardrooms, jammed solid with anxiety over modern problems of scale and complexity, for which they were ill-equipped, rapidly took the point; so did thrusters unsure which way to thrust. One after another the blue-chip names – ICI and the Bank of England, the Post Office and Unilever, Dunlop and the BBC, and so on, and so on – found the McKinsey medicaments irresistible.

British consultants were consumed with jealousy by this American success in winning fat assignments and, adding insult to injury, publicising it. One or two hinted darkly that the follow-up to McKinsey's work was less inspiring than its orders; the dark hints have recently been echoed in the US, with *Business Week* noting that 'the firm has played a major role in advising the managements of such troubled companies as American Express, Digital Equipment, General Motors and Sears Roebuck during their declines'.

The problem is that consultants, in the end, can only be as effective as their clients. Thus, Spillers, then a flour giant, went on a McKinsey course of reorganisation and marketing orientation: its profits then fell by one third in three years. That was merely preparatory work for the vast fall in earnings which led to Spillers' own disappearance – swallowed up by the agriculturally-based Dalgety. Dunlop was another good customer. Just before its marriage with Italy's Pirelli was consummated, Dunlop's pre-tax profits had been stuck for three years running. That merger was probably the most disastrous cross-border liaison in history – for the British groom, that is.

By the time it divorced the Italians, Dunlop had lost huge sums of money on the deal and, far more serious, had lost its way in the technology and marketing of its base business, tyres. Even total capitulation in 1984, selling the bulk of the tyre business to Japan's Sumitomo, couldn't restore Dunlop to health. Later that year, the rump, racked by ruinous debts, was being kept alive only by the bankers – and an unseemly squabble was needed before BTR settled the issue by purchasing the wreck.

Another McKinsey client, the Post Office, set up as a new public corporation, combined big marketing fiascos with huge deficits before management got to work with new consultants and a new approach – TQM. At least, the Bank of England didn't follow this loss-making precedent, since central banks, by definition, can't lose money. But its record in recent years is one of unmitigated boobs, in the course of which national financial disaster was but narrowly averted. Even Shell, after a few years, found the McKinsey scheme of boardroom organisation unworkable.

There are other examples, but their lesson is not that McKinsey's work was bad. On the contrary, its consultancy was no doubt as good as or better than most. The defects were intrinsic to consulting itself – not to consultants. The client company gets for its fee, and for a time, the services and advice of men who (if its choice has been good) have broader experience, superior intelligence, more impressive backgrounds, and sharper all-round competence than most of its executives. But the company doesn't get new management.

Most consultants tell of the assignment where the only essential, but impossible, recommendation was to heave out the boss. One man had a tough job even getting the family chairman to resign the title of chief executive, on which a vitally needed new appointee insisted. The embattled chairman, after many weeks, finally blurted out that he didn't see why he should surrender, not when Henry Ford II (at that time still in the car company's driving-seat) kept his chief executive title. 'Ah ha,' said the consultant, seizing his moment, 'but Henry Ford runs Ford.' They settled the argument by ringing Ford in Dearborn and asking if he ran the company. 'Sure as hell I do,' said Henry, and with that the chairman surrendered.

But consultants don't find it easy to bite the hand that hires them; the weaker vessels are more likely, after cosy months with the board, to unearth unsuspected virtues in the directors. Nor is there any practical point in submitting a report that incenses the customer. First, it won't be accepted, and all the consultant's labour will have gone for nothing. Second, the failed assignment will be bad for the consultant's reputation, and it is on reputation, especially in boardroom work, that a consultant's business depends. The golden rule of traditional consulting, as of advertising, is not just to keep the client happy, but to keep him.

The new emphasis on implementation, funnily enough, is a great help in obeying that golden rule. As noted, it implies that the consultants will stay around for a long, lucrative stretch of time – and never mind the fact that the fashion for implementation springs from consultancy failure, not success. The implementing phase follows hard on the heels of the strategic planning era, and is really Son of Strategy. As Booz, Allen & Hamilton president Jack Lescher explained to *Management Today*, 'A lot of the strategies that were recommended ended up on the cutting-room floor – they weren't implementable.'

Francis Gouillart, a senior vice-president at Gemini Consulting, which now has British Telecom as a top client, recalls that 'The insights you delivered were sometimes impractical. I was probably batting 25% to 30% on an implementation rate.' It was generous of managements to believe that effective implementation would flow from the same people who gave them unworkable plans. But the proposition has established a marvellous line in 'technical-support programmes, manufacturing and marketing enhancement tactics, or a management-information system that will support a company's strategic plans'.

The above words were those of a top Arthur D. Little man, who also observed that 'One trend today is the recognition of the importance of the interrelationships between strategy and operations'. To put it mildly, managements unaware of these connections – and consultants for that matter – should have been in other jobs. John Thackray wasn't being pejorative when he described consultants as 'like golf professionals who have never won any tournament but who are trusted to improve the top players' swing'; after all, Nick Faldo and Nick Price, winner of the 1994 British Open, both pay fulsome tribute to David Leadbetter's work in this respect.

But Thackray notes that in the 1950s, 'the golf-swing analogy would have been laughed at . . . yet in today's climate of general insecurity the idea is evidently plausible'. Probably, this same sense of insecurity had much to do with the literary triumph of *Excellence*. American management, having suffered from a sometimes pitiful loss of confidence before the onslaught of recession and the Japanese, drew comfort and sustenance from a book whose excellent companies were all 100% American, in origin and direction, and whose message reinforced the necessary belief of chief executives that they can shape the destiny of their companies.

Reinforcement is one of the prime commodities that the CEO and his cohorts can purchase for their consultancy fees. Some hire consultants for the most respectable, but now much less common, bad reason – to endorse a decision that, in principle, has already been taken. Very likely, Shell knew that it was fat with surplus middle executives. But the necessary pruning was more comfortable, especially for a company that rejoiced in the avuncular nickname and traditions of 'Joe Shell', when it was done, or seen to be done, on the disinterested advice of efficiency experts. This element in consultancy could be called the Pontius Pilate gambit: the hand-washing comes expensive.

But suppose the Pilate gambit in no sense applies. Assume that the directors are genuinely in a quandary; they know not which way to turn, or how. At first sight, the most sensible action they can take, before going down for the third time, is to clutch at consultancy and hope that it won't prove to be a straw. But what the company needs as well, and urgently, is a top management capable of leading. That's precisely the point that Akio Morita, co-founder of Sony, and father of the Walkman, once made to *Playboy*: 'I think Americans listen too much to the securities analysts and the consultants. American management no longer likes to make decisions. No one takes responsibility. That's why the consulting business is so good in the US.'

To put it more crudely, in the words of a *Harper's Magazine* headline: 'Why do experienced executives pay millions for the advice of young punks in pinstripes who've never run anything?' The rude question has a polite echo in what Bruce D. Henderson, the man who led Boston's spectacular growth, has to say on the salaries paid to those young punks – that is, business graduates, more of whom, attracted by the high initial rewards, go into consulting than anything else. As Henderson said, 'Some clients were not happy at financing, with their fees, these ridiculously high salaries.' McKinsey's Jon Katzenbach noted that 'If I had my way, I'd not pay them that much. A, they're probably not worth it. B, it creates the wrong image with my clients.'

C, he might well have added, it's very hard to argue that the punk in pinstripes can have anything useful to offer that any senior manager worth his stock options doesn't know already – or couldn't find out much more cheaply. That's why the newer breed of consultancies, firms like Kalchas, recruit people whose intellectual equipment is accompanied by real-life business experience. Such firms are unlikely to be large, and even more unlikely to fall into formula solutions. The latter are quite prevalent; the favoured approaches of individual large consultancies can be easily recognised, like hallmarks on old silver, by the cognoscenti.

When a company was told to reorganise into product divisions, install long-range corporate planning, and establish a straight man-to-man pyramid of line executives, with a single chief executive at the top – that was once the authentic hallmark of McKinsey. Today, McKinsey's product mix is different; but it has only changed as necessary to retain its image as the 'high priest of strategic consulting'. Others have changed the brand: BCG has moved on from its once-famous matrix for strategic portfolio planning; now 'time-based competition' has led the firm deep into 're-engineering'.

With that splendid piece of coinage, consultants have successfully relabelled much the same work on improving processes and efficiency that they've always done. CSC Consulting, the coiner of re-engineering, has doubled revenues in three years to $470 million. Whatever their brand, however, few consulting firms are prepared to limit their range of tempting services. One marketing consultant is happy to work on market strategy, new product development, organisation of sales forces, diversification, corporate planning, and so on. Even an enormously successful specialist like Andersen is now strenuously diversifying into strategic and other consultancy.

The dynamic of consultancy, as with any growth business, is maximisation of revenues. Only then can the firm provide its members with the glowing reward and warm job satisfaction that, rather than the grandeur of the organisation, are its objectives. This is a key difference between consulting firms and the industrial corporation, to which organisational grandeur matters greatly – which is partly why many former management consultants find adjusting to executive jobs in industry so tough.

Another part of the trauma hangs on the word 'executive'. The consultant, implement though he may, basically advises; he can only put his own delectable ideas into full practice by quitting the racket. In management, having ideas is wonderfully easy, and buying them, from consultants or anybody else, is not much harder; turning them into reality leads to the pain of ulcers, losses, and angry shareholders. At that point, the top-level consultant is out of the line of fire. If the outcome is disaster, the consultant can always argue either that the client failed to follow through the advice properly, or that the glue would have been still stickier without his advice, an argument that has the great virtue of being wholly irrefutable (and wholly unprovable, for that matter).

If a company wants to employ consultants effectively, it had better use them where effectiveness can be measured. The best reason for using a consultant is because he knows something you don't know. There really are consultants pumped full with all there is to know about 'physical distribution management', i.e. lugging goods about. There are consultants in how to sit, how to sell, how to plan, how to budget, how to interpret market-research statistics: you name it, somebody knows it – and somebody needs it. No management can be blamed for failure to have universal knowledge of the new business technology. But no management can be excused for failure to buy the missing knowledge, or for falling for the idea that general ignorance can be overcome by some single session, even one lasting six hours, at the feet of some guru or gurus.

Whole-day seminars for the board are approximately as helpful to the company as a visit from Billy Graham. But the act of hiring and listening to an apostle of enlightened management is somehow thought to qualify the hirer as an enlightened executive. The intention substitutes nicely for the reality. Moreover, false enlightenment comes cheap. In a situation of hunger – in this case, for enlightenment – the man offering food to the starving has a great bargaining position, especially when even $60,000 a day is a drop in the ocean of corporate waste.

That waste is a subject on which one of the most valuable of all gurus, the late W. Edwards Deming, has forthright views. 'American management on the whole has a negative value – it's like an old refrigerator you can't sell,' he once told *Fortune*. That being so, failing to get a return from Deming's seminars (he gave his last one, aged ninety-three, two weeks before he died) should be fairly difficult. Just mastering the eleventh of his famous fourteen points ('eliminate work standards that prescribe numerical quotas') should be worth many times the cost of attendance. That is one of the many Deming lessons that the Japanese have taken to heart. Observe, though, that this isn't general guidance, but highly specific, with results that can be swiftly and directly measured – just like the Japanese preference in corporate in-house education.

The Japanese not only use the specific, practical advice of consultants. They treat it exactly as they do manufacturing plant or purchased technology; working in partnership, they modify, improve and develop. That's the correct way to use consultants – and they are usable; there truly is a real task in which the business academic, or the professional consultant, can always help. It arises from the same causes that can also negate consulting work – the fact that the consultant, especially one who has real business experience, is outside the company, has the outsider's acute vision, and will play no long-term role in managing the firm.

In any company, no matter how good, internal blindness

becomes a besetting sin. Blinkered by obstinacy, experience, and self-regard, executives can't see their own simple mistakes. The outsider can. But his use as devil's advocate depends on having executives who will listen. Beyond this, the proper use of outside experts, in their fields of expertise, is as rifles aimed to pick off specific identified targets. To use them as shotguns, spraying in all directions, is a wasteful and uncertain method of getting bull's-eyes.

Calling in an expert to install a new management concept is like calling in the computer wizards. Unless the systems within which the new toy works are themselves effective, the toy will give no joy. In other words, it takes a high-class executive to know when he needs a consultant, to get full value, and to take the expert's advice critically and unemotionally. All consultants know that their best work is done with the best companies, a very obvious truth, even if it means that those who most need consultancy use it least and get least out of it.

The high-class executive is also less likely to run for help (or for cover) indiscriminately; it's the lower-class executive who abdicates, who lets the consultants take over, staying in a company forever, moving from one divisional trouble spot to another like Arabs wandering from oasis to oasis. It's been said, cynically enough, that half the time companies employing consultants really need new management, and that, for half the rest of the time, consultants are misused. But whatever the true percentage of proper use by proper managements, the ultimate possibilities, on both sides of the relationship, are defined by the human factors.

Take the case of one super-growth company that had plainly outstripped a rudimentary management system. One of the consultant's remedies was to kick the energetic, pro-consultancy, but elderly, chairman upstairs, in favour of the highest-ranking relative. The chairman's attitude underwent radical change. While preparing to resume the reins, he was heard to mutter, 'I don't think much of these consultants'. That is the problem in a capsule. Often you can't make top-level consultancy work without convincing executives of the error of their ways, and bad ones purely hate to be convinced.

26

The Innovatory
Helter-Skelter

One obsession unites executives right round the world: the urge to innovate. Firms love to boast that such and such a percentage of sales is, or will be, of products unborn five or ten years back. The innovatory quest has spawned new consulting firms, passing gimmicks such as 'venture management', and new areas of aching loss. Consumers are showered with new wonders that they don't want, which don't work, which rapidly disappear – and still executives crave more of the same punishment.

Yet any wised-up executive granted one wish by the great god Mammon would beg not a new product, but one that would become very, very old. The most desirable products, self-evidently, are those that last forever. Most of the world's great businesses earn their bread from just such blessings. The most conspicuous proof is Coca-Cola: when its management sought to change the venerable product's formula, the outcry of outraged consumers forced a volte-face – and original (or 'Classic') Coke remains the backbone of a company worth over $50 billion in mid-1994.

This truth runs counter to a cherished concept of marketing theory, the product life-cycle. Any academic can draw the smooth curve that shows the steep upward rise as the innovation takes off, the flattening-out of profits as competition moves in – before peak sales arrive – then the slow decline through obsolescence to the morgue. From this, any student can mark the spot where new products must pick up the baton if the company isn't to drop out of the race.

The picture is beautiful, beguiling, meaningless. First, theoretical life-cycle charts never have an actual time-scale, and it makes a mint of difference whether the palmy days will last fifty years or five. Second, the phrase 'new product' needs careful analysis. The Mondeo is dazzlingly new compared to the Model T Ford. But the basic technology, as opposed to its refinements, variations and additions, has changed surprisingly little in half a century. This relative stagnation explains a commercial fantasy such as the Volkswagen Beetle, which ran unchanged forty years after its design and twenty-five years after its first sale.

In food, top brands such as Kellogg's Corn Flakes, Nescafé, and Heinz baked beans have been bestsellers almost since introduction. That's true, even though the US alone has been spawning 5–6,000 new food products a year (of which only 1,800 reached the stores and only 500 survived twelve months). In publishing, the *Reader's Digest* has outsold all other magazines for decades. In soft drinks, even Coca-Cola's great challenger, Pepsi-Cola, is no chicken. The common-or-household light bulb of today would be familiar to Edison. The aspirin has been the world's leading analgesic since 1898.

The Mars bar, Vaseline, Kleenex, Levis, Nivea – these are only a few of the legions of products that continue to dominate important markets (and to underpin the revenues of great companies) long years after the proprietorial genius showed them the light of day, or saw it himself for the last time. Nearly all long-lasting products have improved substantially since their dawn. But as technical concepts they are identical. To take the Mondeo again: it's technically superior, more comfortable, more convenient, faster than the Cortina which was Ford's first post-war hit in Britain; but the driver behind the steering-wheel and internal-combustion engine, on top of the four wheels, won't get from point A to point B any faster.

In Detroit's heyday, the products barely altered. Only the outer skin – the packaging – was changed annually at an alarming cost, which was built into the price of the vehicle. This built-in obsolescence opened wide the doors of Detroit to competitors who did vary the concept; minnows from Europe and Japan beat the mightiest American management machines in their own precious market with their own technology. The built-in obsolescence turned out to be, not of the styling, but of the concept. The bungling of the car bosses did not arise from lack of new products, but from missing the effect on old ones of changing tastes and demography – the rapid increase in numbers of working wives, the emigration to the suburbs and ex-urbs, the new interest in fuel economy.

Brands mostly lose market share or wither on the vine, not because they get overtaken by the march of history or the pace of technology, but because executives stupidly neglect them. There is no automatic product life-cycle; there is a mismanagement cycle. A confectionery executive once stumbled on this truth. He had an old line of cachous: a Victorian sweet that any whizzing young brand manager would have shot on sight. Apart from its creaking antiquity, its sales figures were convincingly bad. Over the years they had slid down the life-cycle slope to a quarter of their one-time peak.

The chief executive (who, since the family owned the business, was more possessive than marketing professionals) looked at the figures another way. Certainly, they showed that far fewer people wanted his sweets. But the miracle, for unpromoted, old-fashioned gunk, was that so many still drooled for the stuff. It must have something. So he improved production to cut costs, spent the savings on promotion – and sales doubled.

The mistake, once a company has built a market, is to throw it away. Back in the 1950s, Howard Johnson was almost as symbolic of America as the Statue of Liberty – or rather, of Middle America. The ubiquitous orange-roofed restaurants were as popular with middle-class Americans as the famous ice-cream was with their kids. But Middle America changed, and as it changed, HoJo didn't. On the contrary, for nearly twenty years the company spent not a cent on refurbishing its hotels and restaurants.

After some foolish Britons on the road to dismemberment, the Imperial Group, bought the chain for a fabulous (or fatuous) $630 million, matters deteriorated so far that, even after $350 million of belated spending, ace hotelier Willard Marriott Jr. could pronounce this thumbs-down verdict to *Business Week*: 'Howard Johnson has too much outdated product they can't do anything with.' Howard Johnson wasn't dying from natural causes, note. It had undergone slow strangulation at the hands of the old family management. As the magazine observed, whether the loss-battered Britons sold HoJo or soldiered on, 'it appears that the orange roofs that dotted American highways for sixty years are going the way of wayside Burma Shave signs – and for the same reasons'.

Mind you, the temptation to give in to those seductive arguments, and to go on making an unchanged product until it simply stops selling, is very powerful, on a short-sighted financial view. Old-fashioned car firms like the lamented and lamentable British Motor Corporation, according to their managers, chose to run their wonders, until they and their market dropped, to give the customer continuity. Actually, BMC couldn't afford the whopping investment in new or radically improved models. It also went on making obsolete cars on the specious financial argument that the production equipment had all been paid for with 'depreciation' money.

In reality, the old cars with their antique design and engineering were even more expensive to produce than the new ones – and were stealing the latter's sales. Behind successful cars which seem to change only at long intervals, and then very carefully, like the Mercedes-Benz line, lies a massive investment in both manufacture and R & D: spending which in relation to sales is hardly less significant than the amounts committed by manufacturers in the mass market, where model lines must not only change, but be seen to change.

All businesses need an old product policy – how to make the best of what the company has. After the Second World War, Beecham (whose famous pills date back to 1847) built its considerable fortunes on three oldies: Brylcreem, Macleans and Lucozade. Even at the end of the 1960s, this unglamorous trio – a gooey haircream, a crisp white tooth-paste, and a sickly-sweet glucose drink – were providing, with the genuinely new Beecham penicillins, about two-thirds of the group profits. The old brand has the cumulative weight of years of heavy advertising, of use by (more or less) satisfied customers, of high acceptability and established image.

So long as astute directors improve and upgrade the product in step with the market, and modify the image with the times, the dreaded turning-point in the life-cycle can be put off indefinitely. Because executives get bored or compla-cent with old products, however, they quite unnecessarily condemn them to fast death or slow neglect. Beecham's veterans, Brylcreem and Macleans, had so much life in them that a substantial US business was promoted on their backs. (A newer Beecham condiment, Silvikrin shampoo, failed expensively, however; its name made the unacceptable sug-gestion to Americans that they were going grey.)

One of Beecham's American markets, contrarily, seems to prove the life-cycle: toothpaste, where the old US brand leaders have all been ejected by upstarts. The whole American industry was turned upside down by stannous fluoride. Here was a true technological advance: the first toothpaste whose advertising need tell no lies. It knocked the makers, Procter & Gamble, for a loop (P & G, of course, being a big company, didn't invent Crest – a university did). The hucksters could sing the therapeutic virtues of toothpastes that, hygienically speaking, were no better than any other. They couldn't cope with Crest, which truly was better. After painful false starts, the American Dental Association ended the agony by endorsing the product. A simple, unglamourised advert baldly stating the facts thereupon succeeded superbly, where the traditional ballyhoo had crashed.

While it probably still needs promotion, a great new product has to differ so sharply from any joy already on sale that its qualities – so long as they are good – sell themselves. P & G's competitors made the gratuitous error, when they launched stannous-fluoride toothpastes, called Ace and Cue, of making them almost indistinguishable from Crest. New products fail, and in phenomenally high proportions, because they offer no advantage worth having or, more simply, because they are bad. Even an admirable original (such as xerography or the Polaroid camera) customarily starts life badly: it is clumsy, hard to use, dear, unsatisfactory in its results. But their unique concept allowed Xerox and Polaroid to override initial error.

When similar defects in use attack products that merely vary somebody else's theme, the customers will stand clear in droves. The highest mortality – nine out of ten – is in cigarettes, where the novelty mainly lies in the marketing. Each cigarette is the same as some other cigarette, and those that fail are as good (or bad) as those that win. New-product calamities, in fact, stem from confusion about newness. The pet venture may be a straight or crooked copy; or an attempt to break into somebody else's racket (IBM trying with scant success to muscle in on Xerox, or Xerox, with even scanter success, trying to muscle in on IBM); or the newness may lie in replacing a similar product of your own (like the new detergent formula which set Unilever and P & G at each other's throats in the European market in 1994).

There may be real technological novelty in replacements. But even great 'innovations', such as the Boeing 707, don't produce whole new markets – and don't necessarily greatly expand them, either. People don't shave more because stainless-steel blades are superior to carbon steel, and more airliners would have been sold if the jet engine had never been invented. The complete innovations, like the personal computer and its software, creating whole new markets, thrusting old companies into oblivion and new ones into pre-eminence, are so rare, and so rarely originate from big corporations, that in the past the giants would have been better advised to avoid the chase.

333

Even today, their 'new product' is usually a 'me-too' (an imitation of somebody else's wow); or, far better, some variation on their own themes. The latter pays fine dividends. Stick an extra carburettor, a new paint job and a few fancy extras on the same car, call it the GT or the GTO, and collect a bundle of extra cash from the customers without the financial and technical pain of producing a new super-model. Far better to devise a new method of processing an existing fibre and open up new uses, than to invent a new shoe material called Corfam and embark on a long, expensive failure to foist it on a wary world which prefers leather.

The second, even if it succeeds, only produces a long-haul yield. The former, with minimal fortune, pays off at once, and if it fails, costs little more than some executive's self-respect. Even that bruising will be mitigated by executives' reluctance to remember their failures. Marketing books are full of success stories, but failure has no friends and few case-histories – even though collapse is far more common. On one survey's conclusions, there is an eight-out-of-ten ratio of technical failure, while only one in every three technical successes (meaning that the product works) goes on to commercial triumph.

The lessons of failure are always the more valuable. When executives look back at the successes, like generals brooding over old campaigns, they always rationalise and mistake perfect luck for perfect performance. Triumph often catches its perpetrators completely by surprise, like the runaway hit in the US of two novel 'light' Scotch whiskies, Cutty Sark and J & B. Both were owned by respectable London wine merchants who in those days knew far more about pre-phylloxera clarets than about marketing.

All too often managements under threat – from product obsolescence or competition – react either too slowly or too ambitiously. When Gerber and Campbell's came beefing their way into Heinz's UK goldmine, attacking Heinz's canned foods and ready-to-serve soups with bottled and concentrated recipes, Heinz didn't botch its response. It put out its own bottled baby foods and concentrated soups, just in case the British housewives changed their tastes from cans to bottles and from ready-to-serve to concentrates, and it battered the opposition with massive promotion. Gerber and Campbell's were clobbered.

But more often companies get locked into their technology as well as their management habits – and even more dangerously. 'Maybe Xerox will come first when the inevitable happens,' I wrote long ago, 'and its cumbersome, unreliable reprographic money-spinner is replaced by a more efficient, less unwieldy process. But don't bet on it'. That was sound advice; the Japanese remorselessly attacked every weakness, reducing the giant's market share from nearly 100% to single figures before the one-time champion began a long, arduous and much-lauded comeback.

I added, all those years ago, that 'Xerox shouldn't bet on having the good fortune of IBM'. The first Univac computer (produced by men whom IBM had sent packing) appeared, and made IBM's entire product range obsolescent, four years before IBM got a computer on the market. Univac, however, so crunched up the greatest post-war commercial discovery that IBM, despite its errors and delay, roared past Univac into staggering riches. With later challenges, IBM repeated the process of delay and triumph, all the way to the personal computer. But later challengers and technology gave IBM no space to recover from its errors; by the time the company had woken up, both its total dominance in the world market and its technological leadership had gone for good.

You can bank on the opposition being stupid some of the time, but not all the time. That is the trouble with me-too products. Assuming that the market is established, the me-too executive is gambling that his product will be better and better marketed. This ignores logic. Trying something different is always better than competing directly, for in the latter case, you may lose. The small companies that creep to riches under the skirts of large auntie corporations do so by specialising, by doing something different. Nobody got near Kodak's mass market in conventional cameras and films until the American firm unwisely let the Japanese steal a lead on costs. Before that, though, Polaroid got in under Auntie Kodak by offering a clear difference: instant photos.

335

Self-deception is rampant. No executive confesses, even in private, that the opposition does indeed have a better product (if the opposition has been making the thing longer, it should do). No executive readily concedes that time and other people's money have produced a lemon. Only the most self-aware executive takes honest account of cannibalisation, or robbing Peter to pay Paul; thus a car company's new wonder hits the sales of its next model down, so that total sales don't rise by the numbers of the new winner. Thus Compaq, in introducing low-priced PCs, ran the risk – or rather embraced the certainty – of the new product stealing sales from the established models; gambling, with brilliant success, that total sales would rise enough, even at much lower prices, to offset the consequences.

In the end, Compaq's revenues, market share and profits all recovered to new record levels – the first two spectacularly. By contrast, IBM, in the effort to stop the PC Jr (aimed at the home market) from eating into sales of full-blown office PCs, produced in self-defeating fashion a cheaper model that not only was inferior, but looked it. No wonder the product became the most expensive flop in all IBM history. The logic is inescapable. If the new product is necessary (which Jr wasn't, but Compaq's ProLinea was), cannabilisation is part of the price of progress.

Although such high-technology launches are notorious for high cost and high risks, new products which are lower in technology but high in marketing requirements carry the same heavy burdens. Since maybe only one-eighth of the launches proceed from test market to success, the option of shunning new products looks increasingly attractive – but hardly anybody dares to take it; and rightly. The hectic chase after innovation, which keeps executives busy and advertising agencies in funds, is bound to be expensive, but it isn't a luxury: not any more.

Present prosperity for most companies, and prosperity for a good time to come in the fortunate cases, will rest on old products. But the future, more than it has ever done, must rest on genuine and continuing innovation. The overwhelming reason is that, in a context of sharpened and global competition, fragmenting markets and generally accessible technology, product-leads last too short a time for any leader to rest on its oars. The process of generating new products and processes has to be endless if companies want to stay in the game.

That being so, it makes no sense to stay in the majority: that is, to find three-quarters of your new products failing absolutely, with many of the rest obviously failing in relative terms. Some companies reckon that only 6% of their development money ends up in commercial successes, which is not only perverse but perverted. The condition won't be cured unless the organisation of new product development is made a key activity of the corporation, welded into its structure, springing out of maximum informality and creativity, but then tightly and efficiently controlled to maximise the chances of success.

A crucial point is that, at the current rate of progress, Western companies will have largely caught up with Japanese standards of quality and productive efficiency by the millennium. But catch-ups on these so-called 'hard' factors can't provide competitive advantage. They merely keep you in the new game – and it will be won by the leaders on other, apparently softer ground. The Japanese, usually right on matters of vision, have already marked out that ground. Creativity and innovation, they believe, will win the next century's battles by hard achievement.

Gigantic, corporatic businesses do have alternatives to creative constipation; innovation is a business process that, like any other, can be managed and manipulated to achieve chosen ends. The view is anathema to the romantics, who feel that some people are far more creative than others (true), so that companies in search of innovative fire need simply hire creative talent and wait for the inspired lightning to strike (totally false). Edward de Bono has long taught and shown that any group of people can radically improve the effectiveness of their innovative thought by better methodology.

For instance, the microprocessor with which Intel launched the decisive end-of-century revolution did involve inspiration and genius. But turning the idea into astounding growth and an 80% world-market share took creative management of the highest order. By contrast, IBM's invention of reduced instruction-set computing was the next big breakthrough in microprocessors; but for years the RISC technology was left for other companies to exploit. The failure, unlike Intel's success, lay in lack of brilliant creative management, of disciplined, speedy and determined innovation.

That doesn't rule out the wild card; rather, it supplies a context in which the far-out inspiration will be seized, not rejected by the usual automatic no-reflex. Innovation isn't confined to technologists and scientists, though. On the contrary, unless top management is capable of creative strategic thought, marvellous inventive talent (as at IBM) will run to waste. Unfortunately for their firms, few senior managers see that their positions require special strategic skills which need developing. Mostly, bosses come from operational backgrounds. That helps explain Britain's notorious examples of under-exploited innovations, from penicillin via jetliners and transverse car engines to Sir Clive Sinclair's aborted electronic inspirations.

In too many companies, innovation isn't strategically directed: the task is entrusted to R & D or some other department, instead of being a line management function: access to the decision-makers is the only thing that's tightly controlled, much too tightly; actual execution programmes are sloppily managed, and allowed to run so wildly over budget on both cost and time as severely to jeopardise whatever slim chances they had. That's one way to guarantee that three-quarters of all new products go on failing. But if they do, so will the corporations which perpetrate the failures.

27
The Technology of Techniques

Ask executives what they want by way of improving literature and many will call for a richer menu of management techniques. They don't really want to hear more about barely comprehensible inventions such as Monte Carlo simulation, management by exception, statistical sampling, linear programming, Markovitz Portfolio Selection, and the other contents of the technical basket. Their belief that they should know these mysteries, though, almost suggests that management techniques are like handbooks on car maintenance: master the latter and you save garage bills by doing it yourself; master the former and the business will respond to the magic technical touch.

The analogy breaks down at several points – including the fact that many techniques (among them the most valuable) can't be left to enthusiastic amateurs. Nor can technology. But this raises an obvious and increasingly urgent problem. The advent of the Silicon Age has brought into managers' lives new and complex technology of a type they seldom encountered before. The problems are, of course, especially acute in the companies actually supplying the new technology. So intense have the pressures become in the highest high-tech areas that its prodigies are beginning to talk of a new technology of management itself. Thus Andy Grove, the president of Intel, is fond of talking about VLI2 – meaning Very Large Integrated Investments – and the wholly new concepts that managements in his game must grasp.

The Silicon Valley syndrome is that every decade the microchip markets in which Intel leads become ten times larger: the devices ten times more complex; the density of the circuits ten times greater. The only thing that gets less is the price – again, by ten times. The techniques used by businesses where the key factors don't follow this exponential course simply don't apply, argued Grove, to Intel's situation: a state-of-the-art wafer factory doubled over the second half of the 1980s to twenty times the cost of 1973. The end-of-1980s plant could generate revenues ranging from $300 million (guaranteeing a thumping loss) to $900 million (a smashing profit), depending on whether its operator got the yield and pricing right or wrong – and that in turn depended on correctly judging the ten-times development in applications.

So what's the answer? According to Grove, it's 'process-oriented management', the human equivalent of the advances in artificial intelligence. These, in the shape of so-called expert systems, are now able to give better diagnoses of the meaning, say, of medical or geological information than the human mind can ever achieve. The evolution of a business like Intel's would be a continuous development, constantly modified (maybe eventually by computer) as new information appears, achieving a life of its own, independent in a sense from the managers who are ostensibly in charge. If Grove is right, the apotheosis of management techniques is at hand. Without them, management will become impossible, especially in the world of VLI2.

If so, it truly will be a new world. In the old world, a central difficulty is that of translating technical lore from the page to the battlefield. Imagine the higher executive leafing through a spunky article on the mathematical approach to the product mix (the number and variety of products a company puts out). If the company is typical, several products could be ejected with no harmful effect on profits. In fact, by making room for other lines (not one of which is ever made in the optimum numbers), a bout of slashing must boost earnings.

But the elevating cases in the product-mix article won't exactly fit any other company. And the boss's first reaction will be to call some subordinate's attention to the offending pages. If this beleaguered manager is using the technique, he fires off a brisk retaliatory memo; if not, the defensive mechanisms come into play – and the most valuable of these is sheer delay. This technique, found in no textbook, works wonders, thanks to two main defensive gambits that are diametrically opposed.

Method One is, Don't respond at all until forced. This way (the most common) amplifies the chances that other and weightier matters, like an over-priced bid for another company, will supervene, and the boss will forget all about it. Method Two is to respond at speed in overwhelming and enthusiastic detail. This embarrasses the boss in turn. Now he must make a decision, which he too dislikes, and *his* defensive mechanisms take over. With luck, he will never make the decision at all.

A Method Two twist deserving the admiration of all connoisseurs was applied within one great engineering group. Its new management ordered a full survey of production facilities to find out which could be rationalised (a euphemism of the same order and meaning as 'liquidated' in the undear, dead Soviet Russia). The gigantic tome ended with one short, arresting sentence: 'Nothing can be done until future product plans have been decided.' The incident perfectly illustrates the difference between techniques of management and management techniques.

Techniques of management are used to procure the result a manager really wants – in the above case, inaction. Management techniques are the tools that an executive may or may not use in the pursuit of those real objectives. The true aim of executives who want to bone up on techniques is to feel more efficient, more modern, better equipped. They aren't, like the genuine techniques expert, obsessively interested in applying a mathematical method, such as exponential smoothing or network analysis, to obtain better operational results.

But that – obtaining better operational results – is the name of both their games, and the test of all management activity, high technology or low. Intel's Andy Grove is by no means the only gee-whizz manager, though, to insist that the higher the technology, the higher the technique. Over at Apple, a Johnny-come-lately Silicon Valley hero (until he bit the dust) was John Sculley, who came from Pepsi to the personal computer company's rescue; he used the in-phrase 'management degree zero', saying that 'We're going to purge the word "managers" from the Apple vocabulary'.

For managers, read culture: a 'new culture. We're discovering that we have to make our own models as we go along. Out of this will come new management concepts ... After the end of the [1980s] managing will never be the same again.' He may well have been right in anticipating revolutionary change, though premature in his timing. Without doubt, there's a sense in which management in the new industries is already different; managing new industries always has been. Maybe in Silicon Valley, as Grove says, 'no project will be brought to completion by the same people who started it' as VLI2 enforces its stern laws – and as changes in management style and techniques are enforced in step.

Yet the new jargon does have the ring of old, dead attempts to reinvent the managerial wheel. Remember Harry Figgie and his 'nuclear theory of management' in Chapter 1? Like Figgie and the other conglomerators, the Silicon Valleys of America have had a plentiful crop of flops, near-forgotten names like Osborne and Trilogy. They were brought down to earth not by their inability to cope with VLI2 or failure to create (as Sculley dreamt of Apple) 'a unique learning institution', but by straightforward low-technology management error.

When Honeywell lucked out at Synertek, for example, one of the main problems was that the Minneapolis company, having bought the chip-maker, wouldn't let it use Prime computers. Why not? Because Prime is a spin-off from Honeywell. Inside a year from the takeover, Honeywell had only one of the Synertek founders and officers left on the premises; the affiliate was hopelessly over-dependent (80%)

on Atari for its sales; and a $50 million new facility at Santa Cruz came in too late to forestall the competition. Much the same story of mangled management can be told of the other electronic catastrophes. The Synerteks of the New World don't drop 38% of their sales in three years by modern management failures: good old-fashioned bungling is all that they need.

The new technology has provided plenty of brand-new opportunities for mismanagement, and in a field where the risks are unusually high. Sculley's own cola-to-Apple example proves that non-technical managers can bridge the gap between technologist and management, and in no time at all. But the divide exists all the same. It's a reflection in its way of the conflict, often deadly, between executives and technique experts inside the corporation. Not only do executives get the big money and make the big (and small) decisions; they are also free to use, abuse, or not use the expert's expertise.

To the experts, there is something deeply wounding in being forced to support their surefire cost-saving ideas with voluminous reports, while any nut in the upper echelons merely has a brainstorm in the bath, and the experts promptly have to study its inane implications – in depth, too. The inanity is often immediately apparent. Professor P.M.S. Blackett, the Briton who invented Operational Research to improve bombing efficiency and convoy deployment in the Second World War, wanted to restrict 'systems analysis' (which is the Everest of management technology) to 'calculations that can be done on the back of an envelope'.

Rather than use the same small tool for his simpler sums, however, the executive loads his own failure to clarify his thoughts on to the shoulders of the misnamed management scientist – misnamed because none of the sciences is in any way specific to management, and because the work is seldom scientific, either. The science rests only in applying measurement and logical deduction to established fact, something that executives are supposed to do for themselves.

Take a typical case – the executive who opposes a price rise, or wants to invoke a discount, or open a second sales office in a region, or revamp the corporate image. Rude questions have to be asked: 'If we raise prices by half, how much will sales fall – 10%, 20%, or 30%? At what level of sales and prices will profits drop?' or, 'How much more business will we get through this discount, or new office, or company face-lift alone, and what will it cost?' The cost is always precisely measurable, and you can always work out simply how much in extra sales is needed to cover the overall loss of profit.

Executives fail to make this easy, speedy test, not because they don't know the techniques of simple arithmetic, but because they are dead set on a course chosen for other reasons entirely. One man wants to cut prices because he thinks vaguely that it will help the sales effort; one woman wants to open the new office to widen her empire; another fellow longs to beautify the corporate image – to enhance his own. These are emotional drives. Sitting down with the back of an envelope is a cold-blooded affair that rarely satisfies anybody except the technical expert. And he is too insignificant in the hierarchy for his pleasure to matter.

The greatest operational research calculation of all time was supervised (on a blackboard, not the back of an envelope) by Henry Ford I, whose enthusiasm for management technology was only slightly warmer than his love for unions. The sum showed the economic consequences of raising Ford wages to $5 a day. The calculations proved that elevating Ford workers into potential Ford buyers would leave Henry with enormous profits. Note the sequence of events. Ford had an inspiration, which men of less peculiar genius would have missed or misunderstood. Then, like a good engineer, Ford checked his brainwave by the simplest relevant calculation. Then he put his idea into practice – again like a good engineer.

Engineering is the right analogy. Much management technology is like most production or design technology – the general manager has no necessity to know the details (though a Japanese one probably will), but must know that the technology exists. Mathematical and computational techniques are the machine tools of management, and some are as abstruse as the Cabbala. As one authority wrote, 'Some of these techniques require highly specialised knowledge or equipment for their correct use. Probably only a few dozen people in the country fully understand them ... (others) are as yet barely understood by more than a few experts.' So relax. You wouldn't be able to use them if you tried.

In remaking a factory according to the latest, revolutionary ideas on layout, equipment and flexible manufacturing cells, a good general director decides what to make, but buys an expert to tell him how. The director's judgment then tests the expert's words to confirm (say) that he isn't proposing to use a costly robot when hand-tools will do nicely (or *vice versa*), or isn't using expensive computer time to try some assumption on which no profit hinges. An American chemical plant contractor was disconcerted to find that a British customer insisted on his using the sophisticated, costly technique of network analysis. Back home, it wouldn't have been thought necessary – nor was it.

A second category of techniques is essential to almost any manager; it mostly boils down to applied common sense. Much of this indispensable technology is financial, meaning that the executive (although many will resist it) has to reduce the implications of the actions to money terms. There is always a simple, back-of-the-envelope truth involved, such as the basic discounted cash flow thought – that a pound in the hand today is worth more than a pound in the bag tomorrow. Old-line executives in their ignorance used to rely on pay-back, how long their money took to come home. This assumed, falsely, that money received in three years' time had the same value as today's. The supposedly sophisticated Americans still have a deep sentimental attachment to this ancient concept, and to a considerable degree they are right.

Old-line executives were not as silly as they seemed. Pay-back enshrines a truth. Until you do repocket your capital, the enterprise is financially pointless. Say a firm invests £10 million in a plant that produces a discounted cash flow of £1 million a year for a decade, and then has to be replaced by another plant of equivalent cost; its effort has gone for nothing. The quicker the pay-back, too, the less an executive needs to worry about discounted cash flow or anything else.

Forrest Mars, in creating his confectionery empire, used a crude, but highly effective, measure, judging executives by their return made in real money (with no allowance for so-called depreciation) on the real money that, historically, he, Forrest Mars, had put into the business. In other words, Mars looked at his wealth as an individual proprietor naturally would, and there is more logic (and money) here than in the big bureaucracy's more complex, convoluted measures.

The tycoon grabs hold of a simple, single idea that makes sense to him, and applies it consistently and ruthlessly. But Patterson of NCR, Watson of IBM, Lord Leverhulme of Lever Brothers, Henry Ford, the founding Agnelli of Fiat, and the other emperors had something else; they knew their businesses. Management techniques are adjuncts to management. They don't cope with one basic fact – that the nature of the business partly determines how it is run. You don't have to be a life-long butter-and-egg man to sell butter and eggs. But the lifetime knowledge of those who do know one end of a cow or hen from the other is critical to the success of the business – as turnaround men, or company doctors, often find out, late and to everybody's cost.

The turnaround artist, the expert called in to revive failing firms, is frequently loaded with technical lore. Often the doctor is a renegade management consultant. To judge by several experiences, there is at best a four-year rise-and-fall cycle; the technical touch first produces radical improvement, then yields diminishing returns, and is finally blunted by business troubles. The technically adept executive manager is asked to create an effective, fast-growing, efficient, and professional company out of one that is ineffective, sluggish, sloppy, and amateurish – which is why the *Wunderkind* was called in. But for all his professional equipment, he lacks the one technique that the dozy oldsters all possess: feel and affection for their special market.

Lasting success depends (more than professionals can see, for it reduces their personal marketability) on how fast the newcomers can absorb the facts of a strange market and on how responsive that market really is. Uncovering and eliminating the oldsters' mistakes is the easy bit. One taken-over motor-cycle veteran vehemently opposed dropping a brand name because of its popularity in the Middle East. Enquiry showed that the company's Arab sales could be counted on one maimed hand.

Uncovering and eliminating your own errors is no more difficult, judging by the experience of a group of American industrialists who visited Japan. According to Harvard professor Robert Kaplan, they found that the percentage of Japanese products which didn't need reworking (a hideously wasteful process) went as high as 92%. How much higher was that than the results back home? The awful answer was that they didn't know. Once they had taken the trouble to find out, they discovered an equally awful truth: their figure was also 92%, but in the opposite direction – in their case, that was the proportion *needing* rework.

After being awakened, the industrialists turned their attention to seeking some kind of improvement. Six months later, the no-rework statistic was up from 8% to 66% – and productivity was higher by a quarter. Another example is market share. Whether or not you believe the Boston Consulting Group and PIMS (Profit Impact of Market Strategy) and proceed on the assumption that your profitability will rise with market share, the latter is plainly of considerable significance. But one *Management Today* writer found an executive who took a somewhat different view. He announced 'with great pride that every time the firm put the price up 10%, it lost only 5% of its traffic' – so it still made money.

As the writer observed, 'It needs no mathematical genius to work out that company's doomsday.' This kind of nonsense tumbles out of the woodwork at the first application of common sense or management technique, call it what you will, as in the case of one battery company. It struck its profit at the year-end after simply counting the stock in the warehouse, though its deliveries to dealers were all on sale or return. The professional will settle such follies fast. The harder problem is to discover what the old boys did right, and, still more, to avoid new disasters (which the veterans would never even have imagined) in desperate attempts to overcome inborn defects in the market.

Thus Mattel narrowly survived one disastrous period in its traditional low-tech toy markets (diecast cars, etc) and achieved brief respite in electronic games. Encouraged by this, the management went into home computers as well. Egregious errors in both markets cost shareholders dear; the value of their holdings plummeted by 69% in a single year. Over at Hughes Tool, the core business which made Howard Hughes (and his fortune) a legend, the post-Hughes management tried well-production valves, pumps and services in a bid to expand beyond the golden gusher of drilling bits. The result? The drilling business stagnated, the diversifications ran into an oil and gas recession, sales fell by 35% – and Hughes made its first-ever loss.

As the company retrenched back to drilling bits, *Business Week* understandably remarked that 'Howard Hughes' ghost seems to be saying: "I told you so".' The management technician's skills can stop the rot – thus part of Hughes' new recipe was cutting manufacturing costs by automation. But replacing the fungus with healthy growth requires different aptitudes. No mere technique can solve fundamental problems like Hughes' dependence on a one-product, one-market business, or Mattel's vulnerability to the cyclical, fashion-beset character of the toy trade. Techniques are most valuable for correcting mismanagement. Thus the most important technique, positively guaranteed to wash any business whiter, is challenge.

Since every business is managed badly, in the sense that every operation is capable of improvement, savings can always be made without any loss of effectiveness – and often at little cost. Simple technical analysis will always reveal bad cases of common defects, such as the overheads obsession. One company quite typically maintained a money-losing plant just for its contribution to overheads; it was tying up £4 million for a £65,000 contribution. Another firm kept a large loser going on the same specious grounds – the loss-maker, far from making a contribution, practically was the overheads; substituting a breakeven business for the burden put the company into significant profit at a stroke.

Companies often suffer under the delusion that by juggling costs around the organisation, even with no new money coming in, they can enrich its finances. The best use of technicians is not to chart corporate forays into the remote and uncertain future, but to uncover the errors of its present management. This is unlikely to be popular; it falls foul of a basic lie of management – any mistakes were made by the previous incumbents. The Tenth Truth, however, is that the easiest way of making money is to stop losing it. Dealing with customer complaints once cost Heinz £4 a throw, until some unsung genius thought of issuing a 25p voucher every time a can of beans or tomato soup caused grief. That's real management, and it doesn't need a computer.

The task isn't to understand what is meant by, say, 'a system using doubly exponentially smoothed average demand forecasts with safety stocks being set with a Trigg Tracker and the modules of the Trigg Tracker used to control the parameters of the exponential smoothing'. It is to know rules of thumb such as this: operational research techniques (now very successfully re-christened as 'business process re-engineering') will enable most companies to cut stocks by 30%, saving delicious sums; but eight-tenths of that saving will come from better record-keeping. 'Just-in-time' inventory-sparing systems will provide still greater economies, but most of them, too, come from better organisation – this time of production.

Also (and expert help will show you where), five distribution points will always provide second-day delivery to 80% of a landmass the size of the entire US. Never disparage a good rule of thumb; that digit is as valuable as any computer. But to discover and exploit such verities, you need the ability to challenge, check, and check again. Beyond that, the vital technique of management is the use of analytical methods to picture reality. Managements are always being misled, like the paper company that thought it had developed a great trade in disposable surgical dressings. It applied a much-abused technique (market research) and found that doctors actually used the products as de luxe hand towels.

Luck, that most valuable of all management techniques, had played its usual, indispensable part. If you attribute your success partly to pure luck, you will not only be right, some of the time, but you will be better prepared for the repugnant job of criticising your mistakes, which are plenty. An executive in one of the more efficient retail giants once remarked, 'Anybody listening in on our meetings would think it was the worst-run business in the world.' That is the only safe assumption.

Discontent is commercially divine – the manager's best friend. But like the techniques it employs, self-criticism won't create a wonderful business; the tycoon doesn't need techniques, and can afford self-adulation, because he can think and act along the straight line between a marvellous idea and its realisation. Executives, who are hired hands and tend to think in circles, need all the technical aid they can get – especially from themselves.

28
The Organisational Obsession

The most prevalent organisational blight is organic – the growth of the corporate organism into an end in itself. Executives swear that they exist to make money, sell safety matches, build power stations, market lingerie, or whatever, but insensibly they slide into serving none of these ends. Instead, they serve only the corporation. The business exists to sustain the company. The company no longer exists to do business; it exists to exist.

Consequently, a mind-bending preoccupation of senior executives is with the form of the beloved organism. Like some collector of stamps or rare coins, they fiddle constantly with the object of their love, and they call in other avid enthusiasts (in this case, management consultants) to help in rearranging, pruning, and swapping. Corporate reshuffles are non-events – for everybody outside the corporation. Inside they are of lasting fascination, like a restatement of Catholic dogma. Their initiation alone accomplishes nothing measurable. A bad business can never be swung round to super-growth by redrawing the organisation chart.

Boards huff and puff about strains on the previous structure, about growth imposing new pressures for which the old machinery was inadequate, about it being time for a new look. For the real reasons, read bad trading results, uncomfortable awareness of falling behind the fashion, a

351

takeover bid miraculously concentrating the mind – as at ICI, which suddenly decided to reorganise itself into two separate halves. But the most common cause is simply that introspection, which all bureaucracies enjoy, has to come to a great orgasmic climax at periodic intervals. After their game of musical chairs, the corpocrats, purged and satisfied, settle into their new seats – and carry on much as before.

The revealing contrast is the way in which Japanese companies rise above the hierarchical obsessions and social rigidities which would stultify any Western company. The form is one thing, the spirit is another. But organisational forms can powerfully affect performance in two ways. First, they can actively obstruct effective operation. Second, a change in organisation can do more than anything else to symbolise and thus effect a change in corporate ethos and direction. The difficulties in obtaining these changes can be frightful – simply because the established procedures frustrate even intelligent initiatives.

Thus, IBM carefully worked out processes to ensure that product ideas requested by the marketing operations were, wherever possible, turned into successful products. This required an 'iterative' process, in which the R & D function responded to the initiative with queries designed to tighten up the specification. After some effort, the Europeans established the principle that they, too, could originate new products. But the procedure required that every European affiliate must join in the iterative process. By the time their reactions had been collated, however, the R & D people had moved on to other things.

The net result – intended by nobody – was that the organisation prevented any European ideas from ever becoming concrete. Among other follies, that obstruction negated one eternal, basic principle. Whatever form a company adopts, and for whatever reason, the person who is supposed to manage should manage. It has nothing to do with the letter of the chart, but everything to do with the spirit of the company. The useful purpose of reorganisation is to stop that guiding spirit, whatever it is, from being bogged down in organisational routine. A brisk game of musical chairs sharpens everybody up, the catch being that, if the executives are too slow when the music starts, they will still not be speedy enough at the end.

The sacred scrolls of the organisation's tabernacle are the manuals and, above all, the organisation chart. Like the sacred documents of many religions, these charts often mean very little, even to the initiated. Some iconoclastic managements have tried to stamp them out, with as much success as Nero had against the Christians. In one American multi-national where charts were officially forbidden, the executives drew up unofficial ones. Nothing can destroy the self-preserving desire of the inhabitants of a bureaucracy to know precisely where they stand – or where they don't stand. Many executives are more eager to narrow their responsibilities (which gives them less opportunity for failure) than to widen them.

Very possibly, the unofficial charts drawn up by deprived executives are closer to reality than those blessed by the boardroom. These are abstract art, as highly regarded as Jackson Pollocks. The top management of a big company such as Honeywell was even a bit ashamed that, once upon a recent time, it was chartless. But only the names and job titles are real; the lines of command reflect an idealised truth. The tell-tale symptom is the dotted line; the more dotted the lines on a chart, the less it reflects the way the company actually runs.

A crisp unbroken line is understood by everybody. It means that in theory Executive B reports to Executive A, who in turn supervises, controls, or pushes about Executive B. It does not mean either that B takes any notice of A, or that B manages his segment of the chart at all – A may swamp the fellow entirely. But at least everybody knows what their relationship is supposed to be. Neither A nor B may see it the same way in practice, however. In 134 cases where managers in one US multi-national thought they had told subordinates what to do, the latter were only conscious of receiving seventy-eight orders.

The dotted line, in contrast, is a thing of confused beauty and a joy forever. It fans out from boards to 'advisers' or 'planning units' – staff appointments, often at the highest level, whose work veers across that of the line managers. The chart of one large group, in the days before its untimely disappearance, was festooned with dots of this description. Or dots connect a functional department (engineering, say) with a product division; here dots mean that the two are supposed to work together, all too often a forlorn but pretty fantasy.

If engineers dominate the company (as they dearly love to do) the dotted line is more authoritarian than the solid one. One production manager, invited to reveal his sorrows to a new outside director, pointed out that small differences in fifty virtually identical components forced him to maintain fifty separate production lines. He thought that the technical specification could be met by no more than five variations. The director led him by the hand over to the engineers; they readily agreed that the production manager was dead right. The corporate ethos, or the reality behind the chart, hadn't allowed production considerations, or production men, to intrude on the organisational dominance of the engineers – even to save money.

Other dotted daydreams cover bureaucratic miasmas (see IBM, above) such as independent overseas companies that are controlled by so-called international divisions, but make the same products in the same way as domestic product divisions. Multi-national companies have gone to extraordinary chart contortions to sustain the fiction that their foreign satrapies are independent. They have good reason for telling stories – host countries (another euphemism, meaning the occupied territory) are not fond of reminders that control of large chunks of national markets or assets lies somewhere in the Midwest or even in middle England.

This kind of problem doesn't bother the Europeans one iota. The Swiss of Nestlé and the Dutch of Philips have habitually controlled their overseas companies with a tight-lipped Napoleonic firmness. 'I personally still hold the view,' wrote one of Nestlé's chocolate generals with heavy jocularity, 'that . . . we are rather decentralised. But I am often surprised when talking to our own people in the markets . . . to find that they think the contrary.' As for Philips, an internal wag commented that the electrical giant was the only company in the world where, no matter what your position, there were always more people above you than below you.

When a new man, German Helmut Maucher, took over Nestlé in the early 1980s, he set out consciously to change that heavy-handed tradition. What put courage behind Maucher's convictions was the Swiss giant's worst-ever profit falls. Crisp decisions, including a total retreat out of Libby's canned foods in the US, followed smartly by the $3 billion purchase of Carnation, typified the new style. But more important even than the simultaneous assault on corporate bureaucracy was Maucher's decision, in *Fortune*'s words, 'to give more authority and power to the line managers'. In consequence of all this radicalism, return on sales jumped 60% in three years.

The British are almost certainly more lax, or relaxed, towards managements in other lands. This has something to do with the tradition of empire (unique to the British). By the time bad news got back from India in Queen Victoria's day, it was too late to take any action, and British executives (many of whose companies, such as British Petroleum, grew up as imperially as the British Raj) became used to letting far-flung executives sink or swim. As a result, earnest efforts at home were periodically drowned by disasters in Australia or India, the compensation being that bad domestic results were periodically salvaged by some far-flung miracle.

The American imperialists, even though bad news travels faster these days, have come to share the same experience – the fiascos of Chrysler in Britain, France and Spain were, if anything, more grisly than the company's pre-Iacocca disasters in the US market. As design consultant Wally Olins described it, when Chrysler took complete financial control of British Rootes, French Simca and Spanish Barreiros, 'all names were changed to Chrysler ... The entire range of geriatric English cars, mongrel French cars and Spanish-built inferior American cars was marketed all over Europe. The result was a catastrophe.'

Not that you have to be American to mismanage multinationally. The entire Chrysler European inheritance fell into the hands of Peugeot, which 'started all over again and christened the unsavoury mess Talbot . . . another tale, equally unedifying'. Peugeot had been, as the last family-controlled car firm in Europe, secure in a solid, lucrative, middle-income niche. Its strength lay in clear identity and cherished quality – the Peugeot family even boasted that its workers had the industrious, virtuous habits of the little old Swiss watchmakers who lived nearby (and who have now become yesterday's men because of the electronic revolution).

What drove the company to distraction and vast deficits was that inept swallowing of Chrysler's European interests. Multi-national takeovers simply weren't in its experience, which (apart from Citroën) wasn't long on takeovers at all. The more either Chrysler or Peugeot tried to impose their central will on their new subsidiaries, the worse the latter seemed to perform. Controlling subsidiaries with rods (or dotted lines) of iron may stop some mistakes, but it won't solve the problem, which is fundamentally one of power. The actual management of companies is determined by their power relationships, and these, because they are human and changing, cannot be depicted by anything less than full psychoanalysis.

Like all human relationships, too, they follow no rules. There are only well-known dangers, which you can survive just as you could conceivably survive driving up the M1 on the wrong side of the road. First, if those in charge don't have the power to execute that charge, they probably won't. That needn't be whoever the chart says is in charge, so long as some other executive has the power instead. But if the authority falls into an uneasy vacuum, with overlords sitting on managerial shoulders like so many old men of the sea, the results will be ineffective.

Every manager knows what happens from experience. Some operation is reorganised along all the approved lines, management makes all the right noises, and apparently does all the right things. Yet performance doesn't improve, and may even deteriorate. Indeed, a *Harvard Business Review* study found that three-quarters of 100 companies surveyed were 'unhappy with the results' of twenty-one-plus pro-grammes intended to improve performance.

Britain's governance is another perfectly imperfect example. The reforms sound fine: hiving off executive agencies that have no place in a political environment; requiring responsible chief executives to justify their performance by economic criteria; and expecting public services to achieve the same standards, not least in satisfying customers, as the best exemplars in private business.

Yet the results have ranged from disappointing to near-disastrous. A report into the eighty new executive agencies, commissioned by the government itself, found both their chiefs and the senior civil servants to be unhappy, though on different grounds; the former complain that the latter interfere, the latter bewail the deterioration in values and culture in the agencies. According to the *Financial Times*, the author, a seconded French civil servant named Sylvie Trosa, found 'confusion in the relationship between agencies and their parent departments ... "There is a whole bureaucracy set up to monitor us", one agency chief told Ms. Trosa'.

At February's launch of the Competitiveness Forum by the CBI, Frank Burns, managing director of Premier Exhausts Systems, told how productivity actually fell when half a dozen production workers returned from abroad with new ideas to improve their section's performance. Investigation showed that managers and production experts were interfering to their hearts' content. They were barred – and productivity soared right back up. The principles of decentralisation and devolution work fine, in other words, provided they are allowed to work. But that enablement includes the set-up: the objectives selected, the resources provided, the feedback installed.

Get those three wrong, in business or government, and little can go right. Failed improvement programmes in private companies make the triple threat into reality by a simple method. Very often, the reforms have emanated from top executives, who haven't sought the agreement and advice even of senior managers, let alone the body of employees. The top echelon itself, of course, doesn't submit its own performance to the new disciplines. That helps to damage morale, which is further weakened by the expectation (usually confirmed all too soon) that the programme will lose favour, only to be replaced by another false start – and so on, *ad infinitum* (or *ad* calamity).

There are lessons here from Total Quality Management (high among those initiatives doomed to failure by top-down imposition). TQM involves the famous Deming cycle, PDCA: Plan (goals and methods of reaching same), Do (implement, after training and education), Check (the results), Act (to correct for error). Many companies (just like the British government) plan inadequately, do ineptly, don't check – and don't correct. Where that happens, the fault lies overwhelmingly with the leadership. In politics, that comes down to the one Prime Ministerial person at the apex of the pyramid; in business, generally, to the single chief executive. Is that in itself an organisational error?

The pressures of complexity are leading towards multiple management: not the multiple, hydra-headed variety long favoured by companies like Royal Dutch-Shell or Unilever, still less the troikas of the 'president's office' tried by several American giants, but a genuinely collegiate effort in which primacy doesn't go hand-in-hand with dictatorship. Once again, it's a matter of balance. The organisation must have clear, single, single-minded authority at the pinnacle; but the right to that authority depends heavily on the readiness to relinquish, share and even subjugate it in the interests of effective management.

Where hydra-headed management has grown up over the years, and has become built into the life-style, changing it can be as difficult as altering the whole direction and philosophy of the corporation. Shell found this out after its own McKinsey-advised reshuffle. There one director ended up as something called Director of Co-ordination, Oil. Catch-22 was that Shell happens to be an oil company, the bulk of whose business descended, with backbreaking force, on this one man. His position, like the reshuffle, became quite untenable.

Oil companies such as Shell face in acute form the dilemma of all organisations, which is to resolve the pull between the centre and the lone executive down the line manipulating the physical facts on a day-to-day basis. Because oil is the most homogenous of businesses, the spider in the middle of the web can pull everything in towards it; but what about the happiness and self-esteem of lesser insects around the rim? The decentralise-centralise problem can never be finally resolved. The gibe goes that the management consultant called into a decentralised company says 'centralise'. Show him a centralised company, and he promptly decentralises it. The bigger the company, too, the more likely the consultant is to push the top management upstairs into an ethereal chart zone known as strategy.

But where does strategy begin and tactics end? Did Electrolux rise from sales of $211 million when Hans Werthen took over in 1967 to $4.2 billion in 1983 and $12.9 billion a decade later because of his strategy – buying the biggest share of Europe's appliance market until it accounted for the bulk of turnover? Or were the tactical moves, like exacting high profitability, partly through efficient engineering, the real explanation? And which was responsible for the barely visible profits (0.37% of sales in 1993): bad strategy, incompetent tactics, or both?

The larger a company is, the more often strategy gets locked in by supposedly tactical decisions taken far lower down. By the time most issues have worked their way up the chart to the board or executive committee, the titans at the top may no longer have either the freedom or the time to reverse what some remote underling has wrought. The object of a decentralising reshuffle is to consolidate this unplanned fact into a shining system of delegated responsibility.

But anyone can see the futility of, say, constructing a three-ring circus – the board, a trading board one ring down, and a permanent executive committee of trading directors below that. The overlaps between the three tiers mean that the seven managing executives on the trading board are responsible for their triumphs and misdeeds to a main board that consists mostly of themselves (making life a little easier all round, but also a lot less effective). The astrological complexities of systems like this (taken from the earlier life of British Petroleum), with nine trading executives as satellites of the seven managing executives, and regional and functional orbits crisscrossing all over the planet earth, practically guarantee that the delegated power, like hot air, will rise right back to where it has always resided.

But some secret force makes a company work, more or less effectively, despite the efforts of bureaucracy to turn its management totally inwards. Somewhere in the organisation lurk the 20% of executives who (according to Pareto's law) do 80% of the effective work. Finding the 20% and removing obstacles to their performance is the only proper pursuit of organisational organisers. An idealist might try to uplift the 20% proportion, but this is unrealistic. Maybe the active executives, like worker bees in a hive (only with a king bee or king bees at their head), need a large community of drones. In which case, the chartists should concentrate on keeping the drones in happy, mildly useful and clear relationship to each other, and out of the hair of the workers.

This worker-drone breakdown could be synthesised into a new psychological theory of companies, like the popular contrast between authoritarian Theory X companies and easy-going participative Theory Y firms. The idea of hierarchical managements trying to loosen up is like Soviet reformers trying to give more power to factory directors. It failed because it wasn't what the *apparatchik* bosses really wanted. Styles of management grow out of traditions of companies and styles of people, and there is still, alas, no convincing evidence that Theory Y companies, although much nicer to work for, outperform the Theory X bastards.

All the same, there's more than sheer iconoclasm in the sermon which Robert Townsend has long preached to corporations which are interested in moving in the radical, Theory Y directions he favours. To take one of his stories about the Gore-Tex company, it makes no difference to the efficiency of an organisation whether people have job titles or not; so, if somebody, as one woman did, says she always wanted to be a vice-president, let her call herself anything she likes, as grand as she likes (this Gore lady ended up with 'Supreme Commander' on her visiting cards). Nike, the sporting-shoe company, is another firm which has no respect for titles at all – and just makes them up as it goes along.

The new informality is no more effective in itself than the

traditional ways. But what it stands for is an easier, freer form of association inside the company, from which greater effectiveness should flow. That's why Townsend's favourite steel company, built on a greenfield site by refugees from Big Steel, and now the fifteenth largest in the US, has absurdly large hallways; so that people can meet and argue in them. This freedom of association is actually basic to Japanese managers, whose very souls would generally revolt at the kind of togetherness practised in Nike, Gore or scores of Silicon Valley companies.

But you won't find in Japanese firms the organisational barriers described earlier in this chapter, which stop production from talking to sales from talking to marketing from talking to personnel. The barriers come down because the people on different sides of them, in organisation-chart terms, don't regard themselves as different. They see themselves all as devoted members of the same outfit, with the same basic activity – being businessmen. Thus production, sales, marketing, personnel, planning, etc are all in on all business decisions which affect them all. That's the essence of the famous *ringi* process: not the laborious method by which decisions are reached, stamped and sealed, but the involvement worthy of the best Theory Y culture.

Even where a recognisable Theory Y company is a wow, there is a chicken-and-egg difficulty. As a company succeeds, so its executives, working cheek-by-jowl over the years, develop respect for each other's muscles, wariness of each other's weaknesses, and instinct for a management method that suits them all equally. Call this participation, if you will. But Theory Y can no more be credited for its success than Theory X can be applauded for swimming against the conglomerate tide for a spell under Harold Geneen, a sixteen-hour-a-day dynamo who devised a corporate structure that revolved around him like a top. A manager can make an organisation, and an organisation in turn makes its managers. But if the company falls on evil days, it won't achieve salvation without a change in the management as well as the mechanism.

29
Battle of the Bestsellers

The wondrous boom in management of the post-1973 era quite inevitably meant a wonderful something else: a boom in management literature. Managers desperately needed more knowledge to cover their nakedness, and books are where knowledge resides. Robert Townsend's *Up The Organisation* and Lawrence Peter's *The Peter Principle* proved to be the iconoclastic forerunners of a stream of non-academic tomes which became a spate – and then turned off in a new and unexpected direction. Even *In Search of Excellence* (the book which, as noted in Chapter 25, brought new riches to consultancy) did so in the time-honoured manner, writing about the great and the good.

Time (and honour) have changed, however. Now the great, the good and the not-so-good write about themselves. True, Townsend used his turnaround triumph at Avis as a peg on which to hang his enthusiastic ideas about permissive Theory Y management. But it was still definitely a management book. In 1984, though, the runaway, unprecedented bestseller success of Lee Iacocca's life and good times changed the name of the game. *Iacocca* is a full-blooded autobiography, more in the vein of John De Lorean's literary work – though the latter was the self-justifying effort of a failure with a great deal to justify.

In one way or another, though, all the tycoon texts are as interested in justifying or glorifying the self as in offering precepts for management. Since this vainglorious element is so obvious, what explains the public's appetite for reading the works? One answer is simply that the tycoons (or their publishers) mostly had the wit to employ professional writers, and even to name them. Once upon a time, businessmen confined their literary ambitions to inter-office memos and annual reports, and that's how most of them write.

But beyond the literary professionalism, and far more important, lies the same quest for certainty in an uncertain world that explained the equally unprecedented multi-million sales of *In Search of Excellence*, or the high-rise sales of books promising to reveal the secrets of Japanese business success. The management readers want reassurance; they want to hear that, if they only imitate this marvellous man, or adopt that magical recipe, they can rise above the toughest challenges, as Iacocca did so superbly at Chrysler. But only a portion of Iacocca's amazing sales were confined to managers – and any budding boardroom authors inspired by its success should beware.

Few other executives have lived through such tumult. None has become preternaturally famous through appearing (in 97% of US households, sixty-three times each) in their own commercials ('If you can find a better car – buy it'). Few can tell a story that has so many elements of a *Dallas*-type television blockbuster. The Ford years alone brim with blood and thunder: the ageing 'despot' (Iacocca's word for Henry II) maintaining his cramping grip on a lavish and indulgent court at the price of destroying the ambitious, brilliant, thrusting Crown Prince.

Similarly, Mark McCormack has enough fame as the entrepreneur/agent who made Arnold Palmer into a multi-national, megabuck corporation to give any book a flying start. But celebrity isn't the sole explanation: the sales of his *What They Don't Teach You at Harvard Business School*, of *Iacocca*, of *Managing* (the testament of ITT's Harold Geneen), of Sir John Harvey-Jones's *Making It Happen*, and even of the egregious Donald Trump's *The Art of the Deal* are also symptoms of a general upsurge of interest in the business of business. The issue is whether the books do anything for management other than line the pockets (mostly already richly coated) of their prime authors; whether the readers obtain anything for the expenditure of a few pounds, other than a warm feeling in the heart.

To be fair, that question can be asked of any management book, including this one. The Iacocca phenomenon is no more remarkable than that of *In Search of Excellence* – or that of *The One-Minute Manager* and its sixty-second progeny. That first slim (or minute) volume basically consisted of a crisp lesson as old as management itself, in fact older: 'Don't hire a dog and bark yourself.' Apart from that incontrovertible advice on delegation, and a simplistic three-stage guide to retaining control and motivation while delegating, *The One-Minute Manager* has little to offer except brevity. That's no criticism of the book, though, for the limited range of its lore isn't at all exceptional.

The eight basic attributes, the highest common factors, which the two consultant authors found in their search for *Excellence* among America's leading corporations can also be summed up in one page and read aloud in one minute. That's a vital mark of the business-book bonanza; the essential message, even if the volume, like *What They Don't Teach*, runs to 249 pages, can be expressed in very short compass. Thus, McCormack's argument is that what Harvard doesn't 'teach you is what they can't teach you, which is how to read people and how to use that knowledge to get what you want'. His 'seven-step plan' to supply this academic deficiency occupies just two and a half pages and twenty-four key words ('listen aggressively; observe aggressively; talk less; take a second look at first impressions; take time to use what you've learned; be discreet; be detached').

Good, sound advice it is too. There are other equally pithy summaries *en route* to the epilogue, like how to deal with employees: (1) Pay them what they are worth, (2) Make them feel that they are important, yet (3) Make them think for themselves, and (4) Separate office life from social life.

Again, the words are worth their weight in silver, if not in gold; but they are hardly enough to fill a book. So what does?

The answer in McCormack's case is a wealth of anecdote, much of it inconsequential, and a welter of advice, mostly disconnected. The anecdotes are about sports more than management, for McCormack appreciates better than anybody (he should) the value of dropping a good heroic name, viz: 'I bring up Arnold Palmer's name in business conversations all the time.' But McCormack isn't as original or non-academic as he would have you believe. Some of the lessons he offers are in fact taught at Harvard (like Pareto's 80/20 rule, which lays down that 20% of your customers provide 80% of your sales, etc) and the art of positioning (which tells you where to place and price your offerings in the market-place).

What Lee Iacocca learned in the hard school of Detroit, too, wouldn't surprise any Harvard professor. In the sixteen pages (out of 341) which he devotes to 'The Key to Management', the Chrysler hero advises on quarterly review of subordinates' performance (his favourite nostrum), on decision-making, on motivation, on delegation, on the importance of having a strong ego (but never a large one), and on the vital role of team spirit. The note the Chrysler saviour strikes here is similar to Mark McCormack's, and for similar reasons: both men are great salesmen. Iacocca's management methods – including the review device – derive from managing the salesman and sharing his prejudices; thus Iacocca waxes quite lyrical about the inherent conflict between 'the guys in sales and marketing' and 'the bean-counters'.

The latter are the accountants, a breed of whom Iacocca is wary, even though, as he stresses, the terrifying problems at Chrysler included the fact that nobody was counting the beans properly. Without getting clean, clear financial information about just how and where Chrysler was losing so many hundreds of millions, Iacocca and his team couldn't begin to stem the loss of corporate blood. But Iacocca wasn't really concerned to discuss the finer, or even the coarser points of management. He was far more concerned to demonstrate that the Ford Motor board were deeply culpable for agreeing to the demand of Henry Ford (that 'evil man') for the head of so splendid a president as Lee Iacocca.

You certainly can't argue with at least three of the great man's achievements – anyway, not as he tells them. As the head of the Ford Division ('the happiest period of my life'), he found 'a market in search of a car' and launched the Mustang, which netted over $1 billion in its first two years. That was after killing the Cardinal, a potentially disastrous plan to build a European-designed compact in the US. Later triumphs recorded by their author included the billion-dollar project, another crucial decision, to launch the small Fiesta in Europe. Add the revamp of the Lincoln division with the Mark models (one Mark equalling ten Falcons in profit terms) and you have a terrific track record.

That raises two questions. One, obviously, is why Henry Ford fired the champ. The other is why, with so much Iacocca goodness going for it, Ford failed to emerge as a great, deeply admired, powerhouse super-challenger to General Motors and the world – especially Japan. Iacocca's thesis is that the two answers are linked. Bad decisions by Henry (like his veto of a terrific deal to buy Honda power trains for a US-made small car) offset the Iacocca brainwaves. Furthermore, the latter's good management was vitiated by Henry's bad habits, like firing his brightest and best – including Iacocca's top car man, Hal Sperlich (the hero weakly complied with this execution), and above all Iacocca himself. Yet consider this passage:

> The day after I was fired, Henry sent off a letter to every Ford dealer in the country, trying to reassure them all that they wouldn't be neglected: 'The Company has a strong and experienced management team. Our North American Automotive Operations are headed by talented executives who are well-known to you and who are fully attuned to your needs and the needs of the retail market.' Of course, if that were really true, there would have been no need for the letter.

But if that were not really true, if Ford didn't have a strong and experienced management team, whose fault was that? Iacocca had been president for eight years, after all. Then, consider the Pinto disaster. After 'a number of accidents where the car burst into flames after a rear-end collision', the makers were charged with 'reckless homicide. Ford was acquitted, but the damage to the company was incalculable ... We resisted making any change, and that hurt us badly.' Iacocca himself asks 'Whose fault was it?' and concedes that 'One obvious answer is that it was the fault of Ford's management – including me.'

But surely, again, it was more Iacocca's fault than anybody's, on the basic management principle that the buck stops here – at the desk of the million-a-year man in operational charge. Presumably it was mere coincidence that 'we voluntarily recalled almost a million and a half Pintos in June 1978, the month before I was fired.' But Iacocca conveys a strong impression of taking 90% of the credit for all Ford's feats and little or none for its flops – a by no means uncommon trait among managers at all levels.

What that proves is that super-managers aren't super-human. They feel such common-or-garden human urges as the need to present themselves in the best possible light, their enemies in the worst. Given the chance to write history, they rewrite it to suit (literally) their book. In that they are no different from ex-Presidents of the United States or Prime Ministers of Britain. Just like the White House heroes and the Downing Street heroine, too, the tycoons can now, thanks to the best-seller industry, reap huge financial rewards – even if, as in Iacocca's case, the need for still more personal millions isn't especially apparent.

It's a fair guess that the money motive, even if powerful, comes well behind the passionate drive to justify the self. This essential element of self-justification is as strong, if not stronger, in a book that doesn't even call itself after its hero – *Managing*. To read this work, you would imagine that its author, Harold S. Geneen, was one of America's most successful managers. And so he was, up to a point: that point being when he stepped down from the chairmanship of the company, ITT, of which he was the second founder.

In management, the evil that powerful men do lives after them – and (like Iacocca with Ford) Geneen would have had to shoulder some responsibility for ITT's unhappy recent history, its sell-offs, slump in earnings and general debility, even if he hadn't hung on, Godfather-like, as a powerful and interventionist presence on the board. None of that is recounted in his book, though. The innocent manager would suppose that ITT was still regarded with deepest respect, even awe, at the time of writing. The less innocent manager, though, will guess from Geneen's own account, which does not spare self-praise, how the seeds of defeat were sown in the master's victories, and why they were bound to yield a bitter harvest.

He tells, for instance, of 350 buys, mergers and absorptions, many hasty, most acquired at asking price. Just how do you manage a consequently enormous spread of 250 profit centres? Many, moreover, were bound, on the law of averages alone, to be duds – and expensive ones, at that. In answer, Geneen's overall principle is 'You read a book from the beginning to the end. You run a business the opposite way. You start with the end, and then you do everything you have to do to reach that bottom line.' The bottom-most line was ITT's target growth in earnings per share: 10% per annum compound.

To achieve the bottom line (as he did, remarkably enough), Geneen set up an elaborate, exacting system of budgets, monthly reports and interventionist visits at will by his staff experts anywhere in the company. Geneen calls this invigilation 'open communications'; no doubt, some of the invigilated gave it less pleasant names. But the centrepiece of the system was the General Managers Meeting. All 250 managing directors met Geneen and his cohorts (a strike force of forty-odd executives) once a month, either in Brussels or in New York, for sessions lasting at least twelve hours daily over several days.

In all, says Geneen, ITT management spent thirty-five weeks of every year on planning, budgeting, and the notoriously inquisitorial meetings. Allowing for vacations, 'That left

a scant thirteen weeks of "other time" to run the company.'
Some men cracked under the stress of the inquisitions. But
setting that aside, their still worse defect, shared with the
whole apparatus, was just what the quote implies: most of the
time, Geneen was running the system, not the company. It
was a system, too, which could only be worked by one
brilliant, driven and driving man: Harold S. Geneen. Moreover, it was a system uniquely equipped to seize tight control
of an uncontrolled empire and provide a framework into
which acquisitions could be speedily slotted and where they
could be duly disciplined in turn.

But Geneen, with his concentration on short-term results
and distrust of planning ('There will be no more long-range
planning' is the entire text of one early memo), seems to miss
a vital point – that every business has two bottom lines: the
financial one, of which he was the supreme maestro, and the
organic one, which determines its future. The organic
bottom line would have included such objectives as intensify-
ing ITT's technological power in its base telecommunications markets, instead of allowing it to slip fatally behind. The
ITT giant was in too many businesses to manage them
centrally, but its central system was much too strong for them
to be managed independently.

So long as Geneen was there, his own dynamic performance partially hid this hard truth. With him removed, painful
reality came bursting through – but not into Geneen's self-
perception. He writes witheringly about the man who
'becomes unwilling to accept information which is contrary
to some preconceived notion or image of himself held in his
mind ... [who] believes that he is smarter than everyone
else, that everyone else is there to serve him'. Outsiders at the
time of his personal domination of ITT were led to think this
scathing description of the 'supreme egotist in corporate
life' to be an excellent one of Geneen himself; it's an image
that his book does little to dispel.

Inability to see themselves as others see them, even such
spectacular blindness as Geneen's, isn't confined to managers. As observed in Chapter 16, though, self-deception is a
common managerial vice – and blindness to personal

defects, even worse, easily goes with the avoidance or ignorance of unpleasant truths about the business. Maybe the super-manager memoirs should all be accompanied by an antidote, a commentary supplied by a candid friend, or even an honest enemy, so the reader at least learns that the great man's character and conduct have a side other than the one he chooses to display.

There are also, of course, alternative views of the events the super-manager describes. Robert Townsend's version of life at Avis has been questioned by his co-workers, for example. In a famous passage in *Up The Organisation*, Townsend describes how White Plains was chosen as the head-office site by imagining where 'a man from Mars' would place his chosen centre for a multi-national car-rental business. The revisionists say that the decisive factor came, not from outer space, but from the fact that most of the decision-makers lived nearby. Similarly, one old Avis hand complained that, sure, Townsend (as he reports) had no secretary – but he used everybody else's, and they hated it.

Be that as it may, does it matter? The 'man from Mars' technique – trying to shake free of all acquired attitudes and received ideas before making a decision – is no worse for being based (if it is) on a misleading anecdote. Actually, the idea is very sound, and all the sounder if you gather, from the above historical revision, how difficult it is to be honestly Martian, truly aloof from preconceptions and predispositions. The issue of secretaries, what they are used for, whether they are truly needed, is one that's rarely faced, but should be. The story helps focus the mind, like all parables. And if you find that it may be a fib, that might help you to examine your own conscience for fibs, possibly harmful ones, of your own.

Does it matter any more if the account misleads about actual and important events? If Lee Iacocca wasn't, say, as he has always claimed, 'the father of the Mustang'? In the authorised, or Iacocca version, the project sprang from his brain and was carried to sensational fruition by his energy. According to Ford's chief designer, not so; Iacocca was presented with a completed model on taking over his beloved Ford Division, and then ran with the ball. The truth matters in one sense, because truth always matters. But in terms of the managerial value of *Iacocca,* as of *Up The Organisation,* that worth lies in the inspirational example – and the description of the market analysis that targeted the Mustang's sector is unquestionably valuable, whoever first dreamt up the car.

All the same, the battle of the bestsellers has taken the managerial book far away from the scholarly, deeply researched, thoughtful works of a pioneering writer such as Peter Drucker: far away, too, from a book like *My Years with General Motors,* in which the between-wars super-manager Alfred P. Sloan Jr. wrote, not about himself, but about the history of the great corporation of which he was the architect. It took Sloan 467 pages to tell a story which is still an indispensable management text. No doubt, gilded lilies and misreported events occur in Sloan's narrative, but it's difficult to believe, when reading that careful, dispassionate, fact-filled prose, that the lapses from grace are many.

For that reason, Sloan's magnum opus will probably still be around when today's megasellers and their hectic, 'as-told-to' journalistic prose are long forgotten. That, too, may not matter. As Sloan wrote of the corporation: 'No company ever stops changing. Change will come for better or worse . . . The task of management is not to apply a formula but to decide issues on a case-by-case basis.' What's true of the corporation is true of management in general. Behind the hype and the hoop-la, the bestsellers gain their currency (in both senses of the word) from a direct relevance to real and deep concerns of changing times, even if the relevance isn't too obvious.

There is a strong backlash against the business-school academicism enshrined at Harvard, for instance. There is a powerful reaction against the awful internal and external abuses of corporations like Henry Ford II's Ford or the pre-Iacocca Chrysler. There is, too, a general wave of acute awareness that the mega-corporation has been long overdue for renaissance, for just the kind of managerial renewal that the sage Sloan foresaw. Renaissance heroes – like John Sculley of Apple or Andy Grove of Intel – have even burst into book form while still in the saddle of bucking broncos (which in Sculley's case bucked him right out of the business).

The academics, never easily outdone, have responded to change with a spate of renaissance literature. Elephants are taught how to dance, corporations are reinvented or re-engineered, turned into learning organisations, shown how to create competitive advantage, develop their core competencies, become virtual as well as virtuous; while managers are instructed in 'thriving on chaos' and practising 'liberation management'. Those last two title phrases come from the industrious Tom Peters, with each latest book twice as long as its predecessor. Both he and Robert Waterman, his former co-author, have travelled a long way from the corpocratic examples which so impressed them in *Excellence* days – like IBM.

That company, however, did produce the best of the assisted autobiographies, *Father, Son & Co*, by Thomas J. Watson Jr., who so dramatically improved on his father's astonishing legacy. It's well worth reading, for reasons which apply to the other works. Whatever the motives and misdeeds of the hero-authors, and however many millions their books coin, reading about the experience of other managers is the best (and cheapest) method around of giving naked managers a few more clothes. It helps greatly if they don't fall for the super-manager myths, of course. It helps even more if they learn from their reading not to create myths of their own.

Epilogue:
The Well-Dressed Executive

Next to being told how good they are individually, executives best love to hear how bad they are as a bunch. Any course of myth-destruction services this therapeutic purpose, but at a price: that of building another myth, which is that all executives, being foolish and foible-ridden, make a bad job worse. All that I know about management was learned from executives, some of whom are my friends, many of whom I admire, most of whom deserve respect – clever managers who work hard according to their best lights in circumstances that are often against them. This epilogue is for them. As for the idle, selfish, stupid self-deceivers, this is how to beat them and enjoy it.

The myths keep on coming, and from all directions: from the consultants and the professors, the gurus and the goops, the vain autobiographers and the eager army of business journalists. One grand myth in particular became firmly entrenched in the 1980s, with the aid of all the above interested parties: the idea, akin to the Big Bang theory of the creation of the universe, that there is One Big Solution. Whether it's the One-Minute Manager or the eight attributes of corporate excellence, epilogue fundamental fiction is the same: that Highest Common Factors exist, which you can derive

373

from study of the Highest Uncommon Companies or their executives.

Since you can only find out what happens in corporations by observing their activities, past and present, and drawing conclusions from what you see, it's impossible for any writer about management, including this one, to avoid perpetuating the myth. But the evidence, as savants in other fields would see at once, is purely anecdotal. Parables are marvellous teaching tools. But don't forget that the only thing winning companies have in common is their success – which may well not last: merely look at the loss-making agonies endured, at the hands of the Japanese rival Komatsu, by Caterpillar Tractor, one of the top stars of *In Search of Excellence* and for decades among everybody's top marketing companies.

To get anywhere in understanding management, you have to move from the particular to the general; but don't be led beyond the general to the universal. The temptation to follow those misleading footsteps, though, is well-nigh irresistible. Just imagine finding the secret of successful innovation, the key to market survival, let alone triumph in the 1990s and beyond: surely the key lies among the successful innovators? That's what *Fortune* magazine thought, anyway. It looked at 'Eight Big Masters of Innovation', selected by an exhaustive process, and sought to discover what American Airlines, Apple, Campbell Soup, GE, Intel, Merck, 3M and Philip Morris could teach the sluggards. So what's the Holy Grail of innovation?

Surprise, surprise: 'the management of each of the Eight is convinced of the need to innovate, regarding new ideas as the essence of long-term survival'. That discovery is about as original, and as useful, as announcing that water is wet. Then, 'no matter how dependent the companies are on purely technological advances, they are uniformly devoted to marketing' – again, what else is new? Other glimpses of the obvious are duly sanctified: 'Listening carefully to their customers ... clearly defined cultures ... such mom-and-flag values as product quality, market leadership and (naturally) the necessity of invention'. It's more valuable (but not much more) to know that the Eight 'ruthlessly limit the search for new ideas to areas they are competent to exploit'.

This meagre result is par for the course; and so is the decidedly mixed fate of the Eight. Three of them (American Airlines, Campbell, and Philip Morris) ran into major difficulties after the *Fortune* encomium, and in 1994 there were large question-marks over Apple, Merck and even Intel. What lends the executive peculiar charm and weakness, though, is less the readiness to swallow other people's myths than the inability to recognise one's own nakedness – one's impotence, incompetence and error. So do recognise it; the shock of recognition will improve your performance and give you a lasting start on unshocked competitors. Make things easier for yourself, too, by simplifying everything you can, wherever and whenever you can.

William Blackie, when chief executive of Caterpillar Tractor, never said wiser words than these: 'I deride the idea that an executive's function is problem-solving – it is the bad executive who is up to his neck in problems.' Blackie wasn't thinking of the real, monster anxieties, like those of his own successors as they wrestled (in the end, quite successfully) with recession in key markets, deadly competition from Komatsu and excessive costs in their own plants. He referred to the fact that, in the standard big-company corpocracy, executives stalk new problems with the eagerness of the hunters of the snark. As if ordinary life threw up too few troubles, they invent and invite extra complexity.

Any business situation can be reduced to simple terms. If it is, the solution usually appears from the reduction, and the 'problem' evaporates. The surest way to simplify is to concentrate, to focus. Don't, if you are brilliant at making executive jets (like the late Norman Lear), reckon that you will be an expert hand at cars (especially steam ones). If the company can find one lucrative set of activities or markets in which it functions well, sufficient unto the day be the profit thereof. Concentration and focus also mean that the single-minded company must be single-minded about its overriding objective, which is to be the best at everything from production costs (the lowest) and efficiency (the highest) in serving the consumer (to the latter's greatest pleasure). If you can supply more effectively on a lower cost base than anybody else, you must win.

The more a business concentrates, the less time its executives need to waste. The single-minded, focused company, alas, tends to become monomaniacal as well; its executives are expected to live only for power tools or whatever, and they don't like to buck the system. So every last detail of the business is regurgitated to fill long days of discussion. Even in average circumstances, discussions take up half an executive's time, and interruptions do the rest of the damage.

According to a Swedish study, fourteen minutes is the maximum for which executives are left alone; and nine minutes is the top time without interruption. No wonder they can't think straight. Resist this vice strenuously. The object, as in management generally, is to get the most with the least, the maximum effective management thought and follow-up with the minimum expenditure of hours. Ask of every activity, and especially of every meeting, whether it serves any purpose directly related to the company's profit. Organise the company so that a normal working day will cover normal tasks. And pack executives (including yourself) off home at decent times (that is, unless they don't want to go). Never disturb them after-hours without grave cause, and genuine apologies.

A dangerously narrow line divides a company that wastes no time from a stagnant bunch of idle corporate loafers. The best way to avoid stagnation is to manage young. That is, give people high responsibility as soon as you know that they won't stuff your bank (Penn Square) with a raft of duff energy loans; or pass them on to so many big-bank suckers, that not only does your own bank collapse, but the once-great Continental Illinois is only saved from collapse (and with it the entire US banking system) by a $4.5 billion bale-out. Mozart was dead at thirty-five. So are many living executives.

The one great idea that, if Freud was right, is all anybody is given comes early rather than late. If you wait until men and women are over forty, let alone fifty, to give them their most important job, you will miss their prime – and so will they. Young executives are no more all brilliant balls of energy than old ones are all spluttered-out volcanoes. But the good oldsters were better when they were younger, or would have been, if somebody had given them a chance. And don't kid yourself, either, that you've rejuvenated the company by lowering the average age of the executives from fifty-seven to fifty-three.

That is different in degree, but not in kind, from the octogenarian British chairman who decided to retire to make way for a younger man. He meant his son, a stripling in his sixties. Somebody, preferably that son, should long before have told the old roadblock to clear himself away. But the circumstances of the people almost certainly made serious criticism impossible. Don't let it happen in your company, and don't stay where it has happened. If executives can't be frank with their colleagues and seniors, they won't be frank with themselves either; both sins are equally dangerous.

Never take frankness as far as boasting. The Canadian press tycoon Lord Thomson should have bitterly regretted the day when he described his Scottish television franchise as 'a licence to print money'. So it was; but it didn't take long before the government, alerted and offended, altered the licence drastically in its own favour. It's probable that Gerald Ratner was boasting when describing one of his store chain's offerings as 'crap' to the annual conference of the Institute of Directors. But the resulting fallout decimated Ratner's fortune, cost his job, and eventually destroyed the business.

Remember, as a better example, the Swiss of Hoffman-La Roche, who in many respects have the world's most envied drug company. For years nobody, except possibly its bankers, knew how much money Roche coined. When the facts began to emerge, under the pressure of government investigations, the reasons for Roche's secrecy became even more apparent; it was charging $10 a gram for tranquillisers which cost fifty-six cents to produce. Such conduct is extreme and not to be imitated. But 'speak only when spoken to and avoid vain-glory' is a sounder course than hiring a public-relations army and missing no opportunity to extol your own merits. You may not have any.

For salutary proof of your demerits, follow up a few complaints. No criticism that has reached me in my game, however rude or ignorant, has been without a valuable grain of truth, and your game is no different. In some cases, it isn't just a grain of truth, but a whole Sahara Desert. To be specific, if a company delivers to a customer (probably several weeks late) a product that comes to pieces in his or her hands, and then takes several months of acrimonious correspondence before its offence is put right, then that firm is rotten from top to bottom and needs total overhaul fast. That's trebly true today, when quality isn't a highly valued extra, but a taken-for-granted *sine qua non*.

Don't skate around complaints on the grounds that detail is not your business. The argument that board-level executives, or any executives, should look at the wood and forget about the trees is an incitement to, and an excuse for, unforgivable slackness. The good executive at any level can distinguish between a vital detail and rubbish, and a detail a day keeps the liquidator away. Sometimes, spotting even a beam in your own eye, let alone a few motes, is psychologically difficult. Overcoming this repression is where outside critics come in – so don't be like General Motors and try to wish your own private Ralph Naders away. Like Nader's Raiders, they will, more often than not, be right.

That, true, was in another era, and, besides, the car Nader complained of (the Corvair) is dead. But GM's harassing of Nader's private life fell into the same pattern as the blind eye for its own faults which culminated in dreadful reverses at the hands of the Japanese. GM today is greatly changed, not before time, and not far enough; but it deserved its great punishment for infringing a creakingly ancient moral rule. Do unto others as you would be done by; in other words, behave yourself. Few sights in world business are more unattractive than that of large companies seeking credit and praise for progressive labour policies, or for their anti-pollution, anti-racialism, and anti-poverty programmes – as if they had some right, which they were generously waiving, to foul the environment, or exacerbate social tensions, or grind the workers' faces in the dust.

Executives whose firms have ignored their social responsibilities for decades applaud themselves for doing so no longer. But in fact, the environment is still being polluted. You will still find only slightly more Jews on the boards of US blue-chips than coloured men in any executive role in any European company. Equally awful, you will still find disgracefully few women in senior executive positions anywhere in the Western world (and you can just forget about Japan). The tide of women emerging from the business schools will change this sorry situation – but too slowly for the tastes of many able women. Nobody should tolerate the ridiculous fact that only 0.3% of the top 1,000 US chief executives are female.

The women are voting with their feet. Like the Jewish immigrants before them, or the Asians in Britain today, they are creating their own opportunities as entrepreneurs. But the corporate world will be poorer without them – and serve it right. If prejudice restricts a company's hiring policy, it will miss able people. In many mediocre giants, careers are still not really open to all talents; neither are the talented given every opportunity to rise, and to exercise their rising expertise without let or hindrance. Change that, and you will change the giants, and possibly their mediocrity.

The company's social obligations begin at home. 'In many auto companies life is like a jungle,' said one escapee. 'Among executives, it is dog eat dog.' That is no less barbaric than it sounds, and an uncivilised company is no more worth living in than a cannibal country. Even decent companies are in danger of forgetting that people are not pawns. 'That place is much like being in the army,' an observer said of one giant. 'They rotate people terrifically.' Don't let your company be like either a jungle or the services. Executives are neither animals nor conscripts; they can be made to behave like both, but at dreadful loss in both effectiveness and ordinary humanity.

Employees are not 'Honeywellers' and 'IBMers', as companies like to call them; and it's fortunate for companies, as well as individuals, that changing social norms, the high pressures of high technology and the work of the Theory Y enthusiasts have dispelled much of the aura of the old Organisation Man. Employees produce their best work if they are treated as what they are, individuals. Their loyalty to the corporation is only worthwhile if it is voluntary, non-conformist, and like undercarriages, easily retractable.

The only excuse for being displeased when good executives retract themselves is when the move is a genuine mistake. If the manager is moving to a better job, and you can't outbid the opposition, be happy. After all, the person is supposed to be your friend; and nobody is indispensable (especially you). Huge turnover of executives (or of the whole workforce, for that matter) is a bad sign; someone is either managing or hiring badly. But nil turnover is also a bad sign. The company can't be hiring and developing the ambitious, able, and energetic people it desperately needs; otherwise some of them would inevitably energise themselves out of the place.

Moreover, if holes don't open up, you can't fill some of them with new talent, and that is fatal. This fresh talent need not be imported; it can very often be dredged up from the company's own depths. But only these regular transfusions can save a corporation from the major surgery to which most eventually come. Unfortunately, the surgery only rearranges the same parts. The most effective shake-ups are cataclysmic, not kaleidoscopic. The best thing that ever happened to I.G. Farben, the pre-war German chemical giant, was the break-up by the Allied occupiers of a lumbering, cartel-ridden mammoth into three aggressive and distinct component parts.

The worst thing that happened to Krupp after the Nazi defeat was its preservation intact by a wily owner; that signed the company's death-warrant as a leading European industrial force. 'The first billion-dollar giant that deliberately hives off a few hundred million dollars of superfluous, profitable sales will make history and a fortune for its stockholders.' The last sentence is in quotes because I wrote it a long time ago – years before company after company proved my point by profitably unloading division after division, including some mistakes that had only recently been purchased.

In some cases the grounds were strategic reversal (like BAT, under predatory pressure, selling off stores and perfumes to concentrate on tobacco and insurance): in others, management was repairing past errors (like Coca-Cola abandoning its attempt to lord it over Californian wine, and later selling Columbia Pictures); in others still, the pressures were financial (like the need to reduce vast debts after Du Pont's purchase of Conoco, or after the mega-buy of Esmark by Beatrice Foods). Whatever the motive, the consequences are the same: a business worth more to the shareholders and able, like any tree, to grow more strongly for being pruned.

Size, apart from its other drawbacks, kills homeliness. One common factor of unusually successful firms is their hick quality. They don't have plush metropolitan offices, or, sometimes, plush offices at all. Their heart is in some undistinguished locale such as Goole, Yorkshire. Their bosses know New York and London, but can't wait to get home. Homespun companies such as the boys from Wooster, Ohio, who made Rubbermaid into America's 'most admired' corporation, have built world interests in their concentrated specialities without succumbing to the tempting passion for sophistication and complication. Wal-Mart even became the world's largest retailer without straying spiritually from Bentonville, Arkansas.

Simple principles sound laughably naive; the original J.C. Bamford built his earth-moving business and his fortune on an old-fashioned platform of paying for everything in cash, neither giving nor receiving credit, never borrowing, and staying determinedly private. Non-tycoons, lacking the intuitive quality of business genius, can't afford the same luxury of sticking to principles at all costs. The common-or-garden executive needs flexibility, readiness to change course, even in midstream, willingness to look acidly even at success.

The Apollo programme, hailed at the time, and at the moon landing's twenty-fifth anniversary in 1994, as a triumph of 'good' professional management, is a caution in itself. Because you have made the moon by 1970 for a mere $50 billion, don't assume you've managed brilliantly – maybe it should have been done for $30 billion. Worry more about the worms inside the apple. Then, maybe, astronauts won't be fried alive because of major procedural defects. The real lesson of Apollo is that, if the objective is attainable and there is no limit to the resources available, organisations can achieve almost any task. That is not news.

So don't manage (and many companies do) as if you are NASA. There are always limits to the use of a corporation's resources – first, that it isn't the executives' money; second, that behind the shareholders, the money belongs to the community. Executives are highly privileged individuals. They receive sweeping power over society's economic resources – more sweeping than that of politicians, but entirely in a private capacity – to do with what they will, under conditions of low accountability and virtual permanence. Few executives feel this burden of national responsibility. But they won't do their duty by the country's wealth until they see their work stripped of its mythological trappings and in its true, unflattering light – and thus do it better.

One persistent myth, which the Europeans used to believe about America, is that some other national economy holds the antidote to whatever ails your own country. Americans have now fallen for this comforting idea themselves – the comfort lying in the fact that, if there truly were some magic ingredient that could be imported, a sort of managerial ginseng, economic ailments would be easily curable. The Japanese management model has proved unsurprisingly attractive to US businessmen wondering and worrying about how these ace competitors from the East have captured so many home and overseas markets.

It's true that, just as any sensible company constantly studies or 'benchmarks' its best competitors, and best counterparts in other businesses, to find ways of improving its performance, so much can always be learnt from other countries. But there are no panaceas available, from Japan or anywhere else. The reality of Japan, as the economic setbacks of the 1990s have shown, is that its magic consists of little more (though that's a lot) than dedicated application to clearly defined tasks, founded on the belief that constant improvement (in products, processes, efficiency) is always possible: built around the conviction that a corporation worth working for is worth fighting for; sustained by a tradition of mutual respect; and animated by a non-stop competitive drive. Nothing in Japanese management success should be strange to any European or American manager who has studied the realities of lasting successes in their own cultures – which the Japanese have certainly done.

The Ten Truths of Management given in these pages form a simple anti-myth kit. A wise reader of the manuscript objected that the truths mostly don't apply to executives only, but are common to almost all humanity. He had holed in one. Management is precisely that, a general human activity, to which the best guides are not the management textbooks, but history, sociology, and psychology. The first myth of management – that it exists – seeks to take management away from where it belongs and to put it on a pedestal of pseudo-science. Executives placed on pedestals fall from a great height. If the Ten Truths help to keep you off the pedestal, at least the drop will be much shorter.

1. Think before you act: it's not your money.
2. All good management is the expression of one great idea.
3. No executive devotes effort to proving himself wrong.
4. Cash in must exceed cash out.
5. Management capability is always less than the organisation actually needs.
6. Either executives can do their jobs or they can't.
7. If sophisticated calculations are needed to justify an action, don't do it.
8. If you are doing something wrong, you will do it badly.
9. If you are attempting the utterly impossible, you will fail utterly.
10. The easiest way of making money is to stop losing it.

Another truth lies behind all ten. One of the least attractive myths of management holds that nobody can get rich without at some point being a crook, a con-man, or a mobster. Many crooks, con-men, and mobsters have made great wealth. It does not follow that crookedness is the path to business success, or that executives can throw private morality overboard as they plunge into corporate vice. Ponder, rather, how it is that the Quakers and similar deeply religious gentry made so much worldly lucre. It was because they treated their people honestly and decently, worked hard and honestly themselves, spent honestly and saved pennies, honestly put more back into the company than they took out, made honestly good products, gave honest value for money and, being honest, told no lies. The naked manager can never find better clothes.

Index

Index

276, 278–9; *see also* Geneen, Harold, S.

Jaguar Cars, 17, 120
Japan, 48, 55, 140, 179, 337, 363; CEOs, 169–70, 187, 201, 202–3; competition from, 4–5, 44, 45, 265, 271, 335; Deming influences, 54, 222, 326; education of managers, 38, 314; efficiency, 347; employee relations, 77, 79, 80, 81–2, 83–4; *kaizen*, 239, 299; lead in technology, 61–2, 68, 265, 266, 273; management in, 222, 223, 235, 239, 250, 352, 382–3; *ringi*, 170, 202, 361
Jobs, Steve, 72, 187, 242
Johnson, F. Ross, 28, 141
Johnson, Howard, 330–1

Kaplan, Robert, 347
Katzenbach, Jon, 324
Kay, Emmanuel, 249
Kemerer, Chris, 146
Keyes, Jessica, 147, 148
Kiam, Victor, 31, 32
Kitching, John, 283
Knapp, Charlie, 211
Kodak (Eastman Kodak), 2, 22, 66, 294, 335
Kohlberg Kravis and Roberts, 27
Komatsu, 374, 375
Kreuger, Alan B., 295
Kuenheim, Eberhard von, 169
Kwik Save, 120

Land, Edwin H., 187
Lazell, H.G., 256, 270
Lazell, Leslie, 192
Leasco, 97
Lescher, Jack, 322
'Lestoil syndrome', 61, 62, 64
leveraged buy-outs, 3, 6, 30, 34
Levi-Strauss, 20
Levitt, Theodore C., 46–7, 49
Liebling, A.J., 79
Litton Industries, 22, 276, 210–11, 212–13; decentralisation at, 153, 161
Lockheed Corp., 179, 196; banks confident in, 29, 35; dynamic accounting, 92, 93; Galaxy, 43, 288–9, 291; Tristar, 29, 95, 180, 181, 271–2
Lorenz, Christopher, 303
Love, George H., 31

Lyons, J., 192

Maclean, Sir Alexander, 178
management: defined, 13–14
management by objectives, 226–8, 231–2, 233–4, 300, 301
Mario, Ernst, 143–4
marketing, 49–59; muddled, 158–60; myopic, 46–7; R & D needs, 263–74; selling, 56–7
Marks & Spencer, 176, 189, 281, 310
Marriott Jr., Willard, 331
Mars, 119; Forrest Mars, 346
Maslow, Abraham, 238
Matsushita, 222, 223, 272
Mattel, 348
Maucher, Helmut, 257, 355
Maxwell, Robert, 29, 32, 87, 97, 210
MBAs, 305–6, 310–11, 313
McCormack, Mark, 363–5
McDonald, James, 243
McGregor, Douglas, 238, 247
McKinsey & Company, 50, 165, 168, 188, 228; *Excellence*, 317; failures, 320–1; at Shell, 66, 319–20, 321, 323, 358–9; style, 324
Mercedes-Benz, 331–2
Merck, 374, 375
mergers and acquisitions, 4, 6, 122–32, 216, 249; dangers of, 2–3, 27–8, 51–2, 110, 178–9, 235, 283, 320–1; managing, 16–17, 124–7; price of, 126–9, 130; *see also* conglomerates; diversification
Merrill Lynch, 129
Microsoft, 134–5, 255, 267–8, 296
Midland Bank, 123
Milken, Michael, 213
Miller High Life, 130–1
Mobil, 126
Monitor, 316–17
Monsanto, 231
Moret, Marc, 78
Morgan, J.P., 128
Morita, Akio, 72, 323
motivation, 238–50; ambition as, 241–2; carrot and stick as, 246–8, 249; pay as, 240–1, 243–4, 247, 262
Motorola, 272
Mrs Fields, 148–9
Murdoch, Rupert, 101, 123, 177

Nader, Ralph, 378
Nadir, Asil, 91, 214

388